Lesson Plans

Critical Issues in American Education

Lisa Michele Nunn, Series Editor

Taking advantage of sociology's position as a leader in the social scientific study of education, this series is home to new empirical and applied bodies of work that combine social analysis, cultural critique, and historical perspectives across disciplinary lines and the usual methodological boundaries. Books in the series aim for topical and theoretical breadth. Anchored in sociological analysis, Critical Issues in American Education features carefully crafted empirical work that takes up the most pressing educational issues of our time, including federal education policy, gender and racial disparities in student achievement, access to higher education, labor market outcomes, teacher quality, and decision making within institutions.

Lesson Plans

The Institutional Demands of Becoming a Teacher

JUDSON G. EVERITT

RUTGERS UNIVERSITY PRESS

NEW BRUNSWICK, CAMDEN, AND NEWARK, NEW JERSEY, AND LONDON

Library of Congress Cataloging-in-Publication Data

Names: Everitt, Judson G., author.
Title: Lesson plans : the institutional demands of becoming a teacher / Judson G.
Everitt.
Description: New Brunswick, NJ : Rutgers University Press, 2017. | Series: Critical issues
in american education | Includes bibliographical references and index.
Identifiers: LCCN 2017016359 (print) | LCCN 2017041858 (ebook) | ISBN 9780813588285
(E-pub) | ISBN 9780813588292 (Web PDF) | ISBN 9780813587608 (hardback :
alk. paper) | ISBN 9780813587592 (paperback : alk. paper)
Subjects: LCSH: Teachers—Training of—United States. | Education—Study and teaching
(Higher)—United States. | Teachers—Psychology. | Educational accountability—
United States. | BISAC: EDUCATION / Professional Development. | SOCIAL SCIENCE /
Human Services. | PSYCHOLOGY / Education & Training. | PSYCHOLOGY /
Social Psychology.
Classification: LCC LB1715 (ebook) | LCC LB1715 .E94 2017 (print) | DDC 370.71/1—dc23
LC record available at https://lccn.loc.gov/2017016359

A British Cataloging-in-Publication record for this book
is available from the British Library.

Copyright © 2018 by Judson G. Everitt

⊗ The paper used in this publication meets the requirements of
the American National Standard for Information Sciences—Permanence
of Paper for Printed Library Materials, ANSI Z39.48–1992.

www.rutgersuniversitypress.org

Manufactured in the United States of America

For Jill and our kids

CONTENTS

Lesson Plans

Introduction

Social Institutions and the Professional Socialization of New Teachers

Early in the fall semester, a group of college seniors majoring in math education turn to each other for help on an assignment they have been given as part of their instructional methods course. This is one of a set of classes they are taking together that constitutes the last of their course work intended to prepare them for the final stage of their teacher education program: student teaching in the spring semester when they will be teaching in public schools under the supervision of mentor teachers. Their task for this assignment is to articulate their teaching philosophy in their own words. A number of them struggle with this paper, and the conversation among them that ensues via an online discussion forum reveals a great deal about the realities of becoming a teacher. In response to a classmate asking for help, Lauren[1] posts the following comment:

> Lindsey,
> I also am experiencing a lot of difficulties with this paper. I will have something written, then after thinking about it for a while I will change it. My philosophy is constantly changing, and I believe it always will. I know that I want to be a teacher who fosters an environment that is open for students to share their thoughts and feelings. I know I want to be the teacher that allows for mistakes and learning from those mistakes. I know I want to be the teacher that when a student leaves my classroom for the year thinks, "Wow, that has been my favorite math teacher thus far." Here is the thing though: I change my mind about how to go about making those "wants" come true. I believe teaching is not just about the teacher. It changes when students change. Each year we will get a new batch of kids, with their own new personalities. We have to adapt to each of those groups and I think that each group will modify our thoughts and philosophies on teaching. They will hand us a new set of problems

1

and from those problems comes learning, and from learning, a new philosophy. So back to your question, yes, I am having difficulty, but here's
my advice. I would say create your philosophy from all the classes you
have had from a student perspective and incorporate your field experience. Write the paper knowing that, yes, our philosophy will change, but
write it as if the principal of your school is reading it. Let him/her know
how we want our classroom environment and the reason teachers are
important. Good luck![2]

Lauren has a general sense of what she wants to accomplish as a teacher, but
she remains unsure exactly how that is going to play out with different groups
of students in her future classroom. How could this be? Mere months away from
completing their entire training program and acquiring certification to teach in
public schools, how could teacher candidates be so unsure, so ambivalent about
something so central to their professional craft as a basic teaching philosophy?
Another teacher candidate, Leslie, echoes Lauren's perspective as part of this
conversation, and elaborates further:

I have been trying to figure out what my philosophy is, but like you said,
you have to be able to adapt your philosophy in order to handle different situations. I also agree that until we are out in the classroom on our
own, it's going to be hard to figure out just what our philosophies are. For
now, I want my students to discover all there is about mathematics and
be able to have a creative lesson (whether it involves technology or
hands-on activities)—I don't want to just give them the information, but
I think this is easier said than done. Especially as new teachers who have
to figure out their classroom management techniques, write up lesson
plans, and carry the weight of helping our students succeed—all with the
administration keeping a close eye on us. I think in all of these aspects,
teaching is a game, and we have to learn how to adapt, transition, and
balance everything going on inside our classrooms.

Lauren and Leslie share the view that their teaching philosophy is a work in
progress, and will evolve as they accumulate future experience working with
students in schools. Leslie reiterates Lauren's point about the need for adaptation. Not only will different groups of students shape the way these teachers
think about their work, but other contingencies will too. Covering curriculum
standards, working with administrators, and handling paperwork, for example,
are other elements of future work environments that teacher candidates recognize will shape their philosophies about teaching.
 These teacher candidates' comments reflect a shared sense of ambivalence
and uncertainty in what they know and believe they can accomplish as teachers. As Lauren notes, she frequently changes her mind as to how to make the

things she wants to accomplish as a teacher come true. It would be plausible to conclude that such ambivalence reflects an unpreparedness to enter the job and carry out instruction effectively. Indeed, this has been a frequent and long-standing critique of new teachers and teacher education. But careful attention to these teacher candidates' perspectives, and the ways they express them, reveals a more complex and nuanced understanding about teaching and public education than is often credited to new teachers. To be sure, they are uncertain about the future and how their experiences will unfold as they transition into the work of teaching, but this in itself does not make them different from people transitioning into most any line of work. New experiences retain uncertainty, no matter how much one has prepared or been prepared. Moreover, while these teacher candidates may be unsure how their efforts at instruction will play out at first, they are keenly aware of the competing pressures—and their sources—that will be brought to bear on their classrooms. Different groups of students will require different management and instructional techniques, expectations for student success with standardized curriculum will be high, administrators will be keeping close watch, and planning new lessons day after day will be taxing. As such, Leslie's analysis is sociologically astute when she says, "We have to learn how to adapt, transition, and balance everything going on inside our classrooms."

Understanding teacher education from a sociological perspective is the primary purpose of this book. From this standpoint, we must focus on the ways that people's everyday lives are both enabled and constrained by the social environments within which they find themselves. All social environments are structured. In other words, they have rules, and these rules promote some attitudes and behaviors while discouraging or prohibiting others. In this case, if "teaching is a game," as Leslie characterizes it, then the rules of the game come from the ways that teacher education and public schools are socially structured. These rules of the game are both formal and informal. The formal laws and policies that are relevant for teacher candidates include state licensure requirements that teacher candidates must fulfill, degree requirements in higher education they must satisfy for certification, curriculum standards in K–12 education they must demonstrate they can teach, and existing laws and bureaucratic rules in schools that structure their time and interactions with students. Informal rules are also important, and often take the form of cultural and professional norms for teachers' behavior. These include a strong service ethic and commitment to children's well-being as primary forms of motivation, norms for professional appearance in the ways teachers dress and present themselves, and traditional norms concerning gender that shape different expectations regarding appropriate teacher–student interactions. In sum, teachers have a lot of rules to follow, and most of these rules are externally imposed upon teachers from sources rooted outside the classroom (i.e., state and federal law, colleges and universities, bureaucratic school and district administrations, and preexisting cultural norms).

How do prospective teachers make sense of these multiple and competing forces? Much has been studied, written, and debated about the effectiveness of teacher education,[3] but fewer studies examine how teacher education itself is embedded within, and shaped by, complex interconnections between the broader social institutions of society, or what that looks like from the perspective of people experiencing it. I spent over 15 months going through teacher education with nearly 50 college seniors while they were completing their last year of formal teacher training in a nationally ranked School of Education at a public university in the Midwest, a university that I refer to as "State University." In the process, I documented these teacher candidates' experiences, and the perspectives about teaching that they formed along the way, with a degree of detail that few non-teachers have seen. As I show in the chapters to come, teacher candidates creatively respond to a wide range of conditions that structure the most common routes of preparation and entry into teaching. One of the key themes that emerges in my analysis is the emphasis that prospective teachers— and those who train them—place on adaptation. Indeed, they are trained to valorize the ability to adapt and modify one's course of action depending on what particular situations require, and define ongoing adaptation as a fundamental responsibility of teachers. I call this perspective the *injunction to adapt*, because teacher candidates are indoctrinated into it as both a practical and ethical imperative for effective teaching. I argue that this injunction to adapt is a perspective that emerges out of the processes through which teacher educators and teacher candidates make sense of the "rules of the game" for teachers in education. I also argue throughout the book that it serves as the basis for what I call a *professional culture of ambivalence* among teacher candidates, a shared sense that ambiguity, contingency, individuality, and responsiveness are inherent to the work.

In many ways, the rules for teachers are in flux. With the passage of the No Child Left Behind Act in early 2001 teachers and schools alike have been held more strictly accountable for measured outcomes of student performance on an increasingly standardized curriculum. Since then, other policy changes have come along that have increased pressure on teacher performance. The United States Department of Education's Race to the Top initiative largely shifted accountability to teachers, incentivizing local school districts to measure and evaluate teacher effects on student academic performance.[4] The recent passage of the Every Student Succeeds Act (ESSA) has returned much of the authority in enforcing accountability back to states, but accountability lives on in many ways, including ongoing forms of standardized testing and efforts in most states to link teacher evaluations with measures of student performance.[5] Teacher education programs have been affected by these policy shifts as well. Completing teacher education programs and their certification requirements was the primary means by which teachers fulfilled the mandate of No Child Left Behind that all teachers be "highly qualified." At the same time, university-based teacher education programs have long been criticized for failing to adequately prepare new teachers to succeed, especially in an era of accountability.[6] Alternative training and certification programs have emerged, most notably Teach for America, which recruits academically accomplished college students to commit to a short-term teaching assignment in low-performing schools. Meanwhile, amid all of these changes in the policy landscape, teachers are encountering increasing racial, ethnic, and religious diversity among their students due to ongoing demographic change in the United States. To be sure, beginning a career in teaching in the 21st century means entering a dynamic institutional environment.

However, many of the conditions that structure teachers' work have been around a long time and show little sign they will change. Alongside an increasing standardization of curriculum,[7] public education remains free and compulsory. This forces a great deal of heterogeneity in student skills, backgrounds, capacities, and interests into teachers' classrooms. Despite sporadic and local efforts at team teaching, it remains true that the overwhelming majority of teachers work alone with groups of students in their classrooms (an organizational condition of schools known in sociology as the "egg-crate" model[8]). Despite the growth in popularity of alternative certification programs like Teach for America, it remains true that the majority of people who become teachers obtain certification through university-based teacher education (UBTE).[9] The basic features of these programs are consistent. Most of them require blocks of courses in instructional methods that are informed by educational psychology, and culminate in a student-teaching component where teacher candidates teach full-time in real classrooms. Finally, while student populations are increasing in diversity, teachers are not. The majority are women, and the majority are white.

In the remaining pages of this chapter, I discuss the key institutions that shape teacher education and outline the theory that informs the analysis in this study. I also explain why the sociological perspective I take in this book offers an important alternative to what we already know about teacher education. While this book is not centrally about what makes effective teachers, the empirical findings should inform what we mean when we talk about effective teachers. Rather, this is a book about the social psychology of becoming a teacher, and how that process is shaped by the social environment within which it unfolds.

Teacher Education and Its Institutional Environment

Social institutions can be difficult to define. The word "institution" gets used colloquially with a number of meanings. One might refer to a particular university as an institution of higher education (e.g., Harvard University).[10] In other contexts, people may refer to a historically and culturally iconic place, or even a person, as an institution (e.g., Yankee Stadium or Babe Ruth). While these uses of the concept are informal and often imprecise, they do capture some key elements of sociological definitions of institutions. Namely, institutions stand the test of time, and they represent a cultural ideal that people collectively hold dear. People who have never set foot on Harvard's campus or attended a game in Yankee Stadium know they are sites of academic and athletic excellence, respectively. Likewise, generations of people who never saw Babe Ruth play will routinely cite his stats and retell legendary stories of his heroics on a baseball field. In short, institutions matter to us because they provide enduring meanings for what is important and legitimate in our world.

In more academic terms, institutions are often considered macro-level social systems that are stable over time and stretch across particular locales. The ways they are structured provide the "rules of the game," so to speak, in different arenas of social life. From a sociological standpoint, it is higher education that is a social institution; Harvard is one of many colleges and universities that are part of this institution. Likewise, baseball is an institution; Yankee Stadium and Babe Ruth are parts of the institution, albeit famous ones. The rules of higher education bear striking resemblance across different college campuses. Traditionally, it takes four years to complete a bachelor's degree, students major in particular courses of study, there are multiple degree requirements to fulfill, etc. Certainly, each college and its campus has its own unique culture, atmosphere, and demographics,[11] but the basic academic and governance features are fairly consistent from place to place. To be sure, the caliber and quality of baseball played in Yankee Stadium is distinct from that played on Little League fields, but it is clear that baseball is happening in both places because the rules are the same. Moreover, people tend to take for granted that institutional rules are legitimate. Most college students do not question or challenge the requirement that they must declare a major area of study; they just declare one (or more). Most people who learn, play, and become a fan of baseball do not question or challenge the rule that a batter is out on the third strike. That's just the way it is, and that's the way it has always been.[12]

Most aspects of daily life are institutional. Democracy, capitalism, healthcare, criminal justice, religion, family, and education are all social institutions. Their rules influence different aspects of people's everyday routines in myriad ways. Teachers' work lives, while shaped by a combination of institutions, are most directly impacted by educational institutions. The schools where they work and the teacher education programs where they are certified are embedded within broader social systems of K–12 education and higher education. These institutions structure the responsibilities, expectations, and capacities of teachers, both as individuals and as a group, in ways that people often take for granted as legitimate.[13] Teachers give lessons in different subjects to groups of students in their own classrooms, they praise students for good behavior and discipline them for misbehavior, they give students grades on their assignments, they communicate with parents about their children's progress, and they routinely send kids home with homework to do. That's just the way it is, and that's the way it's always been. Individual teachers certainly vary in their personalities and preferred techniques, but if they are to succeed in this career, they must find ways of fulfilling these institutionalized roles and responsibilities.

Teacher education is very clearly designed to indoctrinate incoming teachers into these institutionalized roles and responsibilities. Though it has not always been the case,[14] UBTE is the most common pathway of training and entry into teaching, and has been for decades.[15] Higher education, therefore, is a key institution that shapes teacher education. For many people, the process of becoming a teacher happens in conjunction with going to college as an undergraduate, fulfilling degree requirements, taking classes from university faculty, and experiencing the social scene of campus life. For better or worse, this means that much of the preparation for teaching is academic in nature.[16] The classes that teacher candidates take as education majors are similar in form to the classes they take in other subjects in departments across campus. Likewise, the content of their classes (i.e., instructional methods, educational psychology, the social and cultural foundations of education, technology in instruction, etc.) is very often the research subject of the faculty and graduate students who teach them. Many education faculty have K–12 teaching experience themselves; many do not. In either case, scholarship and research are central to the mission and broader educational endeavor of UBTE programs, as one would expect in higher education.[17]

Prevailing theory and findings in educational research and related academic disciplines, then, strongly inform the ways that UBTE programs teach prospective teachers about the institutionalized roles and responsibilities of teaching. In particular, student-centered or "constructivist" pedagogy tends to be foregrounded in UBTE. While there are many interpretations of what is meant by constructivist pedagogy, such philosophical approaches to instruction stress the importance of engaging students as active participants in learning, and stress attention to diversity among students in terms of aptitude, interests, predispositions, skill level, and age (as well as racial, ethnic, and cultural diversity). Given such diversity, instructional practice must be tailored to the unique characteristics that each student, or group of students, brings to the classroom in order to actively engage students in a learning process that is relevant to them and empower students to take ownership of their own education, according to this philosophy. This approach to instruction is rooted in research and theory in educational psychology, which often conceptualizes childhood development and intelligence as highly individualistic.[18] It also

dovetails with educational research that underscores the importance of multiculturalism in education to promote racial and ethnic tolerance, inclusion, and
multicultural appreciation among students. Both educational psychology and
multiculturalism are cornerstones of UBTE curricula in Schools of Education in
the United States.[19]

It is through exposure to this type of curricula, and the early training in
instruction it informs, that adaptation first emerges as a fundamental element
of teaching in the perspectives of teacher candidates. In short, they are taught
that it is their responsibility to adapt to the needs of their students, and those
needs are diverse. But the formal curriculum and instruction they receive in
UBTE is only one source of the injunction to adapt. Their experiences inside
public schools, where they both observe other teachers and perform their student teaching, also reinforce this perspective. Public education as an institution provides the prospective "rules of the game" for teacher candidates.
Chief among these rules nowadays is accountability.[20] Indeed, teacher candidates are routinely instructed in the realities of accountability mandates
and standards-based instruction and assessment that await them in public
schools. Another reality of public education—compulsory attendance—adds
to the challenge of standards-based instruction and assessment. To be sure,
compulsory attendance law exists for a number of good reasons, but one of
its effects is that schools and teachers contend with enormous heterogeneity
among the students they are assigned to teach.[21] In many ways, constructivist pedagogy is designed to help address diversity in knowledge, skills, and
background among students, but nonetheless bringing groups of students to
similar levels of academic proficiency is made more complex if students in the
group bring varying levels of proficiency to the classroom from the beginning.
Teacher candidates observe these classroom dynamics firsthand in their training. In conjunction with the ideals of constructivist pedagogy, the practical
uncertainties of classroom interaction and the prospect of having to balance
accountability policies with the instructional complexities created by compulsory attendance also foster an injunction to adapt among teacher candidates.
In other words, teacher candidates are confronted with a dilemma in their
prospective work at hand: how do I teach groups of students who vary widely
in their academic skill and social development in a way that brings them all
to a state-mandated level of academic proficiency? As I show in the empirical chapters to follow, the answer offered them by their formal training is to
continually adapt and modify the ways they teach a standardized curriculum
to meet the needs of different students who often behave in the classroom in
unpredictable ways.

It would be incomplete to examine the ways that the teaching profession[22]
is socially structured without including gender in the analysis. Since the 19th
century, teachers as a group have been dominated in number by women.[23] In

her detailed history of "America's most embattled profession," Dana Goldstein[24] shows how the gender composition of teaching, and women's subordinate social status historically, have long influenced aspects of teachers' work. Persistent gender discrimination has for generations played a role in maintaining stubborn limits on teachers' professional status and compensation.[25] Moreover, traditional gender norms tend to sustain the gender composition of teaching, as people's common assumptions that women are "naturally" well-suited to work with children shape recruitment and retention.[26] In this sense, gender is institutional, as traditional gender norms that have persisted with time shape people's attitudes, expectations, and behaviors in patterned ways.[27] The institutionalized norms and practices related to gender are just as important for understanding how teachers define appropriate work-related action as are the institutionalized norms and practices of education.

By focusing on the role of social institutions, my study offers an important alternative to much of the existing research and policy discourse on teachers and teacher education, which currently focus heavily on their individual capacities. Especially from a policy standpoint, identifying the best teachers and the worst teachers, rewarding and sanctioning them respectively, has become the primary interest in decision-making concerning teachers at the district, state, and federal levels over the last eight to ten years.[28] From a research standpoint, there has been a concomitant proliferation of research studies that seek to measure the qualities of individual teachers and the value they add to student performance.[29] Likewise, the intrinsic qualities of teacher education programs have come under similar scrutiny. There is an intense focus on "best practices" in education research on teacher education, and attention to the various successes and failures of different programs and approaches.[30] Even the most high-profile alternative to university-based teacher education, Teach for America, relies on recruiting individuals with a strong service ethic who are the best and the brightest academically, in the hopes that such a corps of exceptional people can positively impact at-risk students in low-performing schools.[31]

Across the policy landscape—from the United States Department of Education to Teach for America—this emphasis on the value added by teachers through their individual skills and "competencies"[32] is premised upon the idea that producing better teachers is a key means through which we can shape educational institutions for the better.[33] Instead, I examine how institutions shape the ways we produce teachers, and how new teachers make sense of the multiple and competing demands they face in educating students. This is not to say that I reject the idea that schools need good teachers, nor that I reject as futile any efforts to improve teacher education. On the contrary, we know—and frequently hear in mainstream media coverage of education—that teachers are the most influential "school-based" factor affecting student performance.[34] Moreover, the chapters that follow illustrate a number of concrete ways that teacher candidates could be better prepared for their first year of teaching than is often the case. Rather, my aim is to expand upon the prevailing discourse about teacher education and teachers' work by directing attention to issues that have been too often left out of the ongoing public conversation.[35] The intrinsic features of teacher education programs, and the individual characteristics of the people within them, are indeed important, but both the people and the programs are all situated within broader social structures that shape them in patterned ways. Orientation to the institutions that constitute the social environment for teacher education, and the ways that prospective teachers make sense of institutional rules in the day-to-day life of teacher education, helps paint a fuller and more nuanced picture of the realities of becoming a teacher than most people typically see.

Such an analysis comes at an important point in time for teacher education and the teaching profession. Many stakeholders in education policy concerning teachers—district and school administrators, teacher educators, and teachers themselves—are maligning recent evidence of teacher shortages across the country, as well as declines in enrollment in teacher education programs.[36] In addition to the immediate staffing problems this creates in a wide range of public schools, concerns are growing about the future of teaching as fewer young adults are pursuing it as a career path (a reported 30% decline from 2008–2009 to 2013–2014) and more experienced teachers are walking away in increasing numbers (in states such as Arizona, California, Indiana, and Kansas, issuing of teachers licenses has declined as much as 50%, including veterans, from 2009–2010 to 2013–2014).[37] Speculation abounds about the sources of these problems, and debates regarding what to do about them are ongoing.[38] Certain economic trends appear to have had an influence, such as the impact that the Great Recession and its slow recovery has had on the availability of teaching positions, as well as anxiety about growing student-loan debt and the prospects of paying for it on a teacher's salary. But there also appears to be a growing dissatisfaction and resentment among current teachers that their work has become too controlled by standardized testing and the enforcement of accountability mandates at the state and local levels. In the eyes of many teachers, their instructional autonomy has been stripped away at the same time that they have been asked to do more while making less.[39] The analysis in the following chapters reveals key sources of this problem in teaching that has emerged in recent years. In short, the injunction to adapt requires the preservation of at least a degree of instructional autonomy. From the perspective of teacher candidates, adaptation to different contingencies, especially the behavior and interests of students, is an ongoing, dynamic process, one that cannot be uniformly scripted a priori. Because teacher candidates define the injunction to adapt as fundamental to effective teaching and one of their primary responsibilities, work environments that they feel undermine their capacity to engage in adaption cut at the very core meanings that teachers associate with how and why they should do their jobs. I revisit this issue in the concluding chapter, and discuss in further detail that, when understood from a sociological perspective, the current malaise felt by many teachers should come as little surprise.

Creativity and Constraint in Becoming a Teacher

People are both causes and consequences of their social environments.[40] Institutions certainly enable and constrain actions and attitudes, but people actively make sense of the "rules of the game" in their lives. To elaborate on my earlier analogy to baseball, while people take for granted that a batter is out on the third strike, players and umpires alike routinely challenge, interpret, and argue whether or not a given pitch qualifies as a strike or a ball. They do so in inter-action with each other as the game unfolds. The rules of baseball remain con-sistent and players must abide by them, but each game—wherever and among whomever it is played—is contested, contingent, and creative in its sequence of events as well as its outcome. Players even modify and manipulate the rules themselves at times; kids playing ball on a sandlot with no backstop might enact their own local prohibition against stealing a base on a wild pitch or passed ball. Moreover, different players and teams approach similar situations with varied strategies, and they learn a wider variety of approaches to game situations as they accumulate more experience. People interpret the same situations differ-ently in the course of a game. The player who drives in the winning run is a hero to her teammates and fans, but she is a villain to those of the opposing team. In short, baseball transcends time and places, but for it to exist beyond an abstract set of rules and strategies, people have to play it. And when people play it, they actively and creatively reproduce the rules of baseball in each instantiated situ-ation in which they choose to play together.

This is the perspective on social institutions shared by the two theoretical frameworks that inform the study. The first is itself a theory of institutional functioning known as inhabited institutionalism.[41] The second is a theory of socialization developed in the sociology of childhood known as interpretive reproduction.[42] Both attend to the ways that people are active agents whose sense-making through interaction helps enact the larger social structures in which they are immersed, even though they are simultaneously constrained by the same social structures. Engaging both theories in an analysis of professional socialization offers something that prior empirical studies in organizational sociology, the sociology of education, and life course sociology do not. It brings the theoretical precision of how organizations and institutions function into dialogue with the theoretical insight that socialization is shaped concomitantly by multiple social institutions through the ways people make sense of transitions in their lives.

Institutions as Inhabited

Inhabited institutionalism emphasizes the importance of analyzing people's active meaning-making for understanding how institutions and individuals mutually constitute each other. In other words, institutions function reciprocally from the ground up *and* the top down, as people actively construct the meaning of legitimate action via local interactions in ways that are enabled and constrained by the structured conditions of their environment. From this perspective, Tim Hallett and Marc Ventresca[43] explain that while institutions "provide the guidelines for social interactions," they are simultaneously "constituted and propelled forward by interactions that give them force and meaning." Empirical studies informed by inhabited institutionalism have analyzed a wide range of organizations as the specific locales where people inhabit institutions, including public schools,[44] private learning centers,[45] natural foods co-ops,[46] social service agencies,[47] micro-finance,[48] and drug courts.[49] In addition, recent studies examine how people inhabit multiple institutions simultaneously. Lisa Nunn,[50] for instance, shows how the organizational culture of different high schools and the stratified system of higher education are both brought to bear on the ways that high school students define academic success. Likewise, in my own prior work with Bradley Levinson,[51] we analyze the ways that long-standing residents in new destination communities make sense of multiple institutions (i.e., government, labor market, education, and healthcare) in order to respond to local demographic change brought about by immigration. As such, inhabited institutionalism has proven a useful lens for examining the interconnections between different social institutions that people enact and sustain in their everyday lives, interconnections such as those between education and gender that are relevant to my analysis of teacher education.

According to long-standing theory known as new institutionalism, institutional rules are not just guidelines for action. They are also cultural ideals that people tend to rationalize and take for granted as legitimate, something John Meyer and Brian Rowan call "institutional myths."[52] These myths are the formal structure of institutions, and adhering to them is a key way that particular organizations like schools maintain their legitimacy in the eyes of the wider public.[53] Accountability is an institutional myth of public education, as is compulsory education. In the case of accountability, it exists concretely as a set of policies that ties rewards and sanctions to measurable performance of both schools and teachers. It is also a rationalized ideal, as accountability policies are predicated on the notion that schools and teachers should be accountable for their work with students.[54] Likewise, compulsory education as an institutional myth exists in the formal laws that mandate all children go to school. It is also predicated on the widely held value that all children should have equal educational opportunity, and this not only benefits the life chances of all individuals but is essential to sustain a vibrant democracy and prospering economy overall. The degree to which people within particular organizations actually adhere to institutional myths in their daily work practices—also known as "coupling" between rules and practice[55]—tends to vary substantially. Loose coupling tends to stave off the uncertainty and threats to a school's legitimacy in the eyes of the public by masking any potential inconsistencies between what teachers do in the classroom and what they are supposed to be doing (i.e., are teachers actually producing measurable progress in their students' achievement?). In many schools, local enforcement of accountability has greatly reduced loose coupling between policy and practice.

In his study of an urban elementary school, Tim Hallett advances an inhabited view of institutions in his analysis of how "the myth of accountability was made incarnate" when new school leadership authoritatively enforced the standardized curricular and instructional mandates of accountability in the daily practices of the school's teaching staff. Turmoil ensued, as "the recoupling disrupted the routines that had ordered the teachers' world, sparking epistemic distress and a series of interpretive responses that reconstructed a set of meanings and defined the emergent battle."[56] By examining the ways teachers actively make sense of institutional myths, Hallett brings the theoretical insights of symbolic interactionism into analytic dialogue with new institutionalism's emphasis on the ways that institutional myths structure organizational life. From the standpoint of symbolic interactionism, "an institution does not function automatically because of some inner dynamics or system requirements; it functions because people at different points do something, and what they do is a result of how they define the situation in which they are called on to act."[57] Rather than engender standardization, uniformity, and cohesion, as is a chief goal of accountability, this version of its implementation resulted in chaos, uncertainty, and distress among teachers based upon the ways they defined recoupling and its effects on their work. As Hallett explains, "These are the kind of local, constitutive processes that inhabit institutions,"[58] and we must be attentive to the meanings people construct in local settings that serve "as locales for reproducing and revising prevailing institutional myths."[59]

Recent scholarship on educational institutions elaborates on the reproduction of prevailing institutional myths as an inhabited process. Lisa Nunn shows how high school students reproduce both the organizational culture of their respective schools, as well as existing academic hierarchies in transitions to college, through the ways they define success.[60] While Nunn finds that students largely reaffirm prevailing meanings about success that are structured into the routine policies and practices of their schools, she also clearly shows how students are active agents in this process, appropriating existing ideals and using them to craft their own "success identities."[61] My analysis of the injunction to adapt and professional culture of ambivalence among teacher candidates captures a similar phenomenon. Though the injunction to adapt represents a definition of appropriate work-related action for teachers that is structured into various elements of teacher education and school work environments, the ways that teacher candidates adapt in particular situations are unique and innovative displays of their own agency and sense-making.[62] They tend to align their instruction closely with curriculum requirements while continually modifying instructional techniques, a combination of both tight coupling and loose coupling between classroom practice and standards-based policies that has become quite common in the accountability era.[63] As such, the people and processes that inhabit institutions can serve to maintain the stability and legitimacy of institutional myths in some cases, as well as challenge and disrupt them in others.[64]

I advance inhabited institutionalism along these lines by showing how teacher candidates engage in both purposeful and routine forms of action and sense-making as they proceed through their training and respond to institutional myths in education. Teacher candidates take for granted that a variety of rules concerning teachers' work are legitimate, but purposefully modify and adapt the ways they comply with those rules to suit their immediate interests and needs. For instance, a routine part of their training is writing lesson plans in ways that explicitly articulate the "state standards" they will cover with each lesson. They are required to do this as part of their instructional methods courses, and they are expected to document their lessons in their student teaching. Teacher candidates accept as legitimate the need to comply with this formal requirement of accountability, but they also define their discretion and autonomy in determining how they comply with curriculum requirements as equally legitimate. In other words, they know they must cover curriculum standards, but how they do it is up to them, consistent with the institutional myth of compulsory education that prioritizes adaptation to the diverse needs, abilities, and prior skills of students so as to accommodate all learners. Teacher candidates are not homogenous in exactly how they conform to these institutional mandates, but it is still conformity to a great extent. However, through the culture of ambivalence they develop through their professional socialization, I show that teacher candidates define a small degree of failure in their work as an inevitable part of teaching, which is itself a modification of the meaning behind accountability and compulsory education. Viewing institutional conformity as inhabited in this sense is crucial for understanding the roles teachers play in affecting both stability and change in education. Moreover, it sheds new light on an old and perplexing problem for lawmakers and policy analysts in education: documented teacher compliance with reform agendas does not always translate into the reform's intended outcomes.[65]

Femininity and Masculinity as Institutional Myths

Education as a social institution is structured, in part, by the institutional myths of accountability and compulsory education. Gender also operates as a social institution, and we can conceptualize masculinity and femininity as institutional myths that act as the structure of gender as an institution. Like other institutional myths, teacher candidates make sense of femininity and masculinity in a variety of ways, conforming to gender performances based on rationalized meanings in some ways while modifying and challenging them in others. Analysis of gender as an inhabited institution, I argue, offers fruitful insights into the ways professional socialization is a complex process of active gender conformity that can include subtle forms of resistance. At the level of interaction, gender is a social category through which people coordinate behavior with one another.[66] In this sense, Cecilia Ridgeway theorizes that gender acts as a "primary frame" for people's sense-making and interaction, as it provides "cultural knowledge that we all assume we all know" which acts as "rules" for behavior.[67] Gendered behavior is rooted in shared assumptions, and people "do gender" by following these rules for gender performances that play out in face-to-face interactions.[68]

While doing gender is a process that transpires via interaction, gender performances also serve to "sustain, reproduce, and render legitimate the institutional arrangements that are based on sex category."[69] Attention to both the institutional and interactional dimensions of gender "encourages analysis of how institutions and individuals mutually constitute each other," as Patricia Yancey Martin explains.[70] Indeed, gender operates across macro-structural and micro-interactional distinctions.[71] Additionally, the multidimensional qualities of gender facilitate its interconnection with other institutions, and the actors and practices that constitute them. As Ridgeway explains, gender "typically acts to bias in gendered directions the performance of behaviors undertaken in the name of more concrete, foregrounded organizational roles or identities."[72] People do gender as they perform other institutionally defined roles in their lives, such as their professional roles. Much of the literature on the institutional dimensions of gender tends to emphasize the unreflective ways in which people do gender by doing other things in their lives, especially when behavior is gender conforming. Emily Fairchild is somewhat of an exception by showing how the institutional dimension of gender becomes "visible" often when its institutional prescriptions are inconsistent with individual circumstances, motivating people to construct alternative meanings. I argue in the following analysis for the benefits of attending to the purposeful ways people enact meanings about gender and sexuality as they carry out other roles in their lives, even in the analysis of gender-conforming behavior and sense-making.

Educational institutions have long been sites of socialization to the rationalized ideals that structure traditional gender performances. Indeed, C. J. Pascoe documents in vivid and forceful analysis how heteronormative sexualized
meanings of masculinity are intertwined with a wide range of high school
practices and adolescent cultures in ways that subjugate women and repudi-
ate homosexuality.[73] Additional scholarship echoes these findings, and shows
how schools serve as environments for students to creatively reproduce gender norms that valorize sexual aggression among young boys and coerce young
girls to tolerate harassment.[74] Socialization processes in early childhood prime
children for these traditional gender performances as well,[75] and institutional
arrangements in higher education also serve to reinforce these norms and
related inequalities.[76] Likewise, scholars document time and again that adults
who work in educational institutions regularly condone (if not promote) such
gendered behaviors, often viewing them as "normal," "harmless," and things "to
be expected" among children.[77] There is ample evidence that the people involved
in the daily routines of formal schooling accept as "common sense" that men
and boys are sexual aggressors, and that women and girls must adapt their own
actions to account for what is frequently defined as inevitable behavior.

It is well documented, then, that heteronormative sexualized meanings
about masculinity and femininity are widely assumed as legitimate bases for
action in the everyday processes through which schools operate. While these
findings in the sociology of education are consistent with scholarship that
characterizes gender as a social institution, little work has engaged closely with
institutional theory to examine how gender operates as an institution.[78] Much
like other rationalized cultural ideals that often operate as taken-for-granted
assumptions people draw upon as the basis for their actions,[79] femininity
and masculinity typically shape people's active sense-making in unreflective
ways.[80] Moreover, meanings linked with these rationalized ideals endure with
time and span different locales.[81] Elements of masculinity as an institutional
myth include heteronormative sexual aggression, as well as physical toughness,
emotional detachment, and innate capacities for leadership and overall competence. Elements of femininity as an institutional myth include heteronormative
beauty standards for women, as well as sexual purity, passiveness, emotional
responsiveness and intuition, and innate capacities for nurturing.[82] Though
there are clear and persistent patterns in gender norms, no two people "do"
femininity or masculinity in exactly the same ways, nor are people only doing
one set of these rationalized meanings at a time. Rather, people inhabit traditional gender performances through their interaction and meaning-making
in everyday life, making gender fluid in how people enact it. This can include
gender-conforming behaviors and beliefs that normalize gender conformity,
but it can also include behavior and beliefs that modify, challenge, and even
reject rationalized gender norms.

When focused on UBTE, this theoretical lens—one that views gender as an inhabited institution—helps shed light on the complex ways in which gendered meanings undergird the definitions of teaching practice and professionalism that teacher candidates develop. To be sure, rationalized ideals of masculinity and femininity are often expressed as gender stereotypes for behavior. They are not factual descriptions of innate gender qualities. But as institutional myths, they operate as taken-for-granted assumptions that inform everyday interactions in a variety of ways. Rationalized ideals about gender are not "real" in the sense that they reflect essential qualities that different groups of people possess, but they are indeed "real" in the ways they shape people's expectations and assumptions for how people will interact in everyday life. Like other institutional myths, people inhabit them in the ways they modify and reproduce their meanings and relevance in the course of everyday routines and interactions. For teacher candidates, they inhabit gender and education concurrently through everyday instructional routines and interactions with students and other school actors.

Professional Socialization as Interpretive Reproduction

Teacher education is a form of professional socialization, or the process through which newcomers are trained and transitioned into membership within a profession or occupation. This certainly involves the acquisition of technical knowledge and skills necessary to conduct the actual work tasks of the profession, but it also involves indoctrination into the ethics that structure members' behavior and provide definitions of professionalism in the context of their work.[83] Professional socialization shapes people's perspectives and identities as much as it equips them with skills.[84] People learn and develop collective definitions of their responsibilities as members of the profession, but this process is neither rote nor linear. In their classic study of medical student socialization, Becker, Geer, Hughes, and Strauss characterize the professional socialization process as much more complex, driven by the ways students figure out how to confront problems endemic to their medical school training and prospective work as physicians:

> Students collectively set the level and direction of their efforts to learn . . . these levels and directions . . . are the working out in practice of the perspectives from which the students view their day-to-day problems in relation to their long-term goals. The perspectives, themselves collectively developed, are organizations of ideas and actions. The actions derive their rationale from ideas, and the ideas are sustained by success in action. [85]

Professional socialization is a messy process of sense-making about dilemmas unique to a profession (practically, ethically, and emotionally), and this plays out through ongoing trial and error. Becker et al. show in vivid detail that the meanings people construct about their work develop alongside action and interaction as they prepare for, and attempt, new tasks in a new role in new situations in new settings.

Ongoing interpretation is fundamental to socialization processes throughout the life course, but more recent scholarship has focused greater attention on the relationship between people's interpretive processes and the wider social structures that enable and constrain socialization. In William Corsaro's work on the sociology of childhood, he conceptualizes socialization as a process of "interpretive reproduction."[86] According to this conceptualization:

> . . . children are not simply internalizing society and culture, but are actively contributing to cultural production and change. The term also implies that children, by their very participation in society, are constrained by existing social structure and social reproduction.[87]

Such an understanding is not only readily applicable to professional socialization at later life course stages, but it is also remarkably consistent with inhabited institutionalism for understanding the relationship between people's sense-making and institutional rules for behavior. Viewing socialization as interpretive reproduction, we see that even though people are creative agents in how they define transitions in their lives, this does not necessarily mean they always challenge existing social structure or generate novel ideas. At the same time, the fact that people contribute to the reproduction of existing institutional myths does not make the processes through which they do so any less a product of their own agency.[88]

Another benefit of conceptualizing professional socialization as interpretive reproduction is the analytic attention to the temporal elements of social transitions. People draw upon prior experience to make sense of their daily interactions, and they also attend to the future as well.[89] Corsaro's work with Luisa Molinari[90] identifies what they call "priming events" in their research on children's peer cultures. Priming events "involve activities in which children, by their very participation, attend prospectively to ongoing or anticipated changes in their lives." Priming events can include formal activities as well as informal interactions among people. In either case, priming events are observable interactions that engender prospective sense-making. Moreover, they allow for empirical study of what Robert Merton[91] calls "anticipatory socialization," through which people develop the values and perspectives shared among "groups in which one is not yet engaged but which one is likely to enter." Teacher education, like any professional socialization process, is an ongoing set of priming experiences. Teacher candidates are constantly and collectively thinking prospectively, and making sense of how things will be when they are teaching in the future. At the same time, their past experiences inform their presently evolving sense-making about teaching as well.[92] Attention to priming, and how it is situated within people's ongoing experience, makes for a very useful way of examining how teacher candidates inhabit educational institutions via their professional socialization.

A Professional Culture of Ambivalence

While the injunction to adapt is a product of the local organizational culture at State University's UBTE program, it does serve to structure people's sense-making within the local environment. In this sense, it operates as a meso-level organizational lens through which the more macro-cultural institutional myths of compulsory education, accountability, and traditional gender performances are brought to bear on teacher candidates' meaning-making about teaching. As such, teacher candidates also inhabit the injunction to adapt and modify its meaning in the active ways they make sense of its relevance to the practical dilemmas of instruction that they confront in ongoing interactions.

My examination of the social routines in UBTE that prime teacher candidates for future work reveals how the injunction to adapt serves as the lynchpin of meaning for a professional culture of ambivalence among teacher candidates. In other words, the commitment to adaptation teacher candidates develop as they make sense of multiple institutional conditions engenders a concomitant sense of ambivalence about their prospective work. Teacher candidates come to share the perspective that teaching is dynamic work inclusive of multiple approaches; adaptable to different students, situations, and styles; and influenced by a variety of forces beyond teachers' control. As such, from teacher candidates' points of view, there is a wide variety of effective instructional strategies, none of them can be perfectly scripted beforehand, and there are often limits to what any good strategy can accomplish.

I show how this sense of ambivalence is collectively shared and emerges out of the ways that teacher candidates make sense of institutional myths that structure the routines of their training and transitions into their roles as teachers. In this regard, my analysis of professional culture is consistent with prior research on professional socialization that conceptualizes culture as "collective understandings" developed among trainees while playing student roles.[93] It is also consistent with sociological understandings of the role of culture in childhood socialization. William Corsaro defines children's peer cultures as "a stable set of activities or routines, artifacts, values, and concerns that children produce and share in interaction with peers."[94] By bringing inhabited institutionalism into the analysis, we see how broader institutionalized ideals structure the stable sets of routines through which teacher candidates develop values and concerns about the work and responsibilities of teaching, thereby producing a professional culture that is both local and "extra local."[95]

As I show in the chapters to come, this shared sense of ambivalence is not the product of an absence or deficiency in teacher candidates' professional socialization. At least they do not define it that way. Rather, it is rooted firmly in the injunction to adapt, which itself is rooted firmly in the rationalized ideals that structure the institutional environment of their professional enterprise. Moreover, as I argue in the concluding chapter, critically examining the institutional sources of teacher candidates' shared ambivalence about teaching has the potential to illuminate broader societal ambivalences about "the right way" to go about addressing some of our most fundamental and enduring social problems.

Organization of the Book

In the chapters to follow, I present the findings of my ethnographic study on the institutional demands of becoming a teacher. In the analysis, I feature the experiences and perspectives of 49 teacher candidates. They include women and men in elementary and secondary education and across subject matters. All teacher candidates in the sample were white, largely a reflection of the racial composition of this teacher education program in which nearly 95% of total students were white during the year of data collection. Among those in secondary education, the sample includes candidates in the subject matters of math, language arts (English), and social studies. Within the overall sample are two sub-samples. The first—which I refer to as the focal sample—includes 11 teacher candidates (7 women, 4 men) whom I followed throughout a 15-month period, regularly observing their coursework and student teaching and interviewing them multiple times. The remaining 38 teacher candidates (27 women, 11 men)—whom I refer to as the cohort sample—also include people across grade level and subject matters. These were individuals taking the same courses at the same stage of the training process as those in the focal sample. I included them in participant observation and informal interviews, but I did not follow them over the entire window of time in the same way as I did with the focal sample.

The majority of teacher candidates are originally from various parts of the Midwestern state for which State University is the flagship, public university. Seven of the members of the focal sample, for instance, are from State U's home state, and the others are from neighboring states in the Midwest. All teacher candidates were of traditional college age at the time of data collection; as college seniors, they were all in their early twenties. Outside of their formal training to become teachers, their lives were not unlike those of many college students. Some of them were members of sororities and fraternities on campus; nearly all of them worked summers; many of them (though not all) enjoyed aspects of campus life that gave State U its party-school reputation; most of them were staunch supporters of State U's high-profile athletic teams. Though I did not obtain overall academic performance measures from them, all of them reported grade-point averages in the "A" to "B" range with some of them solid

"A" students. Everyone in the focal sample characterized their family socioeconomic background as middle-class.

In sum, the teacher candidates who constitute the empirical focus of this study are in no way idiosyncratic in their demographics, backgrounds, or life-course stage relative to the majority of people who become teachers. They are predominantly women; they are white middle-class; they are local to the region where they trained and planned to work; they are average to above-average students academically; they are young adults enjoying the college experience that coincides with their formal teacher training. To be sure, this group of teacher candidates is not a "representative sample" of the national teaching workforce in the United States,[96] but probability sampling is not an appropriate technique in ethnography. Rather, it is the training process these teacher candidates experienced that is consistent with the training process most people who become teachers experience, and there is little about their social backgrounds to suggest that the ways they make sense of UBTE are somehow idiosyncratic relative to that majority.[97]

The sequence and structure of the following chapters reflect the analytic strategy informed by the theoretical framework of inhabited institutionalism. In Chapter 1, I focus on the ways that the institutional myth of compulsory education, and the instructional philosophy of constructivist pedagogy, are expressed as part of the injunction to adapt in the formal training activities teacher candidates experience in the UBTE program at State University. In Chapter 2, I then focus on the ways teacher candidates inhabit these structured features of their training, and make sense of what it means to them to try to adapt to the needs of all students. In Chapter 3, I then turn attention to the ways the institutional myth of accountability also informs the injunction to adapt and gets expressed through the formal training activities that teacher candidates experience. In Chapter 4, I examine how teacher candidates inhabit accountability and modify its meaning as they confront the routine dilemmas of curriculum coverage and classroom control. In Chapter 5, I examine the injunction to adapt itself as a programmatic response to the competing pressures placed upon teachers by the institutional environment, and how teacher candidates inhabit this organizationally structured part of their training through the diversity of practices they develop in their early teaching experiences. Throughout the empirical chapters, I also examine the role of gender, and the various ways in which institutional myths of femininity and masculinity structure teacher candidates' formal training, as well as how teacher candidates inhabit traditional gender performances in the context of teaching. I conclude with Chapter 6, and discuss the implications of the book's empirical analysis for understanding current and future trends in the teaching workforce, as well as its implications for understanding the limits and possibilities of teacher education.

1

Compulsory Education
and Constructivist Pedagogy

[handwritten annotation: → University-based teacher education]

Research on UBTE has frequently been unflattering of its content and outcomes, and has often served as the basis for various policyholders in education
to level a wide range of criticisms at UBTE programs. Chief among these criticisms is that UBTE programs fail to equip new teachers with skill sets in proven
instructional techniques. Rather, diversity in instructional practices persists,
and new teachers appear to draw upon infinite sources of ideas and approaches
to inform their teaching.[1] It stands to reason that the diversity of instructional
practice among teachers reflects a lack of technical coherence within the profession, and this is driven in large part by formal training and induction processes that are haphazard, inconsistent, and mired in low standards. Indeed,
many people—researchers, policymakers, teachers, and teacher candidates
alike—have drawn such conclusions about teaching and teacher education.[2]
Arthur Levine, for example, characterizes UBTE programs as "governed by a
philosophy of 'let 100 flowers bloom.' Relativism is the rule."[3] However, when
examined in the context of the institutional environment within which UBTE
has developed, and for which prospective teachers train to enter, we begin to
see evidence that promoting diversity in instructional practice in teacher education is the product of a highly rationalized and structured set of responses to
concrete occupational realities, not just deficiencies in UBTE effectiveness or
professional competence.

Rather, the observable diversity of practice that is actively promoted in
UBTE, which can easily be interpreted as incoherence in UBTE curriculum, is
nonetheless quite consistent with prevailing philosophies of constructivist pedagogy. While there are many interpretations of this general approach to instruction, it does have clearly identifiable features. First and foremost, it requires
active participation among students in the learning process, usually in the form
of problem-solving, debate and discussion, or other hands-on activities that

draw upon students' own experiences to facilitate the learning of new knowledge. Second, such approaches to instruction also stress the importance of attention to diversity among students in terms of aptitude, interests, predispositions, skill level, as well as their cognitive, physical, and social development. Instructional practice must be tailored to the unique characteristics each student, or group of students, brings to the classroom in order to actively engage students in a learning process that is relevant to them and empower students to take ownership over their own education, according to this philosophy. Not only is this educational philosophy strongly influential in the teacher education program at State University, it also has a long history that reflects its institutionalization in UBTE more broadly.

From an institutional standpoint, constructivist pedagogy emerged and persists in large part as a programmatic response to the realities of compulsory education. Since the mass education movements that unfolded around the turn of the 20th century, compulsory attendance for all students has been an enduring feature of public education. Today, despite the "school choice" aspect of the accountability era intended to give parents more options for their children's schooling, it remains a legal mandate that children must be schooled. Of course, compulsory education exists for many very good reasons. Whether contributing to economic prosperity, ensuring a vibrant democracy, or sustaining a shared cultural history, the state has any number of interests in maintaining an educated citizenry. In fact, access to a free, public education is enshrined as one of the most basic of human rights, and public education systems have long been viewed as an irreplaceable component of nation-building.[4] As such, the legitimacy of compulsory education is all but unquestioned. Everyone goes to school; that's just the way it is, and that's the way it has been for a long time. Therefore, the historical development of constructivist pedagogy unfolded in a context in which teachers and schools were obligated to educate a population of students diverse in their backgrounds, abilities, interests, and aptitudes. This condition of schooling is universal for prospective teachers and teacher education programs broadly. But its local manifestation in the UBTE program at State University finds expression as an "injunction to adapt," as I call it, and teacher candidates are trained in developing a practical capacity for, and ethical commitment to, ongoing adaptation to student needs, behavior, and abilities.

Teacher Education's Roots in the Discipline of Psychology

Current understandings of constructivist pedagogy have their roots in the "progressive pedagogy" movement in education of nearly 100 years ago. Progressive pedagogy was perhaps most famously (though certainly not exclusively) developed and championed by John Dewey. In what was a radical departure from educational tradition at the turn of the 20th century, Dewey argued forcefully for "child-centered" instruction rather than conventional top-down direction from teacher to student in the form of rote memorization.[5] Himself a philosopher and psychologist,[6] Dewey was especially influenced by the work of psychologist William James, who saw a reciprocal relationship between cognitive processes and action, between thinking and doing.[7] To foster real learning, instruction has to engage students in active forms of inquiry, discussion, and problem-solving so that students can themselves construct new knowledge and understanding of topics previously unfamiliar to them through ongoing investigation of the world around them. From Dewey's perspective, such an approach to instruction not only aligned with scientific understandings of social psychology, but, if widely adopted and implemented in public schools, had the potential to serve as the foundation in preparing future generations of citizens for participatory democracy.[8] Other key figures were just as significant to the development of constructivist pedagogy. One of Dewey's colleagues during his time at the University of Chicago, for instance, was Ella Flagg Young. Young was just as incisive in developing child-centered approaches to instruction, and she was profoundly influential in the advancement of such instructional philosophies among practicing teachers as Superintendent of Chicago Public Schools, the first woman in the United States to run an urban public school district. In addition, W. E. B. DuBois was likewise informed and influenced by William James's work in psychology, and developed a comprehensive educational philosophy, one that was rooted in fostering broad capacities for problem-solving and critical thought.

These scholars and reformers, and the philosophies to which they subscribed, played a key role in shaping the form and content of university-based schools of education. As they proliferated over the years, psychology remained the disciplinary cornerstone of this more academic approach to teacher education than the normal-school model. Ongoing developments in the field of psychology had iterative effects on UBTE as higher education played an increasingly prominent role. In particular, the respective works of developmental psychologists Jean Piaget and Lev Vygotsky became instrumental in the evolution of child-centered instructional techniques. Both scholars theorize that children's cognitive capacities are shaped by complex combinations of their physiological development (physically and mentally) and firsthand experiences they acquire through social interaction. For Piaget, children develop broad mental frameworks (or "schematas") of understanding they then refine through encounters with events and ideas that they try to fit into those existing frameworks. Learning, then, is a continuous process of modifying and building upon mental frameworks through ongoing experience (processes Piaget refers to as "assimilation" and "accommodation"), a perspective in developmental psychology known as "constructivism."[9] Vygotsky places slightly more emphasis on social interaction than Piaget, and theorizes that children possess "zones of proximal development," which represent capacities for understanding new knowledge with the help of "experts." Through interaction with more knowledgeable others, Vygotsky argues children have optimal ranges for learning that can be maximized when adults use children's existing knowledge as the conceptual "scaffold" upon which they help children build understanding of new concepts and ideas.[10] In the case of both scholars' work, experiences and interactions are key for cognitive understanding and development. For instruction to maximize children's cognitive capacities, it must engage them directly as active and thoughtful participants in their own learning.

Based on these scientific accounts of how children learn, "constructivist" models of instruction became, and largely remain, the predominant version of constructivist pedagogy that is taught in UBTE programs. Indeed, the institutionalization of constructivist pedagogy in UBTE, rooted in constructivist frameworks of developmental psychology, is exemplified in the content of popular textbooks for courses in educational psychology which represent required reading in the teacher education program at State University and many other UBTE programs. For example, *Educational Psychology: Developing Learners*, written by Jeanne Ormrod and published by Pearson, is currently in its 9th edition.[11] Much of a foundational chapter in Ormrod's book deals primarily with Piaget's and Vygotsky's theories. Additional developments in the field of psychology have been incorporated into the formal curriculum. In particular, Howard Gardner's theory of "multiple intelligences" has become a hallmark of curriculum in educational psychology. Gardner identifies eight types of intelligence (he later added a ninth), or "modalities," and argues that each individual exhibits distinct combinations of these qualitatively different types of intellectual capacities.[12] The instructional implications of this perspective include viewing child-centered instruction as necessarily accommodating of individual uniqueness, since cognitive diversity among children is hardwired this way according to this perspective in psychology. Finally, accommodation to the cognitive differences of individual children is further institutionalized in instructional practice by federal and state law. The Individuals with Disabilities Educational Act (IDEA) mandates that schools and teachers modify instruction for students with special needs, and these required modifications are documented in "individualized education plans" (IEPs) that must be provided for each student diagnosed with learning or emotional behavioral disorders. Indeed, in addition to coursework in educational psychology, all teacher candidates at State University are required to take a class in teaching students with special needs.

Compulsory education acts as the primary institutional backdrop to constructivist pedagogy that is codified by law. Early developers of constructivist instruction saw it as the philosophical and pragmatic foundation for addressing, equitably, the realities of student heterogeneity that state-mandated mass public education necessarily structures into every classroom in every public school to varying degrees.[13] More contemporary contributors to constructivist

[handwritten margin note: Background]

approaches prioritize responsiveness to diversity in student abilities and aptitudes, as with Gardner's "multiple intelligences."[14] In addition, an important
body of literature on racial, ethnic, and class-based diversity among students
has increasingly influenced UBTE curriculum, and often aligns with constructivist pedagogy in that it similarly emphasizes sensitivity and responsiveness to
elements of social identities and cultural backgrounds that students bring with
them to classrooms.[15] In sum, compulsory education's mandate for all children
to have access to formal schooling makes the multiple sources of individual
variation in learning a central challenge of the teaching profession, and thereby
a central challenge of teacher education. Psychology emerged, and has endured,
as the primary scientific basis for prevailing approaches to instruction that have
become institutionalized in UBTE curriculum. Indeed, this institutionalization
is tied directly to UBTE's residence in higher education. Rooting the practice of
instruction in academic science has been the most common justification for
making teacher education the purview of colleges and universities. Efforts to
professionalize other occupational groups have made similar justifications by
linking professional practice to science, and thus to university training and
credentialing. As Tim Hallett and Matt Gougherty explain, training and credentialing processes have become similar across a wide range of professions
in the ways they are linked to higher education, and these linkages are sustained by the fact that "'scientized' knowledge is upheld as legitimate because
of its university home."[16] In other words, universities are widely seen as key sites
of expertise, and for professional groups to make legitimate claims to unique
forms of expertise, universities must provide the training.

It is within this institutional context that I situate my analysis of UBTE content in this chapter. Teacher candidates are trained to define ongoing adaptation
as a fundamental responsibility of teaching, in part because the scientized knowledge of developmental psychology that informs their training calls for constructivist pedagogy. Constructivist approaches prioritize responsiveness to inherent
diversity among students in their cognitive and developmental abilities with the
goal of engaging students as active agents in their own learning. As such, psychology provides the techno-scientific foundations of the injunction to adapt to
student needs, abilities, and interests. In addition, as an instructional program to
address the institutional myth of compulsory education, constructivist pedagogy
constitutes a key element of teacher candidates' professional culture of ambivalence, as the notion that different students require different techniques becomes
bound up in their definitions of legitimate professional practice.

Priming for Constructivist Pedagogy and a Compulsory System

Many of the formal activities of the instructional methods courses (the "clusters" for teacher candidates in elementary education, or "blocks" for secondary

education) constitute what William Corsaro and Luisa Molinari would call "prim-ing events."[17] Education faculty structure these classes to involve collective activ-ities through which "by their very participation," teacher candidates "attend prospectively to ongoing or anticipated changes in their lives,"[18] in this case, their future work with students in classrooms. It was through these activities that education faculty would model different techniques of constructivist pedagogy, and then allow time for discussion of the techniques, especially how teacher candidates could modify them to accommodate differences in students' abilities as well as engage a wide range of student interests. Through these routine activi-ties, teacher candidates become primed for the execution of ongoing adaption in their prospective instruction, as well as rationalizations for the need to do so. Here, the injunction to adapt is given its most forceful formal expression.

Modeling Instructional Methods, Emphasizing Adaptation

Consistently in their coursework, education faculty encourage teacher candi-dates to choose instructional techniques from a variety of options and adapt them to fit their specific classroom needs. Faculty often model examples of les-sons to teacher candidates, and then discuss ways they can adapt those exam-ples in their prospective work with different types of students. The following excerpt from my field notes offers an example:

> Okay, that was inquiry. Inquiry is a process of problem-solving; it is a method to develop new knowledge. I geared this lesson more toward intermediate students; this is just a quick and dirty way to do it. You can give students other ways. You've got to figure out how to do that. With primary kids, you could do more like what we did with the drawing and visual images; you wouldn't be able to do as much reading with them . . . Think about how you can adapt it. For example, if you had a student with an IEP [individualized education plan] who has a reading issue, you're going to have to find a way to bring that kid in. (Field notes, Instructional Methods Course in Elementary Education)

Teacher candidates are given models to follow, but faculty implore them to adapt the models to the specific classroom conditions they will face. For those in elementary education, one key reason for adaptation is the grade level they will be teaching. In the excerpt above, the faculty member models a lesson geared toward intermediate students, but then gives the teacher candidates additional options for altering the lesson to be more appropriate for primary-level stu-dents. He also gives the specific example of the potential for having students with special needs, and the legal requirement that all such students have an "IEP" that articulates how their individual needs will be met through modified instruction. Lastly, he emphasizes the need to "find a way to bring that kid in," emphasizing inclusion regardless of ability or need. We see teacher candidates being primed through routine class interactions to adapt their instruction to diverse students, as institutional rules of prospective work environments mandate, and such priming is issued in the form of an injunction as faculty tell teacher candidates, "You've got to figure out how to do that."

The curriculum in instruction for elementary education is closely coordinated among faculty responsible for teaching different sections of cluster courses. Four particular strategies that they foreground—Supermarket, Idea Teach, Inquiry Teach, and RAFT—are all constructivist techniques, highly adaptable to different students, topics, and contexts. In an additional excerpt from my field notes of Todd's class, I show in more detail how education faculty model these techniques to teacher candidates, and attempt to prime them for constructivist pedagogy and the ongoing adaptation it entails.

> Today we are doing the "supermarket" portion of the four types of lessons. The big question is where does something come from? I, for one, every day I pack my lunch pail [picks up a plastic, yellow lunchbox]. I've already had my lunch today, but I pack my lunch pail . . . It's got a gorilla in a hot air balloon. In my lunch pail I have this [pulls out a banana]. It's yellow like my lunch pail, and I have it almost every day, but . . . I don't know where this comes from. Do you know where this comes from? I have no idea. Let's look at these statements on the board to see what we know about bananas [several T/F statements on yellow construction paper].
>
> [Todd reads the first statement.] "The bananas we get in the supermarket come from Florida." True or false? [Students reply false, list as false.] False; okay . . . "Bananas are the most popular fruit in the world." True or false? [some different answers]. Well, I don't know; there are a lot of fruits in the world. The most popular fruit in the world? We'll say false. "Bananas grow on every continent." [Several students say false.] False? Why? [Students make one-word replies.] Oh, Antarctica, right . . .
>
> These statements are the "anticipation guide" for this lesson. What we're going to do now, I'm going to give each of you a book on bananas [holds up book], and I want you to look at some marked pages with your group. Then we'll share what we find out about bananas [hands out books]. Have someone in your group be a recorder.
>
> Todd plays some music, "to get us in the banana mood," as he puts it, and begins a recording of the song "Banana Pudding" by Southern Culture on the Skids. The groups read and discuss for approximately four to five minutes. Todd writes two questions on the board:

What are bananas?	Where do they come from?
Plant is an herb	Tropical (equator)
Fruit	Colombia, Florida
Staple (core)	Africa

Todd calls them back and they list some answers under the questions [as written above]. Todd interjects with prompts as they list some things, such as "Where is Colombia?" when that answer is given. He suggests this would be a point in the lesson where a teacher could "pull down a map and show them where on the map it is; also, could talk to students about the equator, or talk about map skills and geography more generally."

Let's return to the anticipation guide. Do we need to make a lot of changes to these statements? [They change one statement on the number of bananas in a bunch.]

Thinking about this as teachers, what else could we talk about here? [Todd repeats student responses.] Trade, transportation, geography, consumerism, that's a big one. The economics you probably wouldn't use with first graders, but definitely with intermediate grades. You could show how there are multiple jobs at each stage of the setup. You've got human resources, capital resources . . . You want to summarize the steps again . . . Health and nutrition as well. So, this attaches to so many different standards. It's a process of investigation to new knowledge. These [holding bananas] are plastic bananas so the younger kids have something to touch, feel, and manipulate . . .

I'm going to hand out a sheet, and I want you to critique the lesson and resources . . . like the books available, the pros and cons with those. For example, what would you do with younger learners and emergent readers? Need to use more visuals. These are the books that I'm going to hand out; there are "True Books" [publisher label] on every topic. Some feel structured, but you can adapt them to your own creative things. Think of ways you can use with K through first grade, those of you who are placed in primary, even third graders, you'll want to use similar things because they're right on the border of intermediate. Somebody note your ideas, and then we'll share with the class. I'll start the music again. (Field notes, Methods Course in Elementary Education)

This excerpt provides a vivid example of what coursework in instructional methods looks like and how it unfolds. Todd simultaneously demonstrates how to execute the "supermarket" technique with an actual lesson on bananas, and he prompts teacher candidates to think about different contingencies to which they might adapt this technique in future situations. We see elements of a constructivist philosophy woven into the specific practices constitutive of the supermarket technique. The "anticipation guide," for instance, is an introductory exercise intended to solicit students' existing knowledge about a topic, object, event, or idea. By beginning the lesson in this way, Todd is modeling the "scaffolding" technique to teacher candidates, consistent with constructivist traditions of Piaget and Vygotsky. Additionally, the anticipation guide activity is inquiry-based. Students are led through discussion and group exercises in which they actively use resources to discover and deduce new information based initially on what they already know about bananas, hence the "changes" to the first round of answers to the anticipation guide. Throughout the discussion, Todd emphasizes the variety of ways that teacher candidates could modify the supermarket approach to different groups of students to better tailor the practice to diverse needs and abilities.

This emphasis on adaptation dominates the subsequent discussion that ensues after teacher candidates have a chance to work on their "critique" of the lesson and resources:

> Todd: Okay, what did you come up with in your critiques? You could develop the process to the lunch pail, yes . . . The books may not be grade-level appropriate. The one we used has a lot of text; it has a lot of pictures, but a lot of text. Probably wouldn't assign a cover-to-cover read, even for fifth graders . . . There is a glossary and index, but we're going to talk about those things later and vocabulary.
>
> There was a lot here . . . You could pick one specific area and dig into that, like Costa Rica, get into the people, the language. What's a source for inquiry? [One student answers "nutrition."] Nutrition, okay . . . [Another student, "the environment."] Environmental issues . . . You could use comparison; a banana doesn't have an opposite, but you could do like an apples/oranges comparison as part of an Idea teach. You have artifacts for these lessons; you don't have to do both, but that's just one way to do it. Make sure you sum up; if you don't, it's not engaging. You can't just give them a stack of books, a stack of pictures. Those are the days when you're not prepared, and you're just in survival mode. That will happen, but you can plan units that are creative. (Field notes, Methods Course in Elementary Education)

The entire discussion circulates around adaptation and modification, thinking prospectively about the potential differences among students that would warrant such modification. Todd emphasizes the academic skills and developmental needs that dictate what is "grade-level appropriate," and how to modify the content of the supermarket strategy to accommodate such student differences. Additionally, there is equal emphasis on student engagement and keeping students actively involved in instructional exercises. At the end, we see Todd characterize adaptation and actively engaging diverse students as imperative, emphasizing that "you can't just give them a stack of books." Rather, he emphasizes, "You can adapt them to your own creative things." Indeed, failure to carry out "creative" instruction that is "engaging" to different students reflects that "you're not prepared, and you're just in survival mode." As such, ongoing adaptation in instruction is something teacher candidates must do to be effective. Moreover, while Todd is prescriptive in the way he insists on adaptation, he is decidedly non-prescriptive concerning specific activities and techniques. The message is clear that there are a wide range of instructional activities for teaching this lesson that could be plausibly equal in their effectiveness (e.g., "that's just one way to do it") as long as they are "engaging." In this sense, adaptation is the rule and ambivalence is the tone, as any number of approaches could work with different students in meeting their needs.

Methods courses for teacher candidates preparing for entirely different subject matter and grade level also revolved around these kinds of modeling activities. Bob was the faculty instructor for the methods course in secondary math that I observed, and the following excerpt from my field notes documents his efforts to model a similarly constructivist approach to prospective high school math teachers.

Bob begins promptly at 4:05, wearing a pair of glasses of which he says, "If I'm wearing these, I'm now Mr. O'Connor." He gives himself 45 minutes, just as they will have, and has a hard cutoff after that time to resemble a class period in a school.

On the board, he has the "goal" for the lesson written: "to understand the properties of logarithmic functions." Bob calls attention to this goal, and then immediately shows them a "starter problem." On the overhead there is a number line with blue numbers along the bottom, and red "signs" at different points along the line. Bob asks them if they can see a pattern in the signs, or if they could make any predictions, for example about what number the sign "6" would be over. The students ponder for a moment, and the only pattern I see is that each sign is over the next number which is twice that of the previous number with a sign (e.g., sign 2 is over number 2, and sign 3 is over number 4, and so on). Based on this pattern, I predict sign 6 would be over number 64. Another student predicts this, Bob confirms. When he asks how they knew that, one student explained it was through exponents and each one was raised to another power of 2.

Bob: "Okay, so what do you have to raise 2 to, to get 64? Any other ways of predicting?"

Another student says it's a log, and Bob agrees this is another way of making predictions. Some students suggest one could "plot" the pattern; again, Bob agrees. Then Bob immediately transitions to the next activity which he explains as a group project to do the same thing. He points to several sheets on the middle table; each one has a similar exercise as the "starter problem" but with different patterns, or "laws." He says that each one is at different levels of difficulty. He wants them to get into groups of three, and each person has a role: one job is graphing, one is reporting, and one is recording. He says he doesn't care how they determine roles, but that each group must have each one. They are each to take an exercise and some chalk (he has thick pieces of sidewalk chalk in multiple colors on the same table as the exercises), and go downstairs to work on the sidewalk immediately outside the building door.

Groups work outside, drawing and discussing their problems. Each group works pretty diligently; one group in the corner does less drawing and stands to talk while all three look at the sheet. Bob walks around to each group to discuss their problems and the solutions they are working on. I walk around too, exchanging commentary with one group in particular, joking about my own difficulties with math. The students are open to me generally. After approximately 15–20 minutes, Bob says all must return to the classroom, and people filter back upstairs. (Field notes, Methods Course in Secondary Mathematics)

The lesson Bob models is very hands-on, active, and problem-based, all consistent with constructivist approaches to constructivist pedagogy. It involves student "inquiry" like the "supermarket" approach for elementary students. Bob uses a "starter problem" as an introduction (not unlike the "anticipation guide" Todd modeled), walking the class through an exercise in the type of math he wants them to do on their own. He then engages students with group work in which all students have a specified "role" to play. The main activity takes the students outside to work on their graphs with chalk on the sidewalk and enjoy the beautiful, early fall weather.

After the 45-minute model lesson, Bob and the teacher candidates break stage to discuss the lesson, primarily how they could adapt it to prospective students.

A student poses a question regarding Bob's plan to go outside with high school kids as opposed to college students.

> Bob: "I've taken high school classes outside. I wonder if it would
> have been different if I'd stayed inside. In some ways, it might
> be even harder to control it in the classroom because students
> might not be as engaged because of the limited space . . . I might
> have advance-planned the roles for particular students the night
> before. Like if I had an ADHD kid, I would have made sure he got
> the graphing role because it's more active."

A teacher candidate asks how someone would approach this lesson with students who had never heard of logs before.

Bob: "I would try to use their language to introduce the term base."

A student raises the point that a group was somewhat confused as to the assignment expectations, especially at the start, and therefore didn't get as much out of it as perhaps others did.

Bob: "Yeah, a general tendency I do have is if I have 3–4 students from whom I get ideas and I take it as a check that everyone's got it. I may have moved on before I should've."

Another student remarks they appreciated that, though; that they felt they were pushed to solve the problem themselves. A student suggests more clearly defining "law," especially if students don't have prior knowledge of logs; also the idea of a practical example of the problem might be useful.

Bob: "Yeah, so put problems in a context for the students. You'll also find some problems work better for some students than they do for others."

Several nod in the affirmative.

Bob: "Yeah, good. The point of these is to also introduce to you all new conceptual knowledge in these lesson plans, and then you can apply them and revise them. The curriculum is very deep, and you all will be learning new things as you teach and make plans."

(Field notes, Methods Course in Secondary Mathematics)

Throughout the discussion, Bob emphasizes adaptation as key to instructional decision-making. This includes tailoring elements of an overall lesson to the needs of particular students, as with making sure the "ADHD kid," as Bob puts it, "got the graphing role because it's more active." But adaptation also includes rationalizing learner diversity as inherent to teaching and learning processes. Some problems just "work better for some students than they do for others," and teachers must be prepared for this reality and respond to it through adaptation to student needs. It also implies a process of trial and error to adaptation in instruction, as teachers must find out which techniques work with which students and which ones fail. That is just the way it is for teachers, so to speak, an ambivalence teacher candidates must embrace.

"Pretend That Everyone Has an IEP"

While responsiveness to diversity in student abilities is institutionalized in teacher education through constructivist pedagogy, legal mandates for individualized instructional modifications for students with documented disabilities add institutional force to the injunction to adapt. Faculty often reference prospective students' "IEPs" and use them as justification for teacher candidates to maintain a constant orientation to potential adaptation and differentiation of instruction.

Moreover, faculty regularly advise teacher candidates that addressing the requirements of IEPs is perfectly consistent with the broader educational philosophies
they are teaching them. One faculty member, Beth, even advises teacher candidates that they should imagine all of their students possessing an IEP:

> Another teacher candidate describes a student in class who has had
> some disruptions; she speculates that the student has some form of dis-
> ability or behavioral disorder. Beth asks her, "Have you asked to see the
> student's IEP?" The student says no, and that she didn't know if "we're
> allowed to know." Beth says that she "always advises asking for that; you
> need to know." She says other teachers will find it "impressive, not inva-
> sive" if they ask to see students' IEPs. Beth asks the class how many have
> seen an IEP. Several teacher candidates raise their hand, but not every-
> one. Beth says, "It doesn't hurt to pretend that everyone has an IEP." She
> says, "The kinds of things that typical IEPs script for students can be good
> for all of them. Treat your classes as if everyone has an IEP." (Field notes,
> Methods Course in Secondary English/Language Arts)

Individualized instruction is universally beneficial, according to the perspective Beth advocates here. Consistent with Gardner's "multiple intelligences"
theory of cognitive functioning and ability, approaching all instruction with the
kind of sensitivity to individuals' specific capacities and limitations that IEPs
formalize and require for special needs students is a recipe for broadly effective
instruction.

Referencing IEPs in this way is common in methods courses across subject
matter and grade-level distinctions. Moreover, education faculty cite IEPs as the
basis for practical instructional decision-making in which adaptation is required.
The IEP, and teaching students with special needs, also informs the ways faculty
advise teacher candidates on what are appropriate and effective ways of diversifying instruction, such as Bob in his methods course for secondary math:

> Another key component of "developing a plan for reaching learning
> goals," he says, is to "think about hypothetical special needs students
> you may have, and how you will make adjustments that avoid stigma."
> He reminds them that "the specific need determines the modification."
> As they've discussed before, Bob says "Special needs is a broad label." He
> gives an example. "Let's say I'm dyslexic; I should be able to do math, but
> reading things I have trouble with. You won't know exactly until you see
> the IEP, but I didn't want you to make a blanket statement that all [spe-
> cial needs students] need more time or easier problems." (Field notes,
> Methods Course in Secondary Math)

Part of an effective strategy for "reaching learning goals" more broadly entails
making "adjustments" to the curriculum that are not only a means of making it

easier, but making it accessible. As Bob puts it, "the specific need determines the modification," and this emphasis on diversity in student needs is rooted in institutionalized assessments of individual cognitive capacities.

Adaptation to "All Students" as Formal Evaluation Criteria

While education faculty train teacher candidates in the need to actively engage students—and continually adapt instruction as a means to do so—the same tenets of constructivist pedagogy are also brought to bear upon formal evaluation protocol for teacher candidates. Figure 1 is the scoring rubric for teacher candidates' supervisors to use when evaluating their performance during their student teaching.[19] For this component of their performance, teacher candidates are assessed on how effectively they carry forward the content of their coursework and put "personalized learning" into practice. The three requirements for evaluation purposes include:

1. "Develops lessons that reflect individual student ability levels resulting in the intellectual engagement of all students."
2. "Develops lessons that are creative, engaging, and are appropriate for the learning community."
3. "Develops instructional activities that address multiple learning styles."

Within these three categories of evaluation, we see expression of both the mandates of compulsory education as well as the tenets of constructivist pedagogy. The first requires accommodation for "all students," a fundamental priority of a compulsory system, with lessons that "reflect individual student ability levels." The second and third evaluation criteria codify constructivist pedagogy in teacher candidates' performance as well, requiring "lessons that are creative and engaging," and include "instructional activities that address multiple learning styles." Indeed, in a compulsory system, students bring varying ability levels and cognitive learning styles with them to the classroom, and teacher candidates are rated based on the degree to which their instruction accommodates and engages these differences in prior skills and cognitive capacities.

A closer look at the scoring rubric reveals more detail. To earn marks of "distinguished" or "proficient," teacher candidates must display evidence of the following:

Distinguished: "Instruction is differentiated for all ability levels . . . Students are challenged and engaged as active participants."

Proficient: "The curriculum is adapted to diverse learners with unique needs and talents through a variety of strategies."

Distinguished: "Lesson plans provide clear evidence of multiple teaching strategies to support all learners in the class."

Unsatisfactory 1	Satisfactory 2	Proficient 3	Distinguished 4
*Develops lessons that reflect individual student ability levels resulting in the intellectual engagement of all students.			
Differentiation is lacking in the instructional process. Students do not understand expectations. One lesson is taught to all students regardless of ability level.	Demonstrates limited differentiation. Students generally understand expectations. Some attempts are made to meet students' cognitive development.	Instruction is differentiated for many ability levels. Expectations are communicated effectively. Successful instruction is demonstrated to meet students' cognitive needs.	Instruction is differentiated for all ability levels. Students individually share in creating and communicating expectations. Students are challenged and engaged as active participants.
Notes/Evidence: Rating ____			
*Develops lessons that are creative, engaging, and appropriate for the learning community.			
Lessons lack creativity. Minimal effort evident to connect curriculum content to the learning community.	Some effort is evident to connect curriculum content to the learning community. Lessons reflect some creativity at a basic level.	Student engagement is reflected both in the classroom and in student work. Through creative activities, lessons reflect the interests of the students.	Lessons demonstrate a strong connection between students' interests and life experiences. Students are inspired to pursue interests through creative lessons that incorporate higher-level thinking skills.
Notes/Evidence: Rating ____			
*Develops instructional activities that address multiple learning styles.			
Depends on one or two teaching strategies that do not meet all learning styles. Lesson plans do not reflect a variety of strategies for diverse learners.	Limited use of teaching strategies. Begins to address the basic diverse needs of students. Lesson plans reflect some effort to meet the needs of diverse learners.	The curriculum is adapted to diverse learners with unique needs and talents through a variety of strategies. Lesson plans reflect a variety of strategies to support learning.	The curriculum is built around the needs of diverse learners. Lesson plans provide clear evidence of multiple teaching strategies to support all learners in the class.
Notes/Evidence: Rating ____			

FIGURE 1. Evaluation Rubric for "Personalized Learning"

We see woven into this rubric the defining features of constructivist pedagogy as well as the institutional myth of compulsory education to address student heterogeneity in ability. First, the rubric is child-centered, requiring that students be "engaged" as "active participants" in the learning process. Second, it requires Vygotskian scaffolding techniques that "reflect the interests of students." Third, it requires adaptation in ways linked directly to meeting the "unique needs and talents" of "diverse learners." Moreover, there are multiple references to "all students," "all learners," and "all ability levels." Demonstrating competence at accommodating everyone regardless of ability is central to the job description as defined by these evaluation schemas, and aligns teacher candidates' prospective work with rationalized ideals of compulsory education that instruction is accessible to all students.[20] It is important to note that although the UBTE program at State University does not conflate cognitive ability and learned skill level among students as the same phenomena, evaluation protocols and course content tended to emphasize instructional adaptation, modification, and accommodation as the appropriate way for teachers to address both phenomena. This evaluation rubric, for example, references "learning styles" and "ability levels," and tends to treat them similarly as preexisting conditions students bring with them to classrooms. These pre-existing conditions, whatever their source, must be accommodated through ongoing instructional modification tailored to particular student needs. Indeed, not only must teacher candidates incorporate ongoing adaptation to earn high marks, they are punished by this rubric with marks of "Unsatisfactory" if they fail to adapt instruction to the various needs of their students:

Unsatisfactory: ". . . teaching strategies do not meet all learning styles."

Unsatisfactory: "Differentiation is lacking in the instructional process . . . One lesson is taught to all students regardless of ability level."

The weight of formal reward and sanction in UBTE is a key component of the injunction to adapt. It is an injunction, an imperative, not just in the ways that teacher candidates' instructors advise them in class, but in the measurable standards for performance that determine whether or not they will obtain certification and to what degree they will earn their supervisors' endorsement for future employment.

Priming for the "Realities" of Gender in Public Education

The institutional myth that education is compulsory and made accessible to all students, when combined with the instructional philosophy of constructivist pedagogy, prioritizes adaptation to, and accommodation of, students' various pre-existing qualities that affect teaching and learning. A very similar

looking beyond individual

set of meanings emerged in my data regarding the ways the UBTE program at State University attempted to train teacher candidates to address issues of gender in their prospective work of student instruction. Likewise, the institutional myths that femininity and masculinity are "innate" qualities that people possess, combined with the instructional philosophy of constructivist pedagogy, prioritize adaptation to, and accommodation of, gendered meanings and behaviors that affect teaching and learning. In other words, the formal UBTE training at State University tended to treat gender in the context of schooling as a type of pre-existing condition among students similar to other forms of student heterogeneity (e.g., skill level or cognitive ability). As such, program requirements for teacher candidates to be responsive and accommodating to gendered behaviors among students were often just as prescriptive as the injunction to adapt to other characteristics among students defined as relevant to teaching and learning. Such requirements were most forcefully and frequently expressed to women concerning how they should and should not dress when working in schools.

 ### Ongoing Warnings to Women Teacher Candidates

Women teacher candidates were routinely reminded by School of Education faculty, administrators, school principals, and teachers alike about what they can and cannot wear when working in schools. Women were prohibited from wearing the types of shirts, skirts, pants, and underwear that reveal parts of their bodies in ways that might be interpreted as a display of being sexually available or alluring. These reminders began for most women teacher candidates during their sophomore year. They increased in frequency and intensity the closer teacher candidates got to their student teaching placements when they were working full-time in schools. Sara describes the nature of these reminders and how regularly they occurred:

Sara: All they talk about is what we can and cannot wear. They start telling us what we can wear with our field experience—that's second-semester sophomore year.

Judson: Do you hear it from administration, from instructors?

Sara: Everyone! *Everyone!* It's like, "Make sure your shirts are long enough, don't wear short skirts, make sure you wear closed-toed shoes."

(Interview with Sara, Elementary Education)

Indeed, teacher candidates did hear these warnings from "everyone," and they heard it repeatedly throughout their training. As Sara describes, women are not to wear clothing that might reveal cleavage, stomach, or much, if any, leg. In addition, they are not to allow any underwear to show. In a separate interview, another teacher candidate, Nicole, at one point expressed dismay that for some women in the program, supervisors needed to "spell it out" for them. I asked her to elaborate:

Judson: So, when they [education faculty and administrators] spell it out, what are some of the specific things that they say?

Nicole: Oh, you know . . . You're not supposed to have a low-cut shirt, you know, and it needs to be long enough so that your underwear's not hanging out your back. And, you know, you're not showing belly. You know, like, no short skirts, all that kind of stuff.

(Interview with Nicole, Elementary Education)

Nicole confirmed what other women experienced regarding the specific components of the dress code pertaining to specific body parts. Additionally, though, she became less comfortable during the interview when I pressed her to explicitly describe the specific components of the dress code for women. She began with "Oh, you know . . ." followed by a long pause, and then enumerated the body parts expected to be covered. In each sentence, she used the phrase "you know" in her description, and concluded with the vague summary "all that kind of stuff." Consistent with how gender scholars theorize that gendered meanings operate in interaction, Nicole assumed I knew what "we assume we all know" about traditional gender performances.[21] When I asked her to be explicit about these underlying assumptions (which required speaking frankly about women's bodies), she became more reticent and halting in her speech when she was typically candid and detailed in interviews.[22] Since the content of these reminders and warnings has become so routine for her and pertains to something as personal as body management, it makes sense that articulating the assumptions behind them could be awkward.

Men were also expected to "dress professionally," but as teacher candidates explain, that has different meaning for men than women:

Judson: Do you feel that's [the reminders] mostly directed at the girls more than the guys?

Sara: Definitely! Because the guys, it's like, you wear pants and a shirt. It's not like they have too many options. Whereas girls can't wear low-cut shirts, they can't wear shirts that are short, they can't wear skirts that are short.

(Interview with Sara, Elementary Education)

Not only do women have different standards and options for what they can or cannot wear relative to men, they must also be more mindful of how their clothes fit:

Judson: Do you think that issue is more difficult for girls than guys who are going into teaching?

Faye: Yes. Boys can have a pair of khaki pants and a button-up shirt. But for girls, it might matter how those pants fit, or what style they are, or how low-cut your shirt is.

(Interview with Faye, Secondary Social Studies)

Women are instructed to cover their bodies and underwear, and are also expected to cover them in ways that do not reveal the form of their bodies (e.g., nothing tight-fitting, especially over or around the breasts and buttocks). There is much closer attention paid to a wider array of details, and options for clothing, about "professional dress" for women. On the other hand, this does not mean that men necessarily have greater freedom than women in their options for satisfying expectations for professional dress. Both Sara and Faye describe the prevailing dress code for men as consisting primarily of khakis and a collared shirt of some kind. Another teacher candidate, Deborah, articulated this point by pointing out my own gender status when I asked her about this difference between women and men: "I'm sorry, but really, how long did it take you to get dressed this morning?" Indeed, I was wearing a pair of khakis and buttoned-down shirt. As I discuss in the next section, this gender difference in dress codes is driven by the same sets of rationalized meanings concerning femininity and masculinity, meanings that tend to reaffirm men as sexual aggressors and women as sexual objects. As such, standards of professional appearance for men are narrowly and rigidly aligned with particular definitions of masculine behavior, and standards for women's professional appearance centrally manage body displays.

Warnings concerning professional appearance are issued by faculty and administrators through routine aspects of the training program. Indeed, the constant reminders were often communicated in cautionary ways and warned of possible repercussions for not conforming to these standards, and were disproportionately issued to women relative to men. An example comes from my field notes observing a teaching methods course in secondary mathematics. Here, the faculty member (Bob) teaching the course issues a "warning" about women's dress when teacher candidates go out into schools to log their field experience hours:

Bob: I spoke with [administrator], especially for the ladies, is a warning about dress codes in schools. Apparently ten principals have complained about what some people are wearing out into the schools for their field experiences. They are threatening to kick people out of their school. So, be really careful about that; you don't want to be the one who gets kicked out of the school for your field experience. (Field notes, Instructional Methods Course in Secondary Math)

Bob's last statement presumes that both the dress codes, directed explicitly at women, and the authority of principals to enforce them, are legitimate expectations for behavior in schools. It also explicitly stigmatizes individuals who would defy the dress code and receive the punishment of dismissal, emphasizing that such a series of events would reflect poorly on women teacher candidates, not schools or their agents who dismiss them. Moreover, Bob's warning presumes his audience knows and understands what the dress code entails for women, and he provides neither detail on what constitutes a violation nor does he speak directly to past or potential offenders. Instead it is a blanket statement to the whole audience. Bob singles out "the ladies" even though he is speaking to an entire class consisting of women and men,[23] reaffirming the legitimacy of institutional standards by reminding all parties involved of the penalties for noncompliance.

Standards for dress were also explicitly, though generically, codified in formal documents administrators used to evaluate teacher candidates' training performance, especially in their student teaching. For instance, prior to student teaching, all teacher candidates had to sign a "Professional Expectations Agreement" that outlined all of the forms of work-related behavior expected of teacher candidates and served as the evaluation rubric for their student teaching performance. Under expectations for "Professionalism" in this agreement, it mandates that teacher candidates "dress appropriately."

The language regarding dress in this document is an example of how Joan Acker[24] argues that formal rules for job evaluation can appear "gender neutral." However, as Acker also argues, when individuals with bodies are put into the jobs being evaluated, this is when gender enters into the evaluation process. We see how meanings about gender and sexuality enter into this process in the actual interactions when administrators reviewed the content of the professional expectations agreement with teacher candidates in the "pre-professional meeting" they were required to attend.[25] Vince Turner, the administrator in charge of student teaching placements and whom I quote in Chapter 3, conducted this meeting. The purpose of the meeting was to prepare teacher candidates for their responsibilities and requirements for student teaching in the spring semester. In this excerpt, Vince is reviewing with them the contents of their "Student Teaching Handbook" and the "Professional Expectations Agreement" included in the handbook:

> Vince tells the crowd that one of the first things they must do is sign and return to the teacher certification office their "Professional Expectations Agreement." The agreement and Vince give similarly vague commands to "behave professionally" at all times, and there are multiple references in the handbook that remind teacher candidates to "dress professionally." He says it's important they take into account the "local context of the school" where they are working to assess what is professional behavior. He then gives an example of what not to do, saying "it's probably a

School of Education   **Office of Teacher Education**

PROFESSIONAL EXPECTATIONS: STUDENT AGREEMENT

Upon admission to the Teacher Education Program, I _____ (student name-please print) understand that I have assumed added responsibilities as a pre-professional education student. I am preparing to become a teacher and to assume responsibilities for children's safety, well-being, development, and learning. I agree to do my best in meeting the professional expectations outlined below in all pertinent aspects of my teacher education program.

As a point of information, the state of _____ has a code of ethical conduct for all teachers in the state (Code Reference #). It is not the intention of the School of Education to define these characteristics; however, local school officials may ask the student to leave the field or student teaching placement for any of the following reasons: Immorality; Misconduct in office; Incompetence; or Willful neglect of duty.

Professional Expectations

Personalized Learning

| respect the ways in which growth and development in individuals may differ | promote engagement for all students | recognize the developmental needs of all students | be sensitive to the external stressors students face | maintain high expectations | encourage independent, critical-thinking skills | _____

Knowledge

| develop informed teaching practices through continual study of theory | supplement the curriculum with authentic resources and activities | be flexible and responsive to individual learner needs | facilitate mastery of skills and concepts | implement multiple ways of teaching and learning | _____

Community

| respect family and student goals, values, and unique identity | promote open communication with the family | value the broad spectrum of cultural diversity and global interconnectedness | encourage democratic principles in both students and colleagues | become aware of and utilize the benefits to education that the community has to offer | ____

Growth and Reflection

| commit to reflective practice and planning | value and pursue opportunities for collaborative work with colleagues and families | pursue personal and professional growth | maximize teaching and learning experiences | _____

Learning Environment

| work toward a learning environment that optimizes student academic, social, physical, and spiritual well-being | use multiple assessments to identify student strengths and refine curriculum | promote a safe and caring environment | appreciate and manage group dynamics that contribute to the classroom | _____

Professionalism

| protect the privacy and confidential information of all students, their families, and teachers unless required by state/federal law | uphold all legal and school obligations including the professional expectations and code of ethics of faculty and staff at State University | dress appropriately | be on time with all scheduled activities and work | be open to constructive criticism and make appropriate modifications upon reflection | communicate to the best of my ability | conduct myself as a professional in all respects when I am working in, or representing, State University by treating others with respect |

I understand that as a student in the Teacher Education Program, I may be withdrawn from the program and/or any field placement including student teaching, for failure to comply with these professional expectations. Other disciplinary actions may include, but are not limited to, an administrative alert, an unsatisfactory grade for course or placement, removal from the Teacher Education Program, and/or dismissal from State University.

Signature _____ Date _____

FIGURE 2. Professional Expectations Agreement

bad idea to walk into your school placement and brag about your unwed pregnancy." Several people utter mild chuckles at this in the audience. He also says that, "to present yourself as a professional is *very* important for you in your classroom . . ."

Next, Vince says they will need to "step up to the professional role." He then goes through some of the expectations associated with the "professional role." He discusses issues of dressing professionally. He gives an example by saying, "When you're in class, and you bend down to help a student [Vince bends down with his back to the audience], I don't want to see any thong song here [waves his hand in front of his backside]." Students in the audience react to this in a variety of ways. Some smile and chuckle, and most of them say things to each other and for a moment, the room is noticeably louder than before. Vince stands up, and tells them to "follow other teachers" when deciding how to dress for school, and "adhere to the local dress code." (Field notes, Pre-Professional Meeting)

Vince's warnings about "bragging about your unwed pregnancy" and seeing a "thong song" are specific to women. The warning that it may be a bad idea to "brag about your unwed pregnancy" is clearly targeted at the women, and characterizes the discussion of women's sexuality as taboo in their future work environments (in addition, the example stigmatizes single motherhood by equating it with sexual promiscuity). Vince also equates these expectations for women with "professional" behavior for teachers. In fact, Vince invokes the ideal of "professionalism" repeatedly throughout the presentation, as he actively defines these specifically gendered and sexualized meanings as "professional" behavior. As such, Vince deploys the legitimacy associated with "professionalism" to define specific ways of monitoring and covering women's bodies as appropriate work-related behavior. Vince is decidedly more specific and graphic than other faculty (like Bob in the previous example) about what not to do, especially his reference to avoiding the display of a "thong song."

Vince places a lot of emphasis on public schools for defining professional behavior for teachers, and implores teacher candidates to "follow other teachers" and "adhere to the local dress code." Vince relays to teacher candidates that these standards for dress are simply a reality of educational institutions, and that prospective teachers should be ready to conform to them. He is telling them how it is, so to speak, and appealing to public schools as institutions to do so. Additionally, that teacher candidates must sign and submit a formal "agreement" in which these standards for behavior are enumerated, imbues the meanings they carry with at least the appearance of rational-legal authority. Through purposeful action such as Vince's presentation at the Pre-Professional Meeting, taken-for-granted meanings about the legitimacy of "professionalism" are actively linked with gendered meanings for behavior.

The Rationalization That "Boys Will Be Boys"

Teacher candidates actively make sense of training experiences such as the pre-professional meeting and interactions in their coursework, and incorporate meanings about gender into their definitions of teachers' work. To be sure, they certainly begin making sense of gender and sexuality long before they arrive in their UBTE program, but through the interactions they experience in their training, they begin linking the ways they should "do gender"[26] to the ways they should do their prospective work as teachers. Women and men consistently shared the perspective that women have different standards than their male counterparts, and that this is something obvious they already know.

Faye: Girls especially, you have to be smart about what you wear. High school boys are high school boys; you can't ignore that. If you don't have any common sense, first of all, you probably shouldn't be a teacher. And second of all, you should realize that you can't wear a mini-skirt to teach. (Interview with Faye, Secondary Social Studies)

From her perspective, Faye is telling it like it is. The reality for women entering teaching is that they must be "smart" about how they manage their bodies through the ways they dress on the job. The reason is, simply, that boys will be boys. Moreover, a basic understanding of this reality for teachers is "common sense," and anyone who does not possess it really should not be a teacher in the first place, according to Faye.

Such a perspective was widely shared among teacher candidates and teacher educators in this study. Faye's comments capture a number of key assumptions and taken-for-granted meanings about gender that teacher candidates actively link to teacher professionalism. The idea that "boys will be boys" is an expression of rationalized ideals concerning masculinity that are heteronormative, and presume men to be "naturally" sexually aggressive. In addition, she also invokes assumptions about femininity as well, asserting that for "girls," a basic understanding of boys' supposedly natural behavior requires they "be smart about what you wear," suggesting women have some "common sense" responsibility to deflect or prevent negative behavior that might result from boys' sexual urges.

Faye suggests that sexual aggression is somehow inherent to boys of high school age by linking women's need to cover their bodies with the statement "high school boys are high school boys." She takes for granted that boys will sexually objectify women, and therefore it is the responsibility of women to cover their bodies so as to deflect boys' essential desires and sexual advances when conducting the routine work of teaching. Moreover, Faye appeals to the "naturalness" of boys' sexuality as the basis for defining body discipline as an inherent, and legitimate, element of teaching practice for women.[27] Faye draws upon interrelated meanings of masculinity and femininity: the idea that boys are innately, and heteronormatively, motivated by sexual urges requires women manage their own appearance as a response to potential behavior defined as normal.

Other teacher candidates echo these similar rationalized meanings about gender as the justification for the strict standards for women's dress.

Frank: I think it's 85, 90 percent geared toward women teachers. So they talk about low-cut, tight pants, not wear trashy jeans . . . I think for girls, I mean, if you're in this class with all these boys going through puberty, like . . . They're gonna be looking for anything! [Frank laughs]. So, I can understand that. (Interview with Frank, Secondary English/Language Arts)

Sara described a similar meaning about boys' behavior in recounting an interaction one of her classmates had during a classroom observation in an elementary school:

Sara: Like I had one girl in my cluster [cohort in the teacher education program] who had an experience with a student, and she's in a sixth-grade classroom, and the student said something like, "Damn! You're fine!" or something like that, and it's like, how awkward is that for her?! That's why they have to say those things. (Interview with Sara, Elementary Education)

In Frank's statement, we see again the assumption "boys will be boys" regarding their sexual urges, and he links them very explicitly to physiological conditions of adolescent development by citing "puberty." As such, Frank "can understand" why teacher educators would constantly remind women they must avoid anything "low-cut" as well as "tight pants" or "trashy jeans." Moreover, Frank invokes assumptions about femininity as well in explaining why this makes sense. The image of one woman "in a class with all these boys going through puberty" implies women teachers' bodies are sexually objectified in the everyday routines of school environments, and therefore women need to be vigilant in staving off the potential sexual aggression that surrounds them. From this perspective, women's bodies are always potentially sexually alluring to boys, and as such, women teachers must continually adapt to the realities of masculine adolescent behavior by dressing in such a way that minimizes the degree to which boys will be able to see parts of their teachers' bodies. Such heteronormative assumptions about the relationships between femininity and masculinity are the basis for Frank's sense-making about the routine reminders issued to his women colleagues as a part of their training, and why it's "85, 90 percent geared toward women teachers." In Sara's account of her friend's experience, she also presumes a relationship between women's appearance and the likelihood of boys making sexual advances toward them. Even among sixth graders, teacher candidates assume sexually explicit or aggressive behavior is inevitable among boys and that all boys will find women's bodies sexually desirable, both assumptions that are widely shared among educators. They thereby justify strict body discipline among women teachers as the legitimate course of action. It is important to note Sara's characterization, "how awkward is that for her," followed by the statement that interactions such as these are "why they have to say those things." She suggests this was just an unfortunate, embarrassing occurrence for her classmate, one that could befall any number of women teachers, rather than foreground the inappropriateness of the boy's comment. She enacts elements of both masculine and feminine ideals to make sense of this routine encounter: women are sexually objectified, commonly evaluated on how they look, and boys are commonly sexually assertive and explicit. For Sara, Frank, and Faye, among other teacher candidates, that's just the way it is, and their perspectives are rife with rationalized ideals of femininity and masculinity.

Conclusion

The injunction to adapt is the centerpiece of the formal curriculum in teacher education at State University. It is a form of technical training, as it involves techniques for instructional modification and differentiation to meet the needs demonstrated by students. It is also a form of ethical indoctrination as well, as teacher candidates are implored by the faculty who train them to commit to the work of ongoing adaptation for the sake of student engagement and accommodation. Throughout my field work, the injunction to adapt found repeated expression in both the content of the courses teacher candidates took and the formal protocol of their performance evaluations. The injunction to adapt is a local and collective interpretation in the UBTE program at State University of the appropriate relationship between constructivist pedagogy and compulsory education. Indeed, there is a coherence in the ways the injunction to adapt both embodies constructivist philosophies and, at least ostensibly, meets the demands of compulsory education. According to the underlying logic, actively engaging students in their education by continually adapting instruction to their unique needs is a recipe for success no matter the type or the source of different students' needs. As such, carrying out the injunction to adapt as a teacher aligns closely with the rationalized ideal that teachers and schools must make education accessible to all students by accommodating, and responding to, whatever pre-existing qualities and skills they may exhibit.

These local interpretations of compulsory education as an institutional myth are filtered through the instructional philosophy of constructivist pedagogy. Local interpretations of masculinity and femininity as institutional myths align with philosophies of constructivist pedagogy with similar emphasis on responsiveness to what people define as innate pre-existing gendered qualities.

Standards for what it means to "dress professionally" are part of the formal program requirements. Part of the hidden curriculum, so to speak, for teacher candidates is that women must adapt and respond to rationalized assumptions that "boys will be boys" by desexualizing their bodies as much as possible in the ways they dress for work in schools. Such findings echo Valerie Walkerdine's analysis in which she shows how the institutionalized discourses and practices of "progressive pedagogy"[28] serve to normalize meanings about the "natural-ness" of boys' aggressive sexuality as students, and according to such discourses "it is the female teacher who is to *contain* this."[29] By treating gender in this way that is complementary and coherent with the injunction to adapt to various sources of student heterogeneity, gender and education become linked through the concomitant ways people inhabit the institutional myths that are their for-mal structure. Indeed, as Cecilia Ridgeway explains, gender "typically acts to bias in gendered directions the performance of behaviors undertaken in the name of more concrete, foregrounded organizational roles or identities."[30] Such overlap between gender and other institutions is facilitated when their respec-tive rationalized ideals align with each other like they do when teacher educa-tors and teacher candidates make sense of constructivist pedagogy and student heterogeneity at State University.

While the injunction to adapt is a key component of the formal UBTE cur-riculum at State University through which education faculty and administra-tors inhabit the institutional environment, teacher candidates also inhabit this environment themselves in even more nuanced ways. In the next chapter, I show how teacher candidates define their own varied responses to the pre-scriptions of constructivist pedagogy for meeting the demands of compulsory education and gender conformity, responses that reveal particular elements of a culture of ambivalence among teacher candidates.

2

The Challenges and Assumptions of Adapting to All Students

The institutional myths that structure education and gender provide many of the "rules of the game" for teachers, and as I detailed in Chapter 1, those rules get communicated to teacher candidates through the injunction to adapt at the State University UBTE program. But teacher candidates are not merely passive followers of those rules. Rather, they inhabit them. Teacher candidates modify and appropriate institutional myths to construct their own definitions of teaching.

Overall, teacher candidates believe in the legitimacy of compulsory education as a mandate of public education, they endorse constructivist pedagogy as an appropriate approach for engaging diverse learners, and they define traditional gender norms as innate human qualities that must be accommodated just like other sources of student heterogeneity. But they also become keenly and incisively aware of certain tensions and contradictions in the rationalized ideals they are expected to fulfill in the daily grind of their prospective work routines as teachers. How they go about trying to reconcile these tensions and contradictions endemic to their work forms the basis of a professional culture of ambivalence among teacher candidates. In this chapter, I show how teacher candidates' sense-making about compulsory education and gender norms shape specific elements of this professional culture.

Ambivalence about Reaching All Students

Virtually no one compelled to enter teaching as a career path goes into it explicitly rejecting the idea that all students are entitled to equality of educational opportunity. But believing in the merits of an ideal and going about the complex work of trying to help deliver on its promises are decidedly distinct phenomena, something teacher candidates confront firsthand throughout their training. They confront this tension first in the ways they engage with constructivist pedagogy and develop plans to carry out their own versions of it, and then subsequently in concrete interactions with different students in classroom settings.

Teacher Candidates' Partial Buy-In to Constructivist Pedagogy

In many ways, teacher candidates buy into the central tenets of constructivist pedagogy and the injunction to adapt. Hillary offers a good example. A teacher candidate in secondary math, here she describes to her classmates a session from a conference she attended:

> One thing I did take away from it was that students work in different ways. They kept saying that it is good to show students multiple ways of doing something and let them decide which way works best for them. It is important to remember that not all students are going to understand one certain way of multiplying, dividing, etc., and if you can be flexible to how they process their work, it will cause you to have a better relationship with that student because you are adaptable to what they need. More importantly, **they are going to be more successful** [emphasis is hers; Hillary put these words in bold]. I would much rather grade work that is done in different ways by different students and have a higher rate of success than have them all do one certain process and not be as successful. (Interview with Hillary, Secondary Math)

Consistent with the emphasis on adapting and adjusting to individual student capacities she has experienced in her methods courses, Hillary endorses being "flexible" and "adaptable to what they need" in her approach to instruction. She links this approach directly to students' potential success in math, and emphasizes this adaptation as a key means to fostering student learning. Moreover, she eschews uniformity in technique, noting that "to have them all do one certain process" could be the very pathway through which some students might "not be as successful."

Other teacher candidates in other subjects endorse differentiated instruction to meet the needs of "diverse learners" as well, and link its effectiveness to the educational psychology. A group of teacher candidates in secondary English/language arts discuss this in the following excerpt from a presentation they gave to their class on a particular lesson they planned together:

> Our presentation is on visualizing and learning, and if you all remember your educational psychology course, you may remember Howard Gardner and his theory on multiple intelligences [shows slide listing the seven original intelligences Gardner identifies: visual/spatial, linguistic, logical/mathematical, bodily/kinesthetic, musical, intrapersonal,

and interpersonal]. What does all of this mean? Whether you buy the theory or not, kids have a range of abilities, and we as teachers need to use as many strategies as possible to reach out to the greatest number of students. (Field notes, Instructional Methods in Secondary English/Language Arts)

As the basis for the lesson they have made, this group cites Gardner's theory explicitly and references the prior coursework all teacher candidates have had in educational psychology in which multiple intelligences is part of the curriculum. That "kids have a range of abilities" is just a fact of life, according to this teacher candidate, and teachers must diversify instruction to accommodate this. While these teacher candidates endorse diversifying instruction, they also signal a degree of ambivalence concerning Gardner's theory of multiple intelligences. Indeed, in this case teacher candidates argue for engaging in practices that align with the scientific theory that prescribes their use, but not in a way that requires 100% belief in the credibility of the theory. One can, and should, differentiate instruction to "reach out to the greatest number of students," but this is achievable "whether you buy the theory or not."

Faculty in the UBTE program sometimes observed teacher candidates' partial buy-in with elements of constructivist pedagogy. In one case, a faculty member, Todd, grew concerned that his teacher candidates were not fully understanding, or committed to, the constructivist strategies he had been modeling to them in class. At the beginning of class one day, he expressed this concern to the class:

He says he thinks they "are not really grasping the concepts . . . behind the strategies." He tells them he thinks this might be "partly my fault, and I apologize." But he says he wants them to get the concepts down so they can improve with practice; he says, in teaching "it's all about practice." One of the biggest problems he says he is seeing in the conferences is a "lack of background knowledge" on the topics they are teaching. Todd asks them if they have gone to the public library to research their topics; nobody answers affirmatively. He says when he was teaching, "the public library, that's the first place I need to go." He gives an example of a time when he did this to teach the American Revolution. He describes walking out of the library with "thirty books, and I would just pore through them." He tells them that he didn't want to do the "typical George Washington garbage, or just traditional stuff, but find those interesting stories." He goes on to say that "without the meticulous research, it couldn't have happened." Todd describes the specific topics and resources he read, such as *1776*, and he would go into detail on things like the duel between Alexander Hamilton and Aaron Burr. He says he wanted to find "relevant, interesting stuff," and that he had to "research and know the ins-and-outs of the topic."

Todd ties the background knowledge to the formats of the lesson plans they have been discussing, saying they need to "really understand the foundations of these four strategies for lessons." The connection to background knowledge is "you can't teach what you don't know." Todd also emphasizes to them the importance of this stage in their training; he tells them, "This is your last chance before student teaching to say, 'I can do this.'" He says they can't just cruise through stuff, that they can't always be in "survival mode." He acknowledges that "I had to survive on occasion, but some teachers do it for the entire year because they have no conscience." Todd relates to them a situation he experienced when he had not slept for two to three days straight, but that he came to work anyway and got through it. He says that on those days when he would just survive, "I had those kids in front of me, I felt guilty." He compares teaching to other jobs where people can come in and log their hours, and that's it because "no one's holding you accountable," but that they can't do that as teachers. He says, "You gotta be genuine, you gotta be real . . . and that comes from your preparation, your emotion for the topic, and the research allows you to do that." Todd says teaching is "not an easy job. It's not a fallback. It's not a safety net." (Field notes, Instructional Methods Course in Elementary Education)

Todd attempts to call his teacher candidates to the carpet, so to speak, on this day in class because he feels they are not putting in sufficient effort in their preparation to realize the potential effectiveness of the instructional strategies he has taught them. In particular, he observes they have not to this point done sufficient research on their own to come up with material to make their lesson plans in social studies interesting enough to meet the level of student engagement these strategies prioritize (recall from the previous chapter the example of the "supermarket" technique, along with "inquiry," constructivist techniques that require student involvement and problem-solving).

Todd actively links the underlying assumptions of the teaching strategies to the effort he expects teacher candidates to put into their preparation. He uses his own prior teaching experience and his observations of other teachers as a means of motivating them to commit to these underlying assumptions concerning student engagement. First, to "really understand the foundations of these four strategies," Todd argues they must do the work to develop their own "background knowledge" in the topics they teach. In this sense, the interaction serves as a reminder to teacher candidates that they need to "find those interesting stories," and emphasize "relevant, interesting stuff" in their lessons as a means of engaging students and motivating their interest in the subject matter.

Todd also warns teacher candidates about the costs of failure to fulfill these foundational principles. If they do not perform meticulous research, their lessons will be little more than "typical . . . garbage" and limited to "just traditional stuff." Todd goes even further with the potential for negative consequences. Not only will prospective lesson plans be poor in quality, such failure amounts to a character flaw in the teachers themselves. To continually "just cruise through stuff" and operate in "survival mode" are the actions of teachers who "have no conscience," according to Todd. Failing to put in the effort to make one's lessons engaging to students should induce guilt, Todd tells them, recounting his own experience, and he appeals to their ethical commitment to the well-being of children as motivation to do the hard work required of them. Importantly, Todd's lecture to teacher candidates on this day in class pertains exclusively to their effort, or lack thereof, in his observation. He does not cite an instance in which teacher candidates have actively resisted or challenged the legitimacy of the principles or assumptions of constructivist pedagogy that undergird the instructional techniques they are planning, nor do any teacher candidates challenge them in this exchange.

Similar to how Todd referenced the specter of teachers who "have no conscience," other faculty used examples of what they defined as poor teaching practice. In one instance, Beth uses a specific example of poor instruction a teacher candidate observes and mentions during class.

> A teacher candidate complains about her experience in that she feels her teacher is not doing a very good job, but she's not in a position to do anything about it.
>
> Beth: "Were you in a position to jump in, what would you have done?" [Teacher candidate says that the teacher is not building on what the students know, so many of them are lost.] "Okay, so it's not set up well, you didn't feel like she was scaffolding enough . . . You would try to do more scaffolding and modeling to students . . . You guys are going to see this; you're going to see how the things you've learned here aren't used, and you're going to see the consequences of not using them." (Field notes, Instructional Methods Course in Secondary English/Language Arts)

Beth takes this opportunity to shape the ways teacher candidates in the class make sense of inconsistencies between what they observe current teachers doing in classrooms and the strategies teacher candidates are learning in their training. In this case, a teacher candidate expresses frustration that, in her observation, the teacher she is observing this semester is "not doing a good job," and students are suffering for it. After the teacher candidate diagnoses the problem at Beth's request, she references "scaffolding" as a technique teacher candidates have learned in training that might work better. In this sense, Beth is helping the teacher candidate think prospectively about how to avoid similar problems in her own future instruction, but she also emphasizes the "consequences" that befall students when "the things you've learned here aren't used." The reference and reminder about a particular technique (scaffolding) that exemplifies institutionalized practices of constructivist pedagogy also comes packaged with a warning about the negative effects of failing to live up to the expectations of the institution.

Such interactions occurred across subject matter and grade-level distinctions for teacher candidates. Another instance comes from a methods course in secondary math:

> A teacher candidate comments on the field experience, and, similar to Hillary's point, that some of class time is used as a "study hall" for the students, which usually doesn't result in student learning. Bob says things like this are examples of "a lot of things that are beyond your control." Another teacher candidate offers a counterpoint that it also matters that the students "didn't use the time wisely." Bob re-emphasizes that there "are a lot of things that don't put students first" in schools, such as teachers who use inefficient practices with students. Also, in their case, their supervising teachers' practices are also beyond their control. (Field notes, Instructional Methods Course in Secondary Math)

We see faculty trying to account for discrepancies between certain routine classroom practices among current teachers and the types of practices they are endorsing in the UBTE program. Instruction that does not keep students engaged as active learners, like "study hall," amounts to one of "a lot of things that don't put students first." Again, there is a kind of moralistic cautioning in Bob's tone in this discussion that serves as a reminder of the core premise of constructivist pedagogy. Throughout their entire training, teacher candidates are indoctrinated into the notion that effective instruction must "put students first." Practices that fail to do so do not produce learning, and an implication of Bob's comment is that teacher candidates should avoid resembling any teacher whose practices do not primarily serve students.

Meanings about constructivist pedagogy, and the underlying institutional assumptions they reaffirm, are not always uniform. In the exchange above in Bob's methods course, one of the teacher candidates offers an alternative meaning concerning the "study hall" practice that Bob claims is an example of common practices that do not "put students first." Instead, this teacher candidate suggests there is an appropriate onus on students to "use the time wisely." The implication is that, in fact, this approach could be useful to student learning if students actively engage themselves in meaningful activities that could fruitfully further student learning. This is a plausible alternative interpretation of constructivist pedagogy, one that assumes an active role on the part of students.

Similar negotiations of meaning emerged in ongoing interaction among teacher candidates. One day in the same methods course in secondary math, two teacher candidates and a doctoral student in math education discussed limitations to "constructivist" approaches in the context of addressing everyday dilemmas in teaching math:

meaning-making [handwritten marginalia]

> One teacher candidate in the group speculates that teaching kids new knowledge like this through group work would be difficult. The doctoral student agrees, and says,
>
> > Ethan: "Sometimes you need to teach, or traditionally explain something to kids . . . We don't want to admit that we need rote teaching."
> >
> > Paul: "That's something people here don't talk about; they focus on the 'constructivist' approach . . ."
> >
> > Ethan: "Kids will come to you crying, saying 'Just tell me what I need to know!'"

(Field notes, Instructional Methods Course in Secondary Math)

In a later interview, I asked the teacher candidate in this exchange, Paul, to elaborate on his comments:

> I feel like there are some [education faculty] that are just really bad, and they have an agenda, and I don't think they're secure enough to admit it. I think there's also some that after we had this conversation would admit that it's really a combination of the two. I would say 50% would and 50% wouldn't. I also feel like, because it's so one-sided—not in Bob's class, Bob's class you can have some real discussions—I feel like in some of my classes it's so explicit! Like if I try to state my opinion, it's like, "Okay, well . . . Moving on." Because it doesn't fit in the agenda. I feel like there's been a number of those, like I said about 50% are like that.
>
> It causes me, at least, to zone out a little bit. It's kind of ironic, I mean, the constructivist principle says that students have to have ownership of what they're doing, they have to process it for themselves to make realizations on their own, yet whenever they teach us how to do that, we can't have real ownership on it because we're not really allowed to evaluate things, and kind of think about it and have some discourse. So in some of my classes, I don't feel like we ever get to take ownership of some of these ideas they're trying to teach us. They don't take a constructivist approach to teaching constructivism.

And the thing is in some of these classes, I know what they want me to say, and I get the distinct impression that if I don't just say what they want me to say, they're not going to give me a good grade, and so I just say whatever and do it. I don't really get much out of it. You know, I've got an interview with a pretty prestigious place, and I think part of the reason I got that interview is because I got a high GPA in a highly ranked program. (Interview with Paul, Secondary Math)

Based on their interactions with students in schools through classroom observations, these teacher candidates observe that there are occasions in which "rote teaching," or teacher-directed instruction, is both appropriate as well as welcomed by students. But this does not fit with the "agenda" of constructivism Paul feels many education faculty espouse in their classes, to the point that he feels his efforts to discuss alternatives in some classes have been unfairly dismissed in class discussions with certain faculty (though he notes Bob is more open-minded).

Paul notes the irony in the common reaction he receives when offering a critique of constructivism. Indeed, "they don't take a constructivist approach to teaching constructivism," because if they did, from his perspective, they would invite this type of evaluation from teacher candidates. Because they do not, from Paul's point of view, he responds in a way that is important for understanding how local sense-making can simultaneously challenge and sustain institutional myths: he tells them what they want to hear. He has been reminded about the tenets of constructivism in ways that are "so explicit," and the institutional rewards of a "high GPA" for compliance are too valuable to challenge constructivist ideals in ways that might sacrifice good grades. As such, Paul complies in his outward behavior with rationalized meanings about constructivist pedagogy, but simultaneously constructs alternative meanings about their legitimacy that will likely inform his own instructional practice in his prospective classroom. As he notes, this is neither a wholesale rejection nor endorsement of constructivist pedagogy ("it's really a combination of the two," meaning student-centered and teacher-directed instruction). Paul sees mixed approaches to instruction as appropriate, but feels his perspective is rejected by UBTE faculty who favor exclusive reliance on constructivist pedagogy.

Teacher candidates subscribe to constructivist pedagogy in many ways, but nonetheless develop their own perspectives about it that are more nuanced than blanket endorsement and uniform adoption. Some retain skepticism about its underlying theories, some underestimate the preparation necessary to execute it, some recognize that it is not universally practiced among teachers in schools, and some feel it is best packaged alongside more traditional forms of instruction. Each of these perspectives can coexist with a commitment to the overall utility of constructivist pedagogy, and for many teacher candidates, they do. Indeed, teacher candidates subscribe to constructivist pedagogy, but they clearly develop a sense of ambivalence about whether constructivist pedagogy is the instructional panacea they feel it is billed to be in their UBTE program.

"There Are Some Kids That Don't Want to Be Reached"

A related element of teacher candidates' ambivalence lies in the perspectives they develop about certain aspects of the student heterogeneity that constructivist pedagogy is intended to address. Especially concerning issues related to student motivation, teacher candidates express profound ambivalence about their capacity to engage all students, regardless of the instructional practices they choose. While teacher candidates bring such ideas with them to their training, they elaborate their meaning through interaction with each other in their coursework and with students in their student teaching. This issue came up in a discussion between teacher candidates in secondary mathematics that occurred via the online discussion forum that was a component of their instructional methods course:

> At some point, it does not matter if you are the best teacher—if students lack the motivation and the concern for their grades, what can you do? I am concerned because as a new teacher, I want to feel like I am really capable of actually being a prepared (and hopefully good) teacher when I graduate college and start my career . . . Students' grades and their success are the most tangible ways to determine how well you are teaching. If one-third to one-half of my students are failing, I know I will be very discouraged and question whether or not I have what it takes to be an efficient teacher (even though my supervising teacher does a great job and has those failing rates). So I guess my question is, how can I engage students who lack the motivation or interest to study math in order to help them succeed, but also keep up with the standards? (Leslie, Secondary Mathematics Discussion Forum Exchange)

One of Leslie's classmates responded to her with the following:

> I agree with you 100% on being concerned with unmotivated students. We as teachers hope that all our students will succeed and love math. But who are we kidding? The way I see it, learning is a two-way street. Students cannot expect us as teachers to carry them through the year. Like we discussed in class, we want our students to struggle and be challenged by mathematical concepts. Sounds like a good idea to us, but that is because we all like math and want to be challenged. I know if I were in an art class and a teacher tried to challenge me, I would tell her where she could go and to just pass me through the class. I have no interest in

art whatsoever. All we can do as teachers is show them the opportunity they have if they work hard now. If they do not want to listen to it, that is not our fault. Like I said, learning is a two-way street, and we as teachers cannot be expected to be a tow truck with all of our students attached behind us. (Chris, Secondary Mathematics Discussion Forum Exchange)

The issue of student motivation arises for Leslie through the classroom interactions she observes as part of her required field experience prior to her student teaching. In observing her supervising teacher (whom she notes is very effective), she grows concerned about the lack of motivation among many students. She relates this directly to constructivist pedagogy in a compulsory system by asking how she is supposed to "engage" all learners when some "lack the motivation or interest." The injunction to adapt calls for teacher candidates to keep experimenting with those students until one finds a technique to engage them, but Leslie's classmate responds with a somewhat different perspective. "Learning is a two-way street," according to him, and "students cannot expect us as teachers to carry them through the year." Moreover, he normalizes low student motivation by citing his own lack of interest in art as a subject. In other words, some students just don't like math, and that's just the way it is. As such, if students "do not want to listen to us, it's not our fault."

Other teacher candidates expressed similar meanings they developed through their student teaching experience, interacting with specific students as they attempted the full-time work of teaching for the first time. Oscar was placed in a school that was ethno-racially diverse and had a high concentration of students from low SES families. He discussed in an interview how his perspective has been shaped by confronting the realities of compulsory education in this context:

I don't think I am as idealistic as I once was. I'm definitely not jaded in any way, but definitely changed my perspective, the way big cities, and inner cities can feel, and all these different ethnic groups and white kids as well as anyone else, there's something [. . . .] There's some [students] that just don't want to learn. And it's kinda like, we're providing a public education, by all means I want to teach all kids, but if they don't want to learn, there's only so much I can do. And I've come to the realization that, God, I want to reach every kid that I can, but there are some kids that don't want to be reached. You can't help those. You can try, and I've tried. You know, it's kind of like slamming yourself against a brick wall. I can see why teachers, because as a student, not as a student teacher, but as a student in the School of Education you can see those teachers and reflect upon the teachers that you've had, and were jaded and had given up on the ideals of teaching. You know, as a student in the School of Ed you're like, "Man, I can't understand why a teacher would be that way." But you know, after tasting the teaching experience, you're kind of like, "Wow, after so many years I can see how this teacher changed their personality and they're no longer, 'Let's get everyone involved and teach and change the world.'" I can see how some, in the environments that they are in, can change. I can definitely see that. (Interview with Oscar, Secondary Social Studies)

Oscar is quick to point out that he himself is "not jaded," but he sympathizes with more experienced teachers in ways he had not before his own student teaching in a school with diverse students and an abundance of behavioral and academic challenges. He emphasizes that "by all means I want to teach all kids," but equally expresses his own limits in achieving this goal "if they don't want to learn." Oscar, like many teacher candidates, is keenly mindful of the limits of his own capacity to "reach" particularly challenging students.

Oscar's experience in his student teaching with the challenges of reaching, or engaging, particular students was nearly universally shared in some way among all teacher candidates. Another example comes from both my field notes from a day in class with Nicole's third-grade classroom, as well as a subsequent interview I did with her after this day in class. First, this excerpt from my field notes captures how these challenges play out in classroom interactions, as well as the practices teacher candidates attempt in real time to address these challenges.

> Nicole keeps reading while walking by and taking a book from Charlotte, who then throws a piece of paper. Nicole keeps reading to the class. Nicole stays close to Charlotte's desk while reading. Two boys begin talking in the back, and Nicole stops, saying "Boys, is there a problem?" They return attention to her. Nicole resumes reading to the class, finishing the relatively short story in a matter of minutes. She says that this is a new "version" of the Cinderella story in which penguins are the characters instead of dinosaurs or dogs like previous versions they've read.
>
> Charlotte hits her desk without warning during this discussion. Nicole says nothing, but walks over and looks at the desk. Nicole tries to continue her question/answer session with the class. She asks, "Is this version a fairy tale?" The class answers collectively, "Yeesss." Charlotte begins kicking the bottom of her desk loudly. She kicks once, then a second time. Then she kicks two more times, very loudly in rapid succession. On the fourth kick, Nicole raises her voice, "Charlotte! I'm not going to put up with you! Go sit on the other side of the door in Ms. Thompson's room!" Charlotte jumps up, and replies scathingly, "I'd be happy to!" Nicole snaps back, "There's no reason for you to act like that!" Charlotte comments over her shoulder sarcastically, "I am so sorry!" She walks

Reminds me of dance class "

out of the room. Nicole resumes the reading lesson with the class. (Field notes, Nicole's Student Teaching)

This day in class was an important priming experience for Nicole in the realities of teaching for many reasons. First, Charlotte was a very difficult student to manage, and she simply insisted on having a temper tantrum in class for reasons completely unapparent to Nicole and myself. That would be challenging enough, but Charlotte is only one student whose behavior Nicole has to manage as she is conducting this reading lesson. She also has to stop the two boys in the back of the room who were talking during the lesson.

It is important to note, however, that Nicole attempts to manage everyone's behavior while also keeping the lesson going. She addresses the class, first reading the story aloud and then asking the class questions, while she also moves around the room taking things from certain students and standing closer to those who are not behaving. Moreover, only when Charlotte becomes so disruptive that the lesson simply cannot proceed does Nicole dismiss her from the classroom. Such a strategy was common among teacher candidates, and these initial experiences in student teaching are the first attempts at enacting the institutional requirement that public schools must educate all comers. Any students that teacher candidates dismissed from class for behavioral reasons eventually returned to class. In fact, it was a common message to teacher candidates from supervising teachers that they should not send many students out of their classroom to the principal for behavior problems. Principals, they were often told, would interpret this as the teacher candidate's inability to manage their own classroom, and it would reflect poorly on the teacher candidate's job performance. Nicole attempted to adapt what she was doing in class to the behavior of her students while moving the lesson along.

These situations are emotionally taxing, and the emotional intensity of their interactions with students heightens the emphasis they place on adaptation as an essential teaching skill. In a follow-up interview with Nicole, I asked her about this day in class and how she tried to manage students like Charlotte and one of the boys in the back of the room who was also disruptive:

Judson: Can you compare how you might deal with other students in your class with how you'd deal with her?

Nicole: It's really hard. He [other frequently disruptive student] is more comical about things; he's more light-hearted, even though he does a lot of the same things, he does them in a different way. Whereas she [Charlotte], she gets mad; she throws fits. So I find myself responding to them in those ways. He's kind of that kid where I can make smart comments, or jokes, and he'll get it. Her, on the other hand, she . . . You really have to get mean sometimes before she's like, "Okay." That's really hard for me.

We did find out from her counselor, when she does those things it's
because she wants the attention from the rest of the class. You know, I kind
of already knew that anyways. It's hard to balance between giving her the
attention she wants and disciplining her. You still need to discipline her
and correct her behavior without letting it become such a big deal where
she's getting what she wants because then you're just reinforcing her negative behavior as opposed to trying to correct it. So, it's really hard.

(Interview with Nicole, Elementary Education)

Even dealing with students who engage in ostensibly similar behavior requires
adaptation. Nicole finds that she can use sarcasm effectively to manage the one
student, but that she really must "get mean" with Charlotte to make it clear that
her behavior is unacceptable. In this sense, we see Nicole employ the injunction
to adapt in another way. In addition to thinking on her feet and responding to
student behavior while continuing the lesson, she uses different behavior modification strategies for these two students based on her observation of how such
differentiation is required by their distinct emotional and behavioral needs. As
such, in several ways, Nicole embraces the injunction to adapt and the constructivist philosophies it expresses.

Despite her best efforts to remain wedded to the injunction to adapt and
work diligently to keep even the most challenging students involved and on
task in her instruction, Nicole still expresses a clear ambivalence about her
efficacy in this effort. She discusses the background information about Charlotte she learned from the counselor who works with her, and how difficult it is
to strike an effective balance between modifying versus reinforcing her negative behavior. Indeed, the steps she takes to adapt to Charlotte's unique needs
to improve her behavior and performance could very well make the problem
worse. Because the relationship between Nicole's effort to adapt and the factors
motivating the student's behavior is so unclear, Nicole emphasizes repeatedly
that "it's really hard" working with such students.

We see teacher candidates develop a shared sense of ambivalence about
their capacity to realize the mandate of compulsory education with all students, and how this emerges through their interactions with students in classroom settings. For some, like Oscar, there are simply "some kids that don't
want to be reached." For others, like Nicole, it is just "really hard" to know
the right course of action to deal with the complicated external factors that
affect student motivation. Such ambivalence is not a wholesale rejection of
the rationalized ideal that teachers must reach all students, but it does serve
to justify for teacher candidates that it is legitimate to partially give up on
a literal interpretation of that ideal. Shared among these teacher candidates
is the sense that there are things beyond their control that affect student
motivation. While they commit to reaching as many students as possible,

they resign themselves to the notion that a partial degree of failure is all but inevitable.

Tensions of Gender Conformity as Teachers

[Book's main Contribution]

Students bring to the classroom a range of pre-existing conditions rooted in different elements of their backgrounds that affect teaching and learning. The injunction to adapt, and the constructivist philosophy it represents, is a programmatic response to the realities that teacher candidates will face in prospective work environments. Teacher candidates inhabit the institutional myth that they must reach all students by developing a sense of ambivalence about their capacity to do so, and this informs their response to the range of these pre-existing conditions that they, along with their teacher educators, define as largely beyond their control. As we saw in Chapter 1, teacher candidates and teacher educators define gendered forms of behavior as pre-existing (even innate) conditions students bring with them to the classroom, and to which teachers must adapt their own actions to accommodate. Teacher candidates inhabit these rationalized ideals about gender in ways that foster a similar sense of ambivalence about their capacity to successfully balance their own gender conformity with the responsibilities of teaching. Much like they define as inevitable a partial degree of failure in reaching all students, so too do they define as inevitable a partial degree of failure in keeping certain elements of their gender identities separate from their professional identities in their interactions with students.

Rationalizing Femininity and Masculinity in Teaching as "Common Sense"

Teacher candidates and their teacher educators assume women are routinely, if not primarily, evaluated in terms of their physical appearance in everyday interactions, and that this entails a heteronormative sexualization of women's bodies. Such a view is consistent with broader cultural ideals of traditional femininity and masculinity, which sustain what Naomi Wolf calls "the Beauty Myth,"[1] and which prioritize narrow definitions of beauty as central to successfully executing traditionally feminine gender performances. When these assumptions are brought to bear on teacher education for women, however, they become the basis for mandates for women to desexualize their bodies as the appropriate professional response to the innate sexual proclivities of boys, the related underlying assumption about masculinity. In the context of teaching, another element of the femininity myth, being sexually virtuous and unattainable, becomes equated with teacher professionalism for women in the ways teacher candidates, faculty, and school personnel make sense of the dynamics of traditional gender performances and their relevance for everyday schooling interactions. As such, women teacher candidates must navigate an inherent contradiction of femininity myths: being sexually desirable without exuding

[why should it be this way?]

sexuality is a defining feature of "successful" feminine performances. The tensions in these rationalized meanings become explicit in UBTE routines through the incessant reminders and warnings to women in the program.

To be sure, teacher candidates take for granted as legitimate the gendered meanings relevant to work-related action for teachers. However, when we examine the active ways that teacher candidates respond to warnings they encounter via professional socialization, we see the ways they make sense of masculinity, femininity, and teacher professionalism are not unreflective. Rather, they actively respond to these messages in ways that involve both compliance with dress codes, as well as modifications to them in the course of routine interactions. Women teacher candidates tend to align behavior closely with aspects of dress code standards that prohibit sexually charged body displays and behaviors, but are more likely to deviate from gendered expectations for dress that they define as loosely coupled with sexuality. Additionally, teacher candidates also interpret inconsistencies between warnings issued by authorities in the teacher education program and what they define as normative everyday dress code practices within the schools where they do their student teaching. When such inconsistencies occur, they define the reminders they hear from UBTE faculty as out of touch with existing realities, and conform to prevailing practices in local schools. Their gender conformity, then, is inhabited, as teacher candidates purposefully enact rationalized meanings about gender and sexuality as they confront practical decisions they must make in the course of everyday interactions in the settings where they are immersed.

We saw Faye in Chapter I define the standards for women's professional dress as "common sense," and she, like Sara and Frank, defined them this way based on their shared "boys will be boys" assumptions about masculinity. Other teacher candidates defined them using the same language. As Nicole said in a separate interview, "I feel like if you have any common sense at all, you're not going to go into a school with half your body hanging out" (Interview with Nicole, Elementary Education).

Men in this study also defined women's professional dress standards as common-sense, legitimate action for teachers:

Judson: Have any of your female friends in the School of Education ever taken offense to that [the standards for their dress]?

Frank: Um . . . No, no. Generally, like people understand why they need to do whatever . . . It's just kinda like a common sense thing, I think.

(Interview with Frank, Secondary Language Arts)

Many teacher candidates found women's standards to be so common-sensical that they expressed disbelief that others would need to be reminded to "dress professionally." Further comment from Nicole:

[Nodding in affirmative] Doesn't that amaze you! You'd think they [other teacher candidates] would know what they can wear and what they can't wear. I really don't see why an instructor should literally have to spell it out for you every single time. It amazes me! And somehow they still wear what they're not supposed to wear. (Interview with Nicole, Elementary Education)

I observed Nicole every week during her student teaching, and she—as well as all women teacher candidates I observed—complied with these standards for their dress and covered their bodies so as not to reveal cleavage, underwear, stomach, or legs, nor did any of them ever wear tight-fitting clothing to teach. Conforming to these standards in behavior and defining them as common sense, teacher candidates contribute to the maintenance of their legitimacy as professional norms for teachers, as well as the legitimacy of the heteronormative institutional myths that inform them. Teacher candidates like Nicole are also "amazed" that there are others who have to be reminded of something that is so obvious to them.

Ambivalence about Gender Conformity and Teacher Professionalism

Teacher candidates also often ridiculed individuals who violated dress codes for women and enforced the standard among themselves. But their conformity was not always wholesale, nor was it an unreflective process of following preexisting rules:

Hillary: I think there's always an issue. Someone's always got their shirt on too low or their bra strap hanging out. Um, I mean, last year it was kind of pointless because we couldn't wear open-toed shoes. I'm like, "Yeah, yeah, that's fine. All the teachers do it." I guess I'm surprised, because I'm like, you walk into these schools and you look sloppy? You look like an idiot! It's you in the end who gets nabbed in the ass.[2] It's too bad for you! I'm surprised at how many comments do have to be made because, it's like, you're twenty-two years old, and you haven't figured this out yet?

Judson: So, it's your experience that there are a lot of students who need to hear that, or that maybe the people in the School of Ed are saying it more than is necessary?

Hillary: In my math block, I think it's more than necessary. Because I know everybody pretty well, and we see each other in our teaching clothes all the time, and I've never seen anybody where I'd be like, "Oh, you don't look very good"—except one time I said something to Lindsay. Um, but I don't know about the other blocks either. It might be more of an influence from there. I feel like to us, it's like, "Okay, we get it now. That's enough."

(Interview with Hillary, Secondary Math Education)

Hillary defines women's professional dress standards as legitimate to the point that, according to her, individuals who do not adhere to such standards "look like an idiot." She describes how she and her peers monitor each other, noting that "one time I said something to Lindsay," when one of her peers dressed in a manner Hillary disapproved.

By and large, Hillary adheres to the dress code and adapts her own gender performance in the context of teaching to accommodate gendered assumptions. But she also acknowledges that minor violations routinely occur as a product of what she characterizes as the normal behavior involved in other elements of traditionally feminine gender performances. As she put it, "someone's always got a shirt on too low or a bra strap hanging out." From her point of view, women engaging in everyday gender performances that are sexually meaningless can nevertheless be interpreted by others as sexually charged displays, and therefore emerge as problematic, albeit accidentally on the part of a teacher candidate. A teacher candidate might view a shirt that she normally wears as appropriate to wear when teaching, but others may define it as "too low." Likewise, a teacher candidate might unknowingly expose a bra strap, but because others might eroticize the bra strap, it could violate dress code standards, according to Hillary. In this sense, because women are so ubiquitously viewed as sex objects, there is always the potential that women's bodies could be sexualized in the context of teaching despite their efforts to desexualize them. In other words, a certain degree of failure to live up to the dress code standards for women is inevitable, a key reason why Hillary thinks "there's always an issue," even though she conforms overall to the dress code and adapts her appearance in response to the assumptions behind it.

In addition, we see Hillary challenge components of the dress code for women. On the issue of "open-toed shoes," Hillary casually dismisses this rule she was told to follow, explaining that it does not square with what she has experienced in her interactions with other teachers in local schools who do routinely wear open-toed shoes. Moreover, this is one element of the dress code that is not as closely linked with sexualized meanings. Exposed toes are much less sexually charged displays than exposed cleavage, bra straps, thongs, midriffs, or legs. Since other teachers frequently wear open-toed shoes, Hillary observes more opportunity to modify the dress code to match her own preferences without risking the same kind of punishment more sexually charged physical displays would likely solicit. The discrepancy between the prohibitions against open-toed shoes within the teacher education program and the daily practices of the teachers working in public schools invites interpretation among teacher candidates in deciding which set of meanings to define as legitimate for their own practice. While teacher candidates are directed by others in positions of authority, they also make their own sense of rules for behavior and actively construct competing meanings through ongoing interaction.

Teacher candidates conform in their behavior to the institutional pressures exemplified in dress codes as best they can while they simultaneously challenge the legitimacy of the UBTE program by ridiculing and often ignoring the ways it enforces the dress codes. An exchange among teacher candidates about the "pre-professional meeting" they had to attend in class one day offers an example:

> Nina, among others, begins talking about the "pre-professional meeting" they have to attend this week. Quintin and others around the room have joined in the discussion of the meeting, and he asks if they're "supposed to dress up." No one thinks they need to, but several of the women in the group note all the times they've heard how they are supposed to "dress professionally." Quintin is in the process of packing up to leave, and as he leaves the room, he says to the group he will see them tonight and, "Be sure to dress skanky; that's how they want it." Several in the group chuckle at this, and others begin packing up to leave. (Field notes, Instructional Methods Course in Elementary Education)

gross

Quintin's joke mocks the UBTE program and its administrators for the incessant warnings issued to teacher candidates, especially women, about the dress code. In this sense, it is a behind-the-scenes challenge to authority figures in the program and their preoccupation with enforcing the dress code. However, his use of the word "skanky" also reifies as legitimate the stigma assigned to women whose gender performances are defined by others as sexually enticing. As such, this exchange contributes to gender conformity even though it is also a jab at the manner in which teacher education continually mandates gender conformity.

Women in the program often defined the constant dress code reminders directed at them in the program as useless, precisely because they defined the heteronormative institutional myths that informed the dress code standards as such obvious, common-sense knowledge.

Nellie: It's just obnoxious that they're wasting our time by saying this for the twentieth time, and they're giving you the old speech, like, "Don't wear a mini-skirt when you teach." It's like "duh." I wish they would tell us who's doing this! Tell those people, because I mean [. . .] I'm so tired of hearing, "Don't let your underwear hang out." Oh my gosh! I wish they would talk to specific people, the ones that are in trouble.

wastes time

(Interview with Nellie, Secondary Math)

Because they are blanket statements to everyone, those like Nellie, who feel they already comply with the rules and understand the assumptions behind them, take offense. Nellie feels as though her own intelligence is insulted and her time wasted. Hillary expressed a similar sentiment earlier in the chapter ("Yeah, okay, we get it."), as did Quintin with his joke to his classmates. As such, teacher candidates' conformity in belief and behavior is often accompanied by mockery and disdain for the manner in which they are monitored and reminded about the importance of compliance. Deborah, in secondary language arts education, articulates a number of these complexities:

Deborah: Now they're talking about, um, closed-toed shoes. I hate closed-toed shoes [Deborah laughs]. So, I don't know how much I'll pay attention to that one.

Judson: Yeah?

Deborah: Men, they're telling them to wear ties. Teachers in the schools, they're not wearing ties. They're worried about the way [university] is represented, because apparently students in the past have not represented them well. They've gotten calls from people.

Judson: That's what I heard in a different methods class, where a faculty member claimed that ten different principals had complained to the School of Education and were threatening to throw people out. Again, it was "dress professionally."

Deborah: The problem with dressing professionally these days, professional clothes have changed. Women are showing more cleavage, skirts are shorter, heels are higher.

Judson: Does it bother you that girls are targeted more than guys?

Deborah: Not really, because it's not like I want to go there showing everything to my students anyway [Deborah laughs]. But, I mean I know how to dress. But, I look at some of the girls, and some of them are a little risky.

Judson: So, some people do need to hear these warnings, but not everyone. Does it bother you that they tell everyone?

Deborah: No, I just don't listen to it. I just choose not to listen to it. [Deborah laughs.]

(Interview with Deborah, Secondary English/Language Arts)

Indeed, many of the women in this study reported they simply stopped listening to reminders about the dress code. Such responses are subtle forms of resistance to formal rules and authority in teacher education, even though teacher candidates mostly comply with those rules in their behavior. When teacher candidates modify the dress code, it is often by the meanings they develop by observing inconsistencies in the norms across different institutional settings. Like Hillary, Deborah plans to ignore the prohibition against open-toed shoes. Likewise, few men adhere to the rule to wear ties. In both cases, teacher candidates view the rule as irrelevant to how teachers actually conduct their work in public schools, and neither are sexually charged modifications for either

he really goes on an an about this...

women or men. Moreover, Deborah observes changes in the norms for women's dress in work environments more broadly as becoming more permissible of the types of body displays for women that the UBTE program and many public schools strictly forbid. She conforms to the dress code, but largely because she has already been socialized to traditional gender performances for women and the contradictions therein ("I know how to dress"). She recognizes, though, the subtle tensions in expectations for "professional" behavior for women in both teaching and other professions. To be successfully feminine according to rationalized gender ideals, women must conform to the ideal beauty standards that sexualize their bodies while simultaneously desexualizing their appearance. Deborah recognizes these contradictions in the prescriptive rules about dress codes and meanings about teacher professionalism in interactions with students. While she herself does not "want to go there showing everything to my students," she is aware that women in teaching could be labeled failures at teacher professionalism for engaging in gender conformity that would be acceptable in other professional settings.

Many women in the program did indeed wear open-toed shoes while teaching, and though this deviates from the dress code, it is still gender conforming for women. Another instance of nonconformity with expectations for professional dress and appearance involved Frank, but was an instance of gender nonconformity for men.

Frank: The thing that gets me every time that I kind of battle with—my ears are pierced. One time, a teacher noticed that I had this in [points to a hoop earring in the top half of his ear; he has one in each ear]. One of the vice-principals said, "You know, you really shouldn't have that in." I'm thinking, it's not going to distract [. . . .] Like, what is one earring gonna do? Well, she asked if I could take it out. And I'm like, "I can't," because I can't take this out without pliers. She's like, "Okay."

Judson: Did she offer any explanation?

Frank: Well, I wasn't going to argue with her. But I think there's this idea about what a teacher should look like . . . But I can understand if I go in and my face is all pierced, and I have pink hair and I'm wearing a dress, I can understand that's going to distract from learning.

(Interview with Frank, Secondary Language Arts)

From Frank's point of view, for a man to wear certain types of earrings is appropriate in school settings, even though administrators have pressured him not to wear them. Frank challenges "this idea about what a teacher should look like" by wearing earrings, and he appeals to the legitimacy of central myths of educational institutions to define his action as legitimate. He argues that his prospective students will not be "distracted" by his earrings, therefore wearing them will not interfere with student learning, a central responsibility of teachers and schools.

Frank deploys taken-for-granted meanings about masculinity as well as institutionalized ideals of teacher professionalism, and links them together to define what teachers can and cannot do as part of performing their jobs in schools. As Frank makes sense of it, men wearing earrings in certain ways violates neither heteronormative standards of gender conformity nor the chief goals of educational institutions; men wearing dresses violate both. Frank resists administrative pressure to remove his earrings, but it is unclear how strongly Frank would have resisted had the threat of disciplinary action been as severe as it often was for women who violated their gendered dress codes (i.e., dismissal from the school). Had he feasibly been able to remove the earrings, he likely would have preferred to avoid confrontation, as he suggests. The administrator relented, though, and Frank wore the earrings throughout his entire 12-week student teaching experience.

Men also experience tensions of contradictory gendered meanings as they inhabit masculinity and teacher professionalism, just with less frequency and in qualitatively different ways than women do as they inhabit femininity and teacher professionalism. While women are expected to manage their own dress and bodies, in part at least so as not to entice the "natural" sexual urges of boy students, men often expect to be under scrutiny for their own behavior. This issue came up in class discussion among teacher candidates and the faculty instructor (Beth) in a teaching methods course for secondary language arts education:

> Dave in the back raises his hand and describes a situation where a female student in his field experience asked him out. A woman teacher candidate, Samantha, in the back of the class interjects, and jokes at him, "You are *such* a stud!" The class laughs, but Dave persists and says it concerned him because he feels like for "guy teachers" it's easier to "make assumptions" about their potential romantic involvement with female students. He says, "To hell with you guys, I was *scared!*"
>
> Beth confirms Dave's point, by saying, "People watch male students [teacher candidates] more closely." She says that for "Men who get into teaching [. . . .]_Society holds men to [. . . .] People keep a closer eye on men." She gives an example of a male teacher who quit because it was rumored he had been sleeping with a student. She says teachers' relationships with students are much more like a parent/child relationship, and to go from that to a romantic relationship is "just weird." She also says that teachers "have a reputation to uphold." (Field notes, Instructional Methods Course in Secondary English/Language Arts)

Dave's concern is commonly shared among men who work with children, and many men do feel as though they are perpetually under scrutiny—if not suspicion—for pursuing sexual relations with minors.[3] Throughout this exchange, though, meanings about men's behavior and sexuality are based on assumptions: Dave did not pursue the student, she pursued him, and the man in Beth's example was only rumored to have had an amorous relationship with a student.

Dave's classmates also reinforce this definition of teacher professionalism, albeit indirectly, via the way they tease him. Samantha cracks a joke at his expense, and many of their classmates laugh at this. The joke, "You are such a stud," ridicules any potential effort Dave might have been making to boast about himself to his classmates by volunteering the story in class. Samantha's sarcasm rebukes the notion that a high school student asking Dave out on a date is somehow evidence of his prowess at traditional masculine gender performances in amorous relationships with women. Whether Dave got the joke or not, other teacher candidates in this exchange manipulate traditional meanings about masculinity and reassert that such a gender performance for men in this context is not only strictly prohibited, but also something to be mocked. In other contexts, especially with other men, Dave's interaction with the girl who asked him out would be praised and reaffirm his dating competence, a common expectation of traditionally masculine gender performances. In this context, as a teacher candidate interacting with a high school student, it is "weird" and inappropriate.

However, Dave's genuine fear is rooted in the knowledge that people assume men to be initiators of amorous relationships with women based on rationalized meanings of masculinity, and this is why "people keep a closer eye on men." For men teacher candidates, they learn they must subdue behaviors they are often socially expected to perform in other contexts. Even abstaining from such behaviors is often not enough to avoid this kind of scrutiny, as both Beth's story of a past colleague who was forced to "quit" and existing scholarship show that men who work as teachers face constant suspicion. In this way, men must cope with ambivalence that is similar in form but different in content to the ambivalence women face concerning their gender conformity in the context of teaching. While women must always cope with the possibility of being sexually objectified despite their best efforts to avoid it, men must always cope with the possibility of being viewed as sexual predators despite their best efforts to avoid it. Because overall gender conformity includes sexualized meanings and teacher professionalism eschews sexualized meanings, teacher candidates face complex contradictions when trying to balance successful gender performances with successful teaching performances.

Conclusion

The mundane routines of everyday life are the empirically observable interactions that create and sustain culture. As I discussed in the introduction, William Corsaro defines culture as "stable sets of activities or routines, artifacts, values and concerns" that people "produce and share in interaction."[4] For teacher candidates' professional culture, adaptation to multiple sources of student heterogeneity and pre-existing conditions beyond their control is an ongoing activity they carry out in a variety of routines and through which their shared values and concerns regarding teaching find expression. When it comes to prospective instruction and interaction with students, teacher candidates inhabit the institutional myths that structure education and gender by developing a culture of ambivalence. Through this shared sense of ambivalence, they modify the rationalized ideals of compulsory education and traditional gender norms in the context of teaching by embracing a quantum of failure as inevitable.

At its core, constructivist pedagogy requires engaging students as active learners. The injunction to adapt holds that if teachers experiment with enough differentiated methods then all students can become engaged, consistent with the equality of educational opportunity that compulsory education mandates. This perspective, however, presumes its own central principle: that students will universally volunteer the agency to be active learners if teachers just find the right way to engage them. In other words, students will be active if teachers effectively motivate them to be. Teacher candidates understand incisively that it does not always work this way. Students are indeed active learners,[5] but that includes their decision whether or not to be active learners in the first place, something that is influenced by myriad factors and that fluctuates on a day-to-day basis. Teacher candidates become keenly aware that factors beyond their control structure student heterogeneity in ability as well as motivation. But teacher candidates do not abandon entirely the ideal of compulsory education nor the philosophy of constructivist pedagogy. They define both as legitimate, and commit to the professional ethic that they must continually *try* to engage all learners through the injunction to adapt even though they know it is unrealistic to expect they *will* engage all learners due to factors beyond their control. Empirical research on teacher effects on student achievement confirms that teacher candidates are right to recognize their own limitations in reaching all students given the many factors that affect student motivation.[6] It is quite rational to respond to unrealistic expectations with ambivalence, and commit effort to the ideal of compulsory education while accepting that the ideal will not be realized in every single case due to different characteristics students bring with them to school.

Teacher candidates develop a similar sense of ambivalence concerning how to engage with the gendered characteristics that students bring with them to school. Rationalized ideals of femininity and masculinity define gendered behavior and displays as innate, and people often assume as much to varying degrees.[7] Consistent with constructivist pedagogy and the injunction to adapt, teacher candidates are then expected to modify their gender performances to accommodate these student qualities.[8] Teacher candidates in this study define elements of femininity and masculinity myths as legitimate bases of meaning for the behaviors through which they enact teacher professionalism. But teacher candidates are constantly striking a balance between competing gendered pressures. For women, to be successfully feminine means, in part, to be sexually desirable. Yet in the context of teaching, they are expected to mute their sexuality as the appropriate adaptation of their own gender performances because they are commonly viewed as sexual objects by boys and men. For men, to be successfully masculine means, in part, to be sexually competent and virile. Yet in the context of teaching, they are expected to completely subdue all sexual urges they are assumed to perpetually feel as the appropriate adaptation of their own gender performances.

Ironically, gender and sexuality are made relevant to the work of teaching by the hyper-vigilance of educators forcefully defining the ways in which gender and sexuality should be irrelevant to teaching. Teacher candidates are caught in the middle of these competing, and often contradictory, rationalized meanings about gender and sexuality that inform the processes through which they define the work of teaching for themselves. Gender conformity for teachers is fraught with both contradiction as well as surveillance, adding to an overall ethos of ambivalence among teacher candidates regarding how to appropriately perform their roles as teachers and deal with the gendered characteristics of their students. Again, it is quite rational to respond to unrealistic expectations with ambivalence. Teacher candidates commit to the professional ethic that they must try to desexualize themselves in interactions with students, but they nonetheless expect that they will, in some cases, be viewed as either sex objects or sexual aggressors despite their best efforts to prevent it. Another collective commitment among teacher candidates to adapt to institutional dynamics they define as beyond their control renders them ambivalent about their capacity to always do so, and they accept a degree of failure as inevitable in how they manage the gendered elements of their interactions with students.

In addition to accommodating and engaging with the student characteristics and the heterogeneity therein that is structured in public schools, other institutional myths that structure education and gender inform the injunction to adapt and teacher candidates' culture of ambivalence. In the next two chapters, I show how accountability in education, as well as other assumptions about gender, influence the ways teacher candidates make sense of their prospective work.

I still think this is missing significant implications and a discussion on how this culture could shift or change. The "so, what?" is missing

3

Accountability and Bureaucracy

To work as a teacher means to work in a school, a condition Dan Lortie calls the "organizational imperative" for teachers, as they have no other options for their work environment.[1] Schools are bureaucracies. They are organized around hierarchies of authority (i.e., principals, teachers, staff), they are structured by codified rules and procedures (i.e., curriculum and discipline policies), and work is conducted through a division of labor (i.e., subject matter and grade-level distinctions). Likewise, UBTE programs are bureaucratic. They are hierarchical (i.e., administration, faculty, staff), policies govern activity (i.e., course syllabi, certification requirements), and work activity is distributed across departments (i.e., curriculum and instruction, educational psychology, language education). Moreover, each type of organization is situated within broader bureaucratic systems: schools within districts and state education systems, UBTE programs within colleges and universities. From early training experiences through whatever point in time one works in education, success in carrying out the work of teaching requires, at least to some degree, that people feel at home in bureaucratic settings.

Feeling comfortable in bureaucratic organizations involves striking a balance between exercising one's own professional judgment and efficiently meeting the formal goals of the organization.[2] Schools as organizations have for a long time been structured in such a way so as to mitigate this tension through what Charles Bidwell calls their "structural looseness."[3] The classrooms that taken together constitute much of the school are semi-autonomous zones for teachers, whose individual instructional activities can vary from those of the teacher next door and may or may not always align closely with the overarching goals of the school. This type of "loose coupling" between work activity and organizational outcomes in public schools is central to how they function, and some scholars have theorized that it enables people to rely on a kind of "logic of confidence and good faith" that schools, and the teachers working inside them, are actually accomplishing the educational goals with students that the public expects them to meet.[4] Loose coupling has also been commonly implicated in a wide range of scholarship as a key obstacle to the implementation of various reform policies in public education over the course of the 20th century.[5] For a long time, the ways that teachers commonly exercised their own professional autonomy seemed to dilute the impact bureaucratic education policy initiatives had on curriculum and instruction in schools.

Accountability brought about substantial change in this regard. Especially in the post-NCLB era, teachers can no longer reduce the influence of education policy by simply shutting their classroom doors. But this change in the policy environment has not eliminated the tensions between bureaucratic goals and teacher autonomy; rather, it has complicated them. Teachers now mediate between the mandates of a standardized curriculum and testing on the one hand and their own teaching philosophies on the other, often privileging elements of accountability that dovetail with their pre-existing worldviews about effective instruction forged through their own classroom experience.[6] When administrators attempt to enforce rigidly the requirements of accountability policies in particular schools, teachers push back and define them as causing much more "turmoil" than benefit when they view them as interfering with their preferred routines.[7] Despite this type of resistance, accountability is a reality teachers must address, a state-mandated increase in bureaucratic authority over their work rooted in the assumption that holding teachers and schools more accountable will more efficiently produce desired schooling outcomes.[8]

The Rise of Accountability in Education

Accountability has been around for some time. It became federal policy in 2002 with the No Child Left Behind Act (NCLB), came to exert more specific pressure on teachers through Race to the Top since 2009, and has been largely delegated back to states with the Every Student Succeeds Act (ESSA) passed in late 2015. But the accountability movement goes back as far as the mid-1980s with the publication of A Nation at Risk. Just as the title suggests, this served as an alarm to policymakers at all levels of government that America's students were falling behind their peers in other countries academically, and we had better do something about it if the United States is to maintain its competitiveness in a global economy going forward into the 21st century. Accountability as an education policy agenda grew out of this alarm. Given the decentralized structure of public education in the United States, not surprisingly, the early versions of accountability policies first emerged at the state level. Curriculum standards came first. Throughout the 1990s, states developed and adopted curriculum content standards. Such reforms were strongly promoted by the National Governors

Association (e.g., Goals 2000), and adoption of standards received federal endorsement through a reauthorization of the Elementary and Secondary Education Act in 1994 (called the "Educating America Act"). By 1998 virtually all states had some system in place to measure and evaluate schools' performance in producing desired student achievement outcomes on a standardized curriculum. Indeed, accountability had arrived even before NCLB became federal law.

Preparing to satisfy the various requirements of accountability policies, then, has been a part of the teacher education experience for nearly 20 years. Teacher education programs must demonstrate they provide training in teaching to content standards for accreditation purposes. Teacher candidates have accountability thrust upon them when they enter their student teaching, as the classes they take over from mentor teachers are in the midst of covering the curriculum that will be on the standardized tests students take. Moreover, by the time of my field work, the teacher candidates in this study had experienced accountability in their own K–12 education, routinely taking standardized tests year after year as students. Consequently, it should come as little surprise that teacher candidates tend to define certain elements of accountability as legitimate, and take for granted that they will have responsibilities as teachers to comply with accountability mandates.

The rise and widespread dissemination of accountability policies across the country (and elsewhere), despite their relative unpopularity among many teachers, is itself evidence of the limits to teachers' power and influence over bureaucratic decision-making in education at the school, district, state, and federal levels.[9] This lack of influence extends beyond the curriculum and testing prescriptions of accountability. In his analysis of these very issues using nationally representative survey data, Richard Ingersoll finds that when it comes to school-level policies concerning curriculum, staffing, scheduling, and even discipline, teachers lack much influence at all.[10] Beyond the selection and performance of specific instructional techniques within the walls of their classrooms, teachers routinely experience a profound absence of influence and control over the conditions of their work environment. Accountability has increased these types of constraints on teachers, first in prescribing curriculum content and forms of student assessment through NCLB, and then later through tying student performance measures to teacher job evaluations through Race to the Top.[11]

Priming for Adaptation to Bureaucratic Contingencies

Anyone who has completed a four-year college degree, especially those who have done so at a large university, can likely sympathize with the challenges posed by the bureaucratic labyrinth one must navigate to satisfy the formal requirements for graduation. Nearly every university has some foundational set of general curriculum requirements that students must complete in some combination, and then of course everyone declares a major field of study (if not more), along with at least one academic minor (if not more). Each of these disciplinary or professional concentration areas is housed within its own academic unit on campus, comprised of a distinct set of faculty with its own specific set of course requirements students must take to complete the major or minor. These different academic units of the university are largely "loosely coupled" from each other, and students must rely on their own initiative and organization skills to coordinate a course schedule over four years that satisfies the range of their degree requirements. Teacher candidates in this study certainly needed such initiative to complete their degrees, and their experiences in the UBTE program at State University served in many ways to prime them for the types of organizational contingencies they were likely to confront as teachers working in public schools.

"It's Your Responsibility!"

Often when administrators would instruct teacher candidates on requirements for their training, they would emphasize that responsibility for navigating the requirements of the program was entirely that of the teacher candidates. In other words, these are the rules and it is your job to follow them. An example of this type of message comes from my field notes observing an orientation meeting that teacher candidates were required to attend:

> An administrator/advisor is speaking to the crowd when I walk in, and is in the middle of discussing the timeline of the last two years of college/teacher education, emphasizing the key tasks and deadlines for the teacher candidates in the audience.
>
> "How many of you have had an advising meeting?"
>
> Approximately one-third of the class raises their hands.
>
> "Okay, the rest of you, what are you waiting for? Last year, we had a senior who was at her student teaching meeting, and we realized that she was one credit short, and she couldn't do her student teaching. It will take a half hour of your semester; come in and have an advising meeting."
>
> [Timeline for two years on PowerPoint.]
>
> "Praxis I and II. Thought you were done with the Praxis exam? Nope; this second exam tests your learning in your education courses. Pedagogy, lesson plans, and assessment, those kinds of things. Did you know you have to tell us you want outta here? You do. You have to apply to graduate, and you have to do it by (date). If you don't, we can't process your application which gets you on the commencement roster. When you show up at commencement in May, you won't be on the list and you won't receive your degree. How are you gonna explain to mom and dad why you're not graduating after they have paid for four years of college? You've got to apply, and you come to the Admin Suite to do that."

[Next slide says in big letters at the top "It's Your Responsibility!" with an image of a finger pointing at the audience.]

"It's your responsibility to make sure you have everything completed. It's not mine; I'm just here to help. Also, if you sleep through your methods classes or you don't attend your required classes, faculty can give an alert on your record, which basically says they have real reservations about you becoming a teacher. This is a big-time problem. We can actually kick you out of the School of Education, which means you're kicked out of State U. How are you going to explain to mom and dad that you're not going to graduate after four years of school? So, it's your responsibility to get everything done. If you have any questions, you can send them to this 'quick question' e-mail address [address is on slide]. It's usually me who gets it, and I will respond. Also, you can monitor your progress to your degree through [State U Software] [pulls up page on screen]. If you're missing required credits, it will show in red [shows example on slide]. If you took a class to fulfill a credit, and it's not showing here, get into our office immediately to address it."

(Field notes, Elementary Education Professional Orientation Meeting)

The office in the School of Education at State University that housed all administrator and advising offices was commonly referred to as the "Admin Suite"[12] by teacher candidates, faculty, and administrators alike. This advisor from the "Admin Suite" spends much of the presentation at this orientation meeting berating the teacher candidates in the audience to take full responsibility for their own path through the bureaucratic maze that is their route to graduation and certification. Ironically, the key way in which this advisor tries to motivate teacher candidates to be responsible adults in this regard is to warn them repeatedly of the disappointment and disapproval of "mom and dad" if they somehow fail. The condescending tone through which this advisor communicates these instructions, however, adds to the overall message to teacher candidates that the elaborate hoops they must jump through to complete their degree is simply a fact of life they must accept. It is an assertion of the legitimacy of the School of Education and its bureaucratic structure to suggest that failure in following all rules and procedures is somehow a sign of teacher candidates' immaturity. Moreover, the advisor instructs teacher candidates to use existing procedures and modes of communication when seeking information or asking questions (e.g., "you can send [questions] to this 'quick question' e-mail address" and "you can monitor your progress to your degree through [State U Software]").

While teacher candidates largely accepted the fact that they were independently responsible for meeting all the criteria of their own degree progress, they also challenged the idea that existing bureaucratic structure in the School of

Education facilitated efficiency like it is supposed to do. Frank discussed his own challenges when attempting to shoulder the responsibility of ensuring all of his course credits counted toward his degree progress:

Frank: When I went abroad, I knew that a lot of classes I took there were not going to transfer to the Ed school because they're very strict about what they allow in their program. And I had to petition before for a credit, and I'm having to petition some more. And it's just a pain in the ass. And I constantly get the runaround from the advisors. Like, "I can't answer your question; you have to go talk to the College of Arts and Sciences' English department, and then you have to come back to us and petition for us." Ridiculous.

So if I could change one thing about the Ed school, it would be like having people in the Ed school communicate with other people at the university. Because they're kind of like their own entity right now. They don't [. . . .] They can't answer questions for me about other, my other interests. It seems like, if you're in the School of Education, you can only be in the School of Education. You can't [. . . .] Like one of my problems, like, as a secondary language arts major, I can't have a minor. There's no outlet for [. . . .] There's no, like specialization, I guess you'd call it. There's no way to do that. So like I had this blanket degree of language arts education; what does that mean? Is that speech? Is that drama? Is that literature? Whatever. So I guess the way . . . I'm the one who chooses how I'm specialized, so like, that's one of the big problems. And then I go to the College people, the English department, or the French department, and I'm a secondary education major, and so they can't tell me about any of my degree progress things, any of their advisors, because like education is so closed-door. So that's a pain in the ass.

Judson: Have you dealt with the same advisor in the School of Ed over time?

Frank: Yeah, I should have changed.

Judson: Did you have any choice in that?

Frank: No. Well, I guess I do have a choice in it, but . . . I tried talking to other people, and I could never really find someone else that would better help me than the person I have. And she's not very good. Because I was in there asking her questions the other day for the second week in a row, and she couldn't [. . . .] She left the office three times to go ask [name of administrator] questions about what I was asking. I'm like, "Can I make an appointment with him?" I've called the School of Education, and they're like, "I'm sorry, he doesn't take appointments." I'm like, "He's the only one who can answer my questions!" And like the English Department advisor, but she told me "Talk to [administrator], he can tell you, answer your questions."

And I *can't*! I can't talk with him. I have to go to an advisor, and ask her a question, who asks him the question. She like left the office, went to his office, then came back.

Judson: Then did she go back?

Frank: Yeah! More than once. Once for the same question and then once for another question. It was just really frustrating. You have to do a lot of leg-work. And that was the other thing, because it was a French credit that I'm trying to get to work for that, I had to go to the French advisor—French department head, who is actually out of the country—so, the Spanish/Portuguese advisor is actually taking over his position. I went to her, and had to get her to look over my syllabus because it's all in French. And my Ed school advisor said they—this is one of the questions she asked him—they couldn't find anyone in the School of Education that would be able to review that syllabus to see if it was worthy of a petition, even though they have French education majors. They couldn't find anybody to, so I had to get her, the Spanish/Portuguese advisor to look over it and then write a letter commenting on it that I'm going to put with my petition letter, and submit it to the standards committee . . . It's like why does it have to be this hard?!

(Interview with Frank, Secondary English/Language Arts)

Hardly a well-oiled machine of efficiency, Frank's experience with the bureaucracy of State University concerning his course credit from overseas study led him through a tangled mess of red tape. In this case, Frank's challenge was not just with the School of Education but rather in the very loosely coupled relationship between the School of Education and the College of Arts and Sciences at State University. While the course in French literature he took in France counted toward a potential degree requirement in the College, it did not in the School of Education and there was virtually no coordination or collaboration between the two campus units on related curriculum. Indeed, this would be one of the key things Frank would change if he could: "having people in the Ed school communicate with other people at the university." Frank certainly performed "a lot of legwork" himself, shouldering the responsibility for his own degree progress in a way consistent with what the advisor emphasized in the orientation meeting I referenced earlier. But he received very little help in the process. In fact, the organizational structure of advising services in the Admin Suite acted more as an impediment to his effort, at one point resembling a scene from a Marx Brothers film with Frank's advisor walking between offices to relay questions to another advisor whom Frank was precluded from speaking with directly.[13]

    Not only were teacher candidates on their own to make sure they were completing the schedule of courses required of them, many of them felt as though they were on their own to teach themselves relevant knowledge and skills that were simply absent from their UBTE curriculum. Teacher candidates in secondary English/language arts education, for instance, routinely lamented the lack of coursework they received in grammar or how to teach it. When this issue came up in class discussion, faculty primed teacher candidates to view their future teaching as self-guided training through which they could educate themselves on how to teach grammar. This came up one day in class the week after many teacher candidates had taken the Praxis II:

> They move on to discuss the Praxis II that most of them just took this past weekend. Most students are worried about it, as several agree it was "so hard." In particular, they talk about some exercises on the test regarding grammar they did not know. Also, several felt very rushed, having to read passages very quickly when they usually prefer to read slowly. Beth tries to reassure them. She says they will learn a great deal once they begin teaching; she says she remembers asking herself, "Six months into teaching, how did I not know that?" She tells them, "You'll be amazed how great you'll be at grammar because you'll have to teach it." Beth again tries to reassure them, "It'll be okay; you'll pass the Praxis." (Field notes, Methods Course in Secondary English/Language Arts)

Beth's advice is to learn-by-doing in prospective classrooms, something she acknowledges she did in her own early days teaching, and she tries to reassure teacher candidates that this approach will be effective for them. Such an approach places the onus for acquiring the relevant knowledge base for teaching the subject matter almost entirely on teacher candidates. Indeed, I observed this methods course every week throughout the semester, and there was no training or instruction in grammar or teaching grammar at all—even though it is tested on the professional exam required for teacher certification and licensure.

While this is a somewhat glaring omission from the curriculum for English/language arts teacher candidates, the phenomenon is not entirely unique to them or the language education component of the UBTE program at State University. Teacher candidates across grade-level and subject matter concentrations found themselves teaching topics and subject matters on which they had received little if any prior training or academic coursework. Social studies education majors frequently found out they would be teaching a period of history with which they were largely unfamiliar. Likewise, math education majors would be assigned particular math classes for which they felt ill prepared. As such, it was not uncommon for teacher candidates to be called upon to teach topics with little background in them, and when that occurred the expectation was they would teach themselves by teaching others (a process one veteran teacher once described to me as "when you're one day ahead of them in the book"). Teacher candidates often confront discrepancies between their subject matter preparation and the actual classes they were called upon to teach, and

this is often a product of the contingent staffing needs of schools as organizations. While this is a common experience for novice teachers early in their
careers,[14] teacher candidates are primed for this reality of working in schools
through the uncertainty that is endemic to the placement process for their student teaching.

The Uncertainties of Student Teaching Placements

Finding a classroom and a supervising teacher for hundreds of teacher candidates every school year is no small task for the people of the Admin Suite in the
UBTE program at State University. In almost every way, the School of Education
is organizationally dependent upon local and regional schools to provide what
is widely acknowledged by teacher candidates and teacher educators alike to
be the most important and formative component of their teacher training. In
every school, there are only so many teachers both able and willing to host a
student teacher; moreover, different principals have varying degrees of interest
and willingness to host student teachers depending on their staffing needs from
year to year. On the School of Education's end, coordinating with a wide range
of schools, principals, and teachers to place several hundred teacher candidates
is a complex process, and more than a few miscommunications and last-minute
changes are all but inevitable.

Teacher candidates await announcement of their student teaching placement with great anticipation. So many conditions of their assigned school,
teacher, and subject matter greatly impact the quality of their student teaching
experience, and for the majority of teacher candidates, the decision about their
placement is entirely beyond their control. Most teacher candidates have few,
if any, contacts among teachers in local or regional schools whom they could
request as supervising teachers, and so they rely upon the School of Education
to find a placement for them. Even in cases, though, when teacher candidates
do have a contact in a local school to request as their supervising teacher, this
itself is no guarantee of placement in that teacher's classroom. Faye faced such a
situation, and her experience captures a lot of the ways in which student teaching assignments are rife with uncertainty:

Faye: So, you get this email, and it's like, "Your placement has been confirmed."
    It's like this really generic, and so you type in your little password online.
    It's through the Ed school, it's just like this web service, I don't know. Type
    in your little password, and I was like, "Hmm; that doesn't say Cloverdale
    North. It says Newton." And like every bad memory I'd ever heard of Newton
    [Faye giggles] came, like, flooding in my mind. And so, I kinda just like took
    that day, and was like, "Oh bummer." And then the next day, I emailed Mr.
    Thomas, and was like [. . . .] I wasn't really that upset over it at first; I guess,
    kinda like, "bummer," you know? But then, I emailed him, and he emailed

back really quickly. I was just like, "I won't be able to student teach with you; I've got my placement in Newton." I said, "Do you know this teacher?" Or, "I'll be teaching world history"—I didn't know I would be teaching that— and "Can I stop by for some resources? Thank you for all your help."

And so he emailed me back, and he's like, "Are you kidding me?! How did they confuse that?!" He got really upset with it. So he emailed me; he emailed Vince Turner. Turner, he kind of went on about how I was rowing, and I think he thought I was going to be rowing this semester, and that was what Turner really got upset with was, "She's not supposed to be rowing, or doing anything extra." So I was like, "Well, actually I'm done rowing, but I still wanna be in Cloverdale." But that was what Turner really caught on, the fact that he thought I was rowing, like, that made a difference where I was going to be student teaching.

And then there were so many confusing things, and like I said earlier, the overseas student teaching thing, I put Cloverdale, but just as a place- ment; like, I'd like to teach there, not a big deal. But on my regular stu- dent teaching thing, I said Cloverdale, Mr. Thomas, Ms. Young; I was like, "Please" you know, whatever, I requested them. But on my student teach- ing thing, it also said I was going to be teaching until November. And so, I emailed my teacher, I emailed the Ed school, and said "I'm going to do my overseas project, and I'm leaving in October, so I won't be able to be there until November." And I was just curious, I guess, about this placement; I was wondering why I didn't get it. And they were like, "Well, you didn't request it in the right form." But, that doesn't really make sense because I requested it. They were like, "Well, we didn't get that form." And I was like, "If you thought I was going to be there for the full semester, that's the stu- dent teaching form where I put Cloverdale." And so it was just like this big email thing, and I just didn't really care that much. I mean, I did care, but it's like, what are you gonna do? Vince Turner didn't leave any room; he's like, "Well, that's where it is; that's where you need to be." So . . .

Judson: So you felt like, "I can't do anything about this"?

Faye: That was it, and, you know, Mr. Thomas emailed them, and I wasn't going to be like, "Can you appeal this decision?" You know? He has other things to do, and my student teaching is not, like, a huge importance in his life. I mean, I was bummed out, and I wish I were [. . . .] But at the same time . . . It is what it is, so . . . I didn't feel like there were any options for me to work around it.

(Interview with Faye, Secondary Social Studies)

In all fairness to the Admin Suite in the School of Education, Faye's was a unique set of circumstances. First, she was a varsity athlete, and as she notes above, there was confusion over how that might affect her availability for student teaching. Second, she was in the overseas study program in the UBTE program, which meant she was to complete an abbreviated version of her student teaching in the fall rather than the full spring semester as is the norm. Bureaucratic organizations are notoriously challenged when it comes to accommodating unique cases since such instances fly in the face of the overall goal of standardized efficiency. Her idiosyncrasies notwithstanding, Faye worked hard and proactively to make her situation easier on the Admin Suite in assigning her to student teaching by filling out the proper paperwork, completing the prescribed steps, and initiating a placement agreement with a teacher in a local school. In part because of her own confusion with the paperwork, Faye actually filled out redundant forms ("overseas student teaching thing" versus the "regular student teaching thing"). On the form the Admin Suite claimed they never received, she requested a particular teacher at a particular high school (Cloverdale North). Despite Faye's inquiry and the support of Mr. Thomas to serve as her supervising teacher, Vince Turner (student teaching supervisor in the Admin Suite) stood firm and insisted that she complete her student teaching at Newton, a high school in a neighboring district.

The unexpected switch to Newton for Faye's placement was a profound one. Newton had a reputation as a poor school with an unwelcoming environment for outsiders. Faye's supervising teacher was minimally supportive, and she did not have nearly as positive a relationship with him as she did with Mr. Thomas, the teacher she requested and who had agreed to work with her at Cloverdale. She also had her subject matter for her student teaching changed at the last minute as a product of the student teaching switch ("I'll be teaching world history—I didn't know I'd be teaching that"), and she had to begin her lesson preparation from scratch. Despite having the most important phase of her training dramatically altered due to an administrative mistake, Faye expresses feeling ambivalent about how to respond. On the one hand, it was demonstrably the mistake of the Admin Suite, and she could have asked for additional support from Mr. Thomas. On the other hand, Turner, the administrator, seemed resolute to her, and it was unclear if further protest would have resulted in favorable change. Ultimately, she resigned herself to simply accept this as beyond her control and adapt to the new, unexpected, and less favorable conditions of her student teaching. As she put it, "I was bummed out . . . But at the same time, it is what it is," and "I didn't feel like there were any options for me to work around it." She opted for adaptation over advocacy when confronted with a forceful expression of bureaucratic authority.

Last-minute changes to student teaching placements were not uncommon, but many teacher candidates knew their placement a semester in advance. Also, like Faye attempted to do, many teacher candidates worked proactively to make contact with their supervising teacher and get as prepared as possible for what would be expected of them prior to the start of their student teaching semester. Nonetheless, many conditions of their student teaching remained outside their control, and they had to adapt to a variety of contingencies as they learned about them. Betsy's experience preparing for her student teaching offers an example of how teacher candidates first encounter the transition into a classroom that is not their own:

> So, I took one of the days off we had at State U, and I went down there. And I told her [supervising teacher], "Hey, run me through your schedule, what kind of stuff do you do, you know, what do you want me to do." She's like, "Yeah, sure I can do that. Keep your entire day open, stay here the entire day." I'm like, "Alright, cool."
>
> So, I go, and I'm all excited. I get there, she's like, "Hi . . . Who are you?"
> I'm like, "Your student teacher; you told me to come visit you."
> "Oh . . . Well, just grab a seat in the back, I'll be right with you."
> You know, I thought maybe no big deal, maybe she forgot. At the end of class, she took five minutes to show me her China stuff because that's the one thing we have in common. And then she gave me the book, and the workbook, and the atlas, and she's like, "Here you go."
> I'm like, "Okay . . . Well, what do you want me to do with it? Is there something you want me to teach?"
> She's like, "Oh, anything you want. I don't ever use the book, I don't ever use the workbook, but you can use them if you want."
> "Uh . . . Okay. Will I teach the first day?"
> "Oh yeah, you're just gonna jump right in."
> "Oh . . . Okay. Do I need to come up with my own set of rules?"
> "If you want."
> "Okay . . . What's the grading policy? What's the attendance policy?"
> She's like, "Ummm . . . We just got a new principal, it's kind of laid-back. Do what you want the first couple of days, and we'll cater to it if it's wrong."
> I'm just like, "Oh my god, I'm working with a moron!" I expected to work with someone like the teachers I had in high school. I expected to work with someone who was on top of it. This woman was the farthest thing from it!
> But, I don't know. I found out my placement early enough, so like when I had to do all of my unit plans and everything for my methods courses, I was just like, "Okay, I already know what I'm teaching, I might as well do it."
> (Interview with Betsy, Secondary Social Studies)

In Betsy's case, the Admin Suite had her placement squared away on time and there were no last-minute changes, but she discovered on her first meeting that her supervising teacher would offer her virtually no mentoring or guidance. Moreover, she did not have what some supervisors did for their student teaching (and what was advised by the UBTE program), which was a gradual transition into taking over the full-day teaching schedule. Rather, she was told, "you're just gonna jump right in." In addition, she was given no guidance on school policy. Explaining that the "new principal" is "kind of laid-back," her supervisor instructs her to "do what you want," with the caveat that they may need to make accommodations and adjustments later "if it's wrong." Betsy immediately commits herself to adapting to the new contingencies she learned about at this initial meeting. Knowing she would be on her own to perform her student teaching, she incorporates this knowledge into how she goes about completing her instructional methods courses so as to use it to prep as many of her instructional units that she knows she will teach in the spring. Despite the utter lack of support she would receive, she at least knew about this lack of support ahead of time and made adjustments to prepare for it.

Not all teacher candidates displayed the kind of initiative and wherewithal that Betsy or Faye did, and for them, the contingencies built into the student teaching placement process could prove very challenging, at times even derailing their training process. A handful of teacher candidates enrolled in the methods course for secondary English/language arts that I observed were also in the special education training program for secondary education. Their program required teacher candidates to identify and contact their own school and supervising teacher, and make arrangements for their own student teaching placement. Many teacher candidates in this program, especially those from outside the geographic region where State University is located, had no idea where to begin this search process, and they had a limited number of special education teachers in the area to solicit in the first place. This came up in a discussion among teacher candidates in class at the very end of the fall semester:

> I ask Lilly, who is earlier in the program than most in the class, "You're not doing your student teaching next semester, right?" She says no. Lilly then asks the woman to her right, Mary, where she's doing her student teaching. Mary says with a nervous giggle that she doesn't know. Lilly and I look at each other with surprise, as it's the end of the semester and student teaching will begin in January. Lilly asks her what happened. Mary is also in the special education training program, and must find her own supervising teacher. She says that she still does not have one, but it is unclear why this has happened. She says that she's uncertain what she's going to do, and that the Admin Suite has not offered her much in the way of help or advice. Mary says that at this point, she doesn't know who to ask or how to find a supervising teacher. (Field notes, Methods Course in Secondary English/Language Arts)

Everyone was concerned for Mary, including the faculty instructor for this course. While her situation was the most urgent given how close she was to her last semester, all teacher candidates in the secondary special education program faced similar uncertainties and challenges in locating their own student teaching placement (indeed, Lilly was similarly at a loss, but had more time to resolve the issue than Mary since she was earlier in the program). This was not just a matter of dereliction on Mary's part; the rules of the program explicitly placed the burden of securing a site and a mentor for student teaching on teacher candidates in secondary special education. While other teacher candidates received more institutional support for scheduling their training than those in the special education program, they similarly learned that in many ways, they were on their own to adapt to whatever contingencies they may face as they transitioned into the training and work environment of public schools.

"I'm Looking for Teachers Who Are Adaptable and Flexible"

Administrators and faculty in the School of Education make sense of the teacher education process from their own vantage point, and from the perspective of many of them, the uncertainty that is baked into the transition into student teaching is an important learning experience for teacher candidates. In an interview I did with Vince Turner, the administrator who directed the student teaching placement process, he explained what teacher candidates learn as a product of the placement process:

> I try to do a very good job of that when they go to the Pre-Professional Meeting, saying, "You're a guest. And what you find out there is there to help you. It may not be what you agree with, it may not be what you like, but that's the way it is" [Vince chuckles]. We're not there to evaluate, we're not there to tell people how to do their jobs. We're there to learn . . . Going in, and wanting to try all of the things they've learned, and finding out that they're constricted by the environment. And that whole variation of practices among all the teachers in [State] versus the way that we teach it here at State University. I think that shatters the expectations. (Interview with Vince, administrator in the State University School of Education)

For Vince, it is an important learning experience for teacher candidates to "find out that they're constricted by the environment" in public schools, and "that's the way it is." In this sense, the teacher candidates need to be primed to their subordinate status as a reality within the context of public schools, and he suggests their training in the School of Education does not provide that in the same way as immersion in the daily life of schools.

Teacher candidates interact with other administrators during their training who attempt to prime them for what life will be like prospectively in schools.

Frequently, current or former school principals served as adjunct faculty for courses in the UBTE program designed to help teacher candidates navigate the job market post-graduation. I attended one of these courses, and the following is an excerpt from my field notes taken during one day in class:

> When writing your objectives, there are some key characteristics you want to include about yourself. When I'm looking through applications, I'm looking for teachers who are adaptable and flexible. There was one teacher who I had who was terrific like this. Anytime I needed someone to do lunch duty, I could walk into the teachers' lounge, and say "I have a meeting I have to attend, I can't do lunch duty; can anyone fill in?" She would always volunteer to help, even if she were in the middle of her lunch . . . That teacher, I would do anything for her. If the babysitter couldn't come, she could bring her kids to school, anything. That really means a lot. Things always come up, and I'm looking for teachers who can adapt. From one year to the next, I may need teachers to teach different grade levels; even if you've never done it before, those teachers who are willing to switch to another grade are the most helpful. So, adaptable and flexible are the most important. (Field notes, Course on Job Search Strategies for Beginning Teachers)

In this case, teacher candidates hear from the horse's mouth, so to speak, that adaptable and flexible are the key characteristics to employability as a teacher. Not only that, they can reasonably expect quid pro quo from their principal if they are flexible and cooperative in addressing various staffing contingencies ("I would do anything for her"). Indeed, unforeseen changes to the daily and yearly schedules are the key reasons this principal cites for needing teachers able and willing to adapt. On this day in class, this principal primes the teacher candidates that signaling their capacity for adaptation and flexibility to potential employers will make them more attractive as teachers. Moreover, in her explanation as to why this is so important, she primes teacher candidates for the realities of prospective work environments: unforeseen things come up routinely, and your principal will need you to adapt.

Priming for Accountability in Public Schools

As I discussed in Chapters 1 and 2, education faculty emphasize the injunction to adapt in the instructional methods courses they teach in ways rooted in constructivist pedagogy that are responsive to the student heterogeneity of a compulsory education system. Accountability adds two more elements to the injunction to adapt that education faculty incorporate into their instructional methods courses and that are codified in formal training documents. First, teacher candidates are taught they must align the content of their teaching very explicitly with state-prescribed curriculum standards (commonly referred to as "state standards"). Second, accountability adds institutional force to the ideal that teachers must impact all students. While this second element overlaps with the ideal of compulsory education, accountability—especially NCLB, which was the guiding federal law during data collection—more explicitly ties teachers and schools to what students learn. In other words, while compulsory education mandates that all students go to school and receive equal educational opportunity, accountability mandates that all students achieve minimally similar educational outcomes.[15] As such, the injunction to adapt requires teacher candidates to effectively address the student heterogeneity structured by compulsory education in a manner that produces the standardization in content and outcomes mandated by accountability.

Incorporating Standards into the Injunction to Adapt

We see the institutional myth of accountability find expression and formal codification in the UBTE program through evaluation rubrics for teacher candidates' performance similar to the ones discussed in Chapter 1. Figure 3 is the scoring rubric intended to measure teacher candidates' demonstrated "knowledge" in the field evident in their classroom teaching. Note the manner in which compliance with state accountability standards is packaged with differentiated instruction and adaptation to diverse student learning needs we saw in Chapter 1. The three categories of "knowledge" that teacher candidates must demonstrate include:

"Demonstrates knowledge of student learning and development."
"Demonstrates knowledge of content, state standards, and resources."
"Demonstrates an understanding of a variety of assessment strategies."

Indeed, to earn marks of "Distinguished" across these three categories, teacher candidates must show that they can make sure the "level of content is appropriate and is differentiated consistently to address a range of abilities," while also making sure "instruction is aligned creatively with state standards." These statements articulate what teacher candidates are ultimately able to do in their instruction by the completion of their program.

Throughout their training, teacher candidates are primed to figure out how to sufficiently address a standardized curriculum while they adapt instruction to different students. A common priming exercise for teacher candidates in their coursework was to craft their own prospective lessons using lesson plan templates like the one illustrated in Figure 4. This template was issued to all teacher candidates through their required orientation meetings and their coursework. Note the prompts on the template that teacher candidates must address in the course of designing their lessons. They are prompted to articulate the "connection to state standards" their lesson will cover. All lesson plans required that the

Unsatisfactory 1	Satisfactory 2	Proficient 3	Distinguished 4
*Demonstrates knowledge of student learning and development.			
Level of content is inappropriate for most students. Minimal knowledge of student development is evidenced.	Level of content is appropriate for most students. Some activities and assignments demonstrate understanding of differentiation and student development.	Level of content very appropriate for the majority of students. Activities and assignments often address the needs of individual learners as well as whole group.	Level of content is appropriate for all students and is differentiated consistently to address a range of abilities. Activities and assignments incorporate all cognitive levels.
Notes/Evidence: Rating ____			
*Demonstrates knowledge of content, state standards, and resources.			
Insufficient content knowledge. Instruction is not aligned with state standards. There are few quality resource selections. Inaccurate, out-of-context, or outdated information is presented.	Basic understanding of academic content as well as state standards. Lesson plans reflect the intent to tie instruction to standards. Uses limited variety of resources.	Strong content knowledge. Instruction aligned with state standards. Encourages diverse perspectives and engages students in the material through multiple resources.	Extensive, enriched content knowledge. Instruction is aligned creatively with state standards. Encourages diverse perspectives and engages students in the material through multiple resources.
Notes/Evidence: Rating ____			
*Demonstrates an understanding of a variety of assessment strategies.			
Assessments not matched to instructional objectives and include little variety in assessment strategies used. Little or no feedback is provided to support student learning.	Assessments matched to instructional objectives and include some variety of assessment strategies utilized. Adequate feedback is provided to support student learning.	Assessments matched to instructional objectives. Multiple assessment strategies and constructive and timely feedback are utilized effectively to support student learning.	A broad range of formal and informal assessment strategies, matched to instructional objectives, utilized. Interactive and constructive feedback is ongoing and timely to maximize student learning.
Notes/Evidence: Rating ____			

FIGURE 3. Evaluation Rubric for "Knowledge"

material presented was aligned with state curriculum standards, and teacher candidates were reminded of this frequently in their coursework. But notice also the formalized way in which adaptation in practice is promoted in the lesson plan template. Under "Preparation," the template says, "Identify techniques to be used to motivate students"; likewise under "Application," it says "Identify activities to be used to engage students." While the template formally codifies adherence to constructivist pedagogy as well as content standards in teachers' planning, it also allows a high degree of autonomy and discretion for teacher candidates to figure out how they will both engage students and connect to standards. Teacher candidates could choose any number of techniques and activities to accomplish these goals of a lesson—even on the same subject matter topic—and the specific selection of practices is left largely to the discretion of teacher candidates, allowing for a great deal of variation among teachers in how they teach a curriculum.

Variation is not only permitted, it is encouraged. Faculty teaching courses on instructional methods coached teacher candidates in how to adapt their instruction to both standards and student needs when using lesson plan templates to plan instruction. Bob, a faculty member teaching methods for secondary math, advised his teacher candidates in the following way:

> When writing these, make sure your objectives are "truly learning objectives" and you include a broad range of [State] standards . . . multiple content standards. I want you to include some NCTM standards with technology standards. For the unit plan, you need three lesson plans that are linked together . . . You want to think about how each lesson plan is linked to the others to meet your overall unit goal. You have to have flexibility to adapt as you go. You have plans, and you anticipate how things will go, but you have to be responsive to how your students react to it and modify as you go . . . For the last part of your grade, I will be looking for how insightful, creative, and cohesive the unit plan is, and how it all ties together. (Field notes, Instructional Methods Course in Secondary Math)

Bob is a stickler for standards, and insists that teacher candidates address multiple standards in their lessons and units. Yet he emphasizes that teacher candidates cannot take a one-size-fits-all approach to teaching standardized content. Through prospective iterative processes, he implores them to "be responsive" to students and "modify as you go." The standards get taught, but their content gets packaged and repackaged in multiple ways depending upon teacher candidates' sense of their students' reactions to the material and the way it is taught, which requires teacher candidates "have flexibility to adapt as you go." Bob tells these teacher candidates up front that they will be evaluated by how "insightful" and "creative" they are in their plans to address curricular standards. On a later day in class, Bob reiterated the need to adapt curriculum standards to the ways

Lesson Plan Example 1

Subject Area:

Grade Level:

Unit Title:

Lesson Title:

Performance Objectives:
Upon completion of this lesson, the student will be able to . . .

Connection to State Standards:

Materials:

References:

Preparation:
Identify techniques to be used to motivate students, summarize the previous lesson, explain the importance of the lesson, and tell students the order of the lesson presentation.

Presentation:
Note instructional topics to be presented, items to be sure to remember in the presentation, and an explanation of the preparations for the application section of the lesson.

Application:
Identify activities to be used to engage students in the use of presented materials.

Assessment/Evaluation:
Explain how students will be checked for their understanding of the presented materials.

Closure:
What method of review will be used to complete the lessons?

Assigned Student Work:

FIGURE 4. Lesson Plan Template

students receive it. He spoke with a group of teacher candidates discussing the diversity of "ability levels" among students:

> The group sitting next to me has one student who poses the question, "How do you teach students with so many different ability levels in your classroom?" His colleagues at his table agree this is a good question. Bob walks over to their table as discussion proceeds. Bob says, "I imagine your lesson would be very different in here than in the schools. You might think about changes you could make, and the differences in the people you were trying to teach." In response to a follow-up question on "content," Bob says, "Well, I think content comes from the students. You might have topics, but the content is how the students respond to it." (Field notes, Instructional Methods Course in Secondary Mathematics)

Bob encourages teacher candidates to think about this ahead of time, and what kinds of "changes you could make" to address the needs of different students. He concludes his advice in this exchange with an invitation to view "content" as malleable rather than static, advising that it "comes from the students" and how "students respond to it," requiring adaptation among teacher candidates to the range of student responses as they go.

Similar types of priming for adaptation to state standards occurred in methods courses for elementary education as well. On a day in class near the end of the fall semester, teacher candidates are asked to discuss the applicability of the instructional techniques they have been learning to their prospective classrooms. At one point in the conversation, the faculty member asks them how they will address standards.

> Todd breaks the silence by asking, "How about standards?" Liam answers that his approach to lesson planning changed; whereas before he would "write the plan and see what standards fit, later I was writing the lesson plan to get the standards." Denise says that in her field experience, their "teacher gave us the topic . . . we hit some of them [standards], and we got lectured for it [not hitting enough standards]." Brent raises his hand and says that if you're somewhat "creative" he thinks it's pretty "simplistic and easy to apply them [the standards]." Several women in the room scoff at this comment. Todd interjects and says that you can "play the interpretation game" when articulating how lesson plans address standards. (Field notes, Instructional Methods Course in Elementary Education)

While addressing standards is a ubiquitous part of their training, these teacher candidates discuss their different approaches they are developing as they accumulate more experience. We see again the external pressure to meet content standards. In writing a lesson plan for a class they were observing, some students describe being pressured by supervising teachers to more closely and explicitly align their instruction to state standards. Moreover, Liam describes how his process of writing lesson plans has become more driven by standards over time. Brent, on the other hand, emphasizes creativity, and argues that with some creativity, covering standards is pretty straightforward. Importantly, this is the point that Todd, the faculty member, validates in the discussion, advising teacher candidates that tailoring instruction to content standards is an interpretive process. While Brent claims adapting his instruction to standards is straightforward for him, others find this more challenging as indicated by the scoffs that Brent's comments solicited.

Nonetheless, advice akin to Todd's that teacher candidates can "play the interpretation game" when it comes to articulating how their instruction aligns with state standards was widespread according to teacher candidates. Moreover, they received such advice from both their faculty instructors as well as the supervising teachers they worked with prior to student teaching. Frank describes the overall message concerning standards he received in the methods courses he took:

> I think I was lucky with the professors that I had, because they were like, "Come up with what you think the students should be learning at this point, and then mold the standards to that." Like, take the standards and apply them to the lesson rather than the other way around. (Interview with Frank, Secondary English/Language Arts)

While somewhat more cavalier with addressing state standards than Todd or Bob advocated for in their classes, Frank reports a similar orientation to accountability standards among the faculty who taught his courses in English/language arts. The institutional force of accountability is inescapable in the training Frank has received; he cannot ignore the standards, even if he still retains a degree of agenda-setting power in determining content for his classes. But he is trained that the standards are malleable to interpretation in a manner similar to how Todd counseled teacher candidates in his elementary methods course. Though intended to structure uniformity in subject matter, teacher candidates are trained to treat accountability standards as content they can and should manipulate as part of their broader effort to adapt material to the needs, interests, and skill levels of their students. As Frank puts it, he needs to "come up with what you think students should be learning at this point, and mold the standards to that." Such a perspective is also similar to how Bob coached teacher candidate in secondary math that "the content . . . comes from the students."

In addition to education faculty, supervising teachers often echoed a similar perspective about the malleability of state standards, especially in how teachers should proceed through the prescribed content. Oscar describes how the teacher he observed as part of his field experience hours prior to student teaching advised him on addressing state standards: "Mr. Carter told me going in as I was watching him teach, 'Yes, there's a ton of stuff to cover, but there's always tomorrow that you can get to it'" (Interview with Oscar, Secondary Social Studies).

According to Oscar, Mr. Carter expresses another way of reconciling adaptation with accountability. While "there's a ton of stuff to cover" that is prescribed by state standards, as long as you cover it all, how you cover it all is up to you. Again, we see teacher candidates advised that there is no way around state standards ("Yes, there's a ton of stuff to cover"), but they are routinely reminded of their autonomy, in this case in their classroom, to decide how to address the standards.

Required texts are another element of the content of their instructional methods courses that emphasized adaptation and creativity in the context of teaching standards. One teacher candidate in secondary English reacts to one of the required readings in a post to her classmates on their online discussion forum:

Becky: In Chapter 14, Whitaker discusses the issue of standardized testing. One thing he says is that "effective teachers don't let standardized tests take over the entire class." In the past I have thought about how hard it could be to not focus on the tests when the teachers are under a lot of pressure to have the students do well on them. However, I do not think this is a huge problem, as there are always ways to teach skills needed for the test in creative ways that help the students too. I think the bigger problem that I have seen is how some schools are classifying students based on their test results. At some schools in the area, they have whole classes that are for students who have not passed [standardized test]. Although I see it is important for these students to pass the test, wouldn't it be better to actually teach these students the skills needed to do well on the test rather than on how just to pass it? Also, by classifying these students in this way, and grouping them together in one classroom . . . is this harming the students more than it is helping them? (Online Discussion Forum Entry, Methods Course in Secondary English/Language Arts)

Becky describes having arrived at a point in her ongoing sense-making about teaching standards where she now defines adaptation as legitimate. She used to think it unavoidable to fixate on test content, but now believes "there are always ways to teach skills needed for the test in creative ways." At the same time, she anticipates other problematic aspects of the standardized testing under accountability systems, namely classifying students based on testing outcomes. She has seen this in her own observational experiences in particular schools, and questions the practice here. She thereby challenges this feature of accountability, at least as she has seen it performed in particular locales. Despite this challenge, she still defines testing as legitimate, emphasizing "it is important for these students to pass the test." We see Becky, then, define accountability, as well as teachers' adaptation of test content, as legitimate. At the point of concluding their coursework, many teacher candidates define accountability as compatible with the injunction to adapt consistent with the manner in which the UBTE program trains them.

Conclusion

The UBTE program at State University put the realities of accountability at the center of the formal curriculum for teacher candidates. Moreover, teacher candidates were routinely primed for the related realities of working within bureaucratic organizations more broadly. Indeed, completing degree and certification requirements within the UBTE program at State University was its own crash course in navigating bureaucratic environments. Teacher candidates are taught that there are routine bureaucratic contingencies beyond their control to which they must continually adapt. Teacher candidates are also taught that they must strategically modify standardized curriculum to accommodate particular student needs and responses. Taken together, the ways teacher candidates are formally evaluated, taught, and advised in how to prepare for accountability and bureaucracy reinforce and further elaborate the injunction to adapt.

Overall, teacher candidates embrace and endorse the meanings that constitute the local wisdom about accountability, and how teachers should handle it in their classrooms, in the State University UBTE program. At the time I was in the field, addressing standardized curriculum and preparing students for assessment on said curriculum was the predominant element of accountability as an institutional myth in public education. In the middle stages of the NCLB era (2006–2007), aligning standardized curriculum with state-based assessments for the purposes of measuring school quality was accountability's central goal at the federal level.[16] As such, teacher educators could reconcile long-standing commitments to constructivist pedagogy with new accountability mandates in public schools through the injunction to adapt. Especially when they transition into their student teaching, however, teacher candidates confront concrete dilemmas in complying fully with the demands of accountability that play out in the local interactions of classrooms and schools. In the next chapter, I show how making sense of these dilemmas lead teacher candidates to modify meanings about accountability and bureaucracy in ways that contribute to their culture of ambivalence.

4

Dilemmas of Coverage and Control

The UBTE program at State University primes teacher candidates to incorporate accountability into the injunction to adapt. They enter their student teaching expecting to align the content of their instruction with state standards. But they elaborate their own understanding of what this means as they encounter the instructional dilemmas that arise in the everyday routines that unfold within the organizational conditions of classrooms and schools. In their student teaching, the schedule of classes and school-wide activities, student groupings that comprise their classes, and policies concerning curriculum and discipline are all externally imposed with little input, transparency, or information in advance. As such, contingency becomes bound up in the process for teacher candidates, an element of teachers' work they often define as something they must accept as a fact of life and to which they must continually adapt. The institutional myth of accountability in the bureaucratic settings of schools adds another element to the injunction to adapt for teacher candidates. In short, they do not have a choice but to commit to ongoing adaptation to contingencies beyond their control as they try to cover the curriculum standards prescribed for them.

Teacher candidates grapple with the tensions that arise between elements of the organizational environment they do not control and the elements of their jobs they are expected to control virtually all on their own in their respective classrooms. In particular, challenges emerge out of the daily schedule and within particular classroom dynamics that interfere with teacher candidates' ongoing efforts to effectively cover their curriculum. Nonetheless, the responsibilities of complete curriculum coverage, as well as effective classroom control, falls entirely to teacher candidates. Left largely to their own devices to fulfill these expectations, teacher candidates creatively draw upon their own experiences, ideas, and identities to adapt to ongoing organizational contingencies.

Attention to these processes reveals additional ways in which teacher candidates inhabit rationalized ideals about gender—especially with regard to displays of authority—alongside those of education as they learn to cope with the competing pressures that constitute their formal job descriptions.

Organizational Conditions and Covering the Standards

The Daily Schedule

When teacher candidates transition into student teaching, they have curriculum guides and textbooks prescribing their course content that is aligned with state standards. Pressure to maintain a predetermined pace of coverage often comes through the supervising teacher, as it is their jobs and their schools are evaluated based in part on these students' performance on standardized tests. Faye describes her experience with coverage in an interview:

Judson: So you didn't realize the pace at which you had to work?

Faye: Not at all. I looked at the time on the lesson plans, and I'm like, "Okay, four periods on one thing, that seems like an average." No, no, no. It's not the average at all. There's a book [curriculum guide] that goes along with the textbook, and it says how long you should spend on each section. And it's like, "A day on the Aztecs and the Mayas." That's how the book spells it out. At first I was spending too much time on, apparently, trivial things. [Faye chuckles.] And he [Faye's supervising teacher] was just like, "I'm just concerned that you're not getting to everything." So, the first thing I did was make a schedule of where I wanted to be, to make sure I would get as far [. . . .] Because he's like, "You need to be here when you're done."

(Interview with Faye, Secondary Social Studies)

Faye is under pressure to cover the curriculum as it is formulated in the textbook she must use, and these textbooks were closely aligned with the state curriculum standards. Not only does she have that to reference, but she gets persistent pressure from her supervising teacher to ensure she is covering enough of the required material, forcing her to move at a faster pace than she would prefer. Teacher candidates frequently expressed frustration during their student teaching that they could not go into more depth with certain topics due to the pressure to cover a large amount of curriculum content.

The message to embrace adaptation remains consistent, as supervising teachers coach them to adjust to ongoing contingencies. The daily schedule itself is constantly subject to change, and school events and activities frequently intrude on instructional time in ways unanticipated by teacher candidates. Nicole's supervising teacher, Ms. Lacy, referenced this as one of the key things with which Nicole had to learn to cope and adapt to.

Ms. Lacy: Probably . . . time limit. I have to teach this subject, and oh, I have to teach reading, I have to do math, and I have to get language in. Setting a time table to get everything in. She said that was really hard, she mentioned that. When she went to college, they show you how to teach this, but they don't say, "Okay, you have 45 minutes to do this." Or today you have an hour to do it, so tomorrow you'll have to make it shorter to get everything in. And then the interruptions where things come up, "Oh, today we have a program." And Nicole said, "How am I supposed to do this?!" I said, "Well, you'll just have to fit everything around it." That was a couple of big things she had to learn. (Interview with Ms. Lacy, Nicole's supervising teacher, Elementary Education)

Ms. Lacy accurately points out that the training teacher candidates receive in their UBTE program on lesson planning rarely, if ever, requires they factor in administrative interruptions or infrequent school-wide activities that take time away from classroom instruction. These types of events, though, are bureaucratic mainstays of public schools, and teacher candidates scramble to account for them in their planning during student teaching. Such experiences were ubiquitous among the teacher candidates in this study, similar across grade level, subject matter, and school setting. Faye describes from her own experience how these often unpredictable interruptions play out in the daily grind of school life:

But then, there's things like state testing which take away three days. And things like fire drills and picture days and whatever, that just like take away so much time. For example this morning, I think every student in my first period class was called down to the office. There are five interruptions right there. So we didn't get to play our review game today. (Interview with Faye, Secondary Social Studies) Frustrating

Intrusions upon instructional time can come from a variety of sources. Some are predictable; the three days lost to "state testing" is on the calendar. But many interruptions are administrative actions that come with little, if any, warning. Teachers might know a week or a day in advance about fire drills and picture days, and student teachers often have even less advance warning since their supervisor often has the school calendar instead of them. Finally, an administrative voice can unexpectedly interrupt class at any moment through the intercom in each classroom through which principal offices can communicate with each teacher. Students can get "called down to the office" for any number of reasons (e.g., disciplinary reasons, health reasons, a parent is picking them up early, special activities, etc.).

On any given day in any given class period, this could constitute "five interruptions right there." Teachers and teacher candidates are powerless to prevent such interruptions; they cannot simply turn off the intercom, they cannot refuse an administrator's request to see or excuse a student, and they cannot abstain from school-wide activities, drills, or exercises. As such, this represents another condition of the environment to which teacher candidates learn they must continually adapt as they manage the time they have, and the time that gets taken away, for instructional activities they plan. This poses an ongoing challenge to the successful completion of the full range of instructional activities teacher candidates plan to cover their subject matter. In the face of this, Nicole pointedly asks her supervisor, "How am I supposed to do this?!" to which she is met with the reply that she will "just have to fit it in." In many cases, though, teacher candidates are forced to adapt by leaving out certain activities. Faye scraps a review activity she designed to help her students prepare for the next exam because she did not have the anticipated time in that period due to administrative interruptions.

These types of interruptions are not evenly distributed across the school day or the wider calendar, which requires teacher candidates to adjust instructional plans either with different groups of kids or different subjects that are differentially affected by schedule contingencies. Oscar, for instance, discusses how this was initially a major challenge for him in student teaching:

> I always felt like I was running out of time, and the hardest thing for me or I guess it was, I have a better handle on it now, but trying to get those classes that I had all equal. So telling the same thing to all of the three other classes. And that was really difficult for me to do and I worried about it a lot. (Interview with Oscar, Secondary Social Studies)

He improved this balancing act with experience, but meeting the organizational goal of uniformly covering the same curriculum with all students was initially challenging for Oscar, among many teacher candidates. While external interruptions could affect some class periods and not others, different classes could have internal disruptions and delays also. Oscar, for example, tended to allow students to veer off topic for the sake of class discussion. A similar dilemma emerged for other teacher candidates, but for different reasons. Dennis had difficulties gauging the pace at which students could perform different tasks in his class of fifth graders:

> I basically, like when I was planning, I'd look at the standards and see what I had to get in, and I used the textbook along with that too. And, um, I was kinda [. . . .] The textbook goes lesson 1, lesson 2, lesson 3 for a chapter, so, I gotta get through lesson 1 and halfway through lesson 2 this week, and try to get all that done. It's hard gauging how long an activity might take or if they're gonna be able to get it done in one day or if it's a two-day thing. So, it's just constantly being on your toes and adjusting [laughs].
>
> (Interview with Dennis, Elementary Education)

Different groups of kids learn different topics at different rates. As I discuss in more detail in Chapter 5, Dennis struggled to figure out the appropriate pace at which his fifth graders could learn. As a result, he often had to readjust his plans, and he lost quite a bit of instructional time due to his need to review previously covered material with his students. Other teacher candidates had similar problems, but for the opposite reason. Nelly underprepared for one of her math classes, as she underestimated the speed with which a particularly talented group of her students could cover new material.

Nellie: Probably my fourth-period class, the pre-algebra. I thought, "Okay, we'll just focus on one thing at a time, and we'll get through it and it will be great. And I can really push them in this sense." And they just zipped right through it. I did not plan enough stuff for them to do. I think especially fourth period, I couldn't give them enough to do. Finally, the last two weeks of class I finally got it down where they had enough to do but weren't overwhelmed. That was probably the biggest surprise was realizing just how much these kids can understand. You guys are 13 years old and I can give you two or three lessons and you guys just swallow it up. So, I think learning to balance that out. And I really thought the kids would struggle with the previous stuff we were talking about, so I planned for two days of material and I covered it all in one day. So, I was like, "I've got to rearrange . . ." (Interview with Nellie, Secondary Math)

To be sure, a key reason that Nellie, as well as Dennis, needed to "rearrange" and "readjust" with these students was their own lack of experience. However, Nellie only misjudged the pace for one of her classes, and Dennis only misjudged particular topics with his fifth graders. In both cases, it was the particular grouping of students assigned to the classes they taught that was the source of the pacing contingency to which they had to adapt. Student assignment and class composition are administratively assigned, and such work conditions require adaptation beyond just issues of timing and schedule.

Class Composition and Time-Consuming Student Behavior

[handwritten annotation: !!! So impartant to consider]

In Chapter 1, I discussed the ways teacher candidates are trained in constructivist pedagogy to make them responsive to the learning differences of individual students. When they transition into student teaching, they also confront the need to be responsive to different group dynamics of the classes they are assigned to teach, and the collective of students that comprises each one. Again, these student groupings are administratively assigned; teachers and teacher candidates have little if any input into how students are grouped together, but this is a key contingency to which they must adapt their instruction. Organizational practices of schools, namely ability grouping or "tracking," results in the segregation of high- and low-performing students into different class groupings.[1] Nellie's high-performing fourth period I just discussed is an example; they were, as a group, so high-performing that she had to rearrange the sheer amount of material she presented every day. The converse of this type of situation can be found in many low-performing tracked classes, which not only house low-performing students academically but students that tend to have more behavioral problems. Moreover, beyond tracking practices, administrators have a habit of concentrating students with histories of behavior problems in the same class sections. Nellie, Frank, Nicole, and Oscar all taught classes grouped in this way across their grade-level and subject-matter differences. Classes grouped in this way often require different instructional and management techniques as the frequency of interruptions—both by students as well as by teachers attempting to manage the disruptions[2]—vastly exceeds that of other classes. Teacher candidates earn high praise from supervisors when they display a capacity to effectively adapt to classes with high proportions of disruptive students. Nellie's supervisor, Mr. Bower, discussed her success in managing an "extremely tough" class in ways distinct from how she managed his other class sections:

> We had a tough period with period 5. Period 5 was extremely tough. And so that gave her a sense of what it's like if you have a class or two of, not necessarily lower-level students, but just students who struggle time to time, and they choose to cause more discipline problems than anyone else. She was blessed in a way by having an opportunity to teach in all the different levels.
>
> But I was still impressed with the way she went about it. She never gave up, she tried something different all the time. She actually developed a discipline plan for period 5 only, and she implemented that and it seemed to work out well. So, I was impressed with her effort; she never got down on herself. You know, it can be very frustrating at times, but she did a great job. (Interview with Mr. Bower, Nellie's supervising teacher)

Though "very frustrating," Nellie was "blessed in a way by having an opportunity" to gain experience in how to deal with such a class, according to Mr. Bower. This blessing is a reflection that such organizational practices in schools are just a reality of the environment that teachers must face, and the sooner they develop their own strategies for managing such classes the more prepared they will be. Other supervising teachers made similar statements about the benefit their teacher candidates gained by having collections of students in the same class with frequent behavioral problems. Ms. Lacy commented in an interview that if Nicole "can handle this class, she can teach any class." In Nellie's case, what "impressed" Mr. Bower in particular was her persistence in experimenting until she found a strategy that worked with this group of students. Nellie discussed how the process unfolded:

Judson: You mentioned fifth period, and they were the tough group. What was the first day where you realized, "Okay, I got to go back to the drawing board with these kids." Describe that day to me.

Nellie: Really, I feel like it wasn't until almost halfway in, because the first three weeks were kind of like the honeymoon period, where they were like, "Okay, we're going to be really nice and respectful," and then they got used to me and were like, "Oh, we can push her buttons here." Or, "Oh, we can say that we're going to the restroom and then go out and walk in the halls for half an hour." So, probably almost five to six weeks in where I couldn't get them to be quiet, and kids would come up to me and say, "These people are cheating," or "I can't learn." So that's when I talked to Mr. Bower more, and had him sit in on it. But, of course when he sits in on the class they're a little bit better, but . . . So I talked to [school principal], and said, "This is what I'm thinking, what do you think about it?" So, that's when we dropped our little discipline plan about the warnings, and just go straight to the office.

Judson: And that was just for fifth period?

Nellie: That was just for fifth period only. I never had any other trouble like that with any other class.

Judson: So Mr. Bower was supportive, but was the principal also supportive of your plan?

Nellie: Oh yeah! He knows this group of kids. Because they all take similar classes, they all get clumped together, so he's used to dealing with all of them on a daily basis. Yeah, he was definitely supportive, like he was like, "This is almost too light; make it a little more strict." It was nice to have that conversation and have that support system.

Judson: And so there was a real improvement after that?

Nellie: Not at first. I handed it out on a piece of paper, and said "Guys, this is the new discipline plan. I'm sorry for those of you to whom this doesn't apply to." So we had that conversation, and it was really good the first couple of days, and then they went right back into their little . . . I was like, "Okay." So I wrote three referrals [to the principal's office] after two or three days. Then they were like, "Oh, okay so this is what's going on." And then it was really good.

(Interview with Nellie, Secondary Math)

Nellie developed a discipline plan tailored specifically to her fifth-period class, one she did not implement in any other class. The unique behavioral challenges of this class dynamic and collection of students required a more regimented approach than other classes. Not only did she have Mr. Bower's support, she

how common is principal support?

this is interesting but also sounds like a unique experience also had her principal's, who was keenly aware of the discipline problems linked with this group of students, in part because they were referred to him often and in part because he and his staff grouped them into the same class sections. His support—indeed, even his advice that she could be harder on them—is no doubt in appreciation for Nellie's effort to cooperate with administrative practices of the school by adapting her management techniques to better accommodate the class composition structured by the organization.

While the new discipline policy for fifth period enabled her to make more student referrals to the principal's office, Nellie still had to manage abundant disruptions in class largely owing to the concentration of students with histories of disruptive behavior. The following exchange occurred while Nellie was trying to cover the previous night's homework assignment with one of her math classes at the beginning of class:

> A student on the far right side of the classroom continues to hit his calculator repeatedly on his desk. A student answers number six, and immediately after confirming "25%" as the correct answer, Nellie raises her voice to the student with the calculator, saying, "Stop banging your calculator!"
>
> Lance instantly calls out, "Who's he bangin'?!"
>
> Students laugh raucously at this comment; all but a couple of students are laughing. Nellie reacts quickly and angrily, walking toward Lance and pointing to the door as she shouts, "Lance, go to the office right now! That is uncalled for!" Lance does not get up to leave, and students around the room continue laughing, some uncontrollably with tears streaming down their cheeks.

Cringe

(Field notes, Nellie's Student Teaching)

Nellie tried hard to keep the review progressing despite continuous small disruptions that preceded Lance's joke. Only when Lance's comment brought the class to a standstill did Nellie stop what she was doing and dismiss the student from class.

Managing unpredictable student behavior like this is an ongoing challenge of adaptation for teacher candidates, and adds to the complexities of covering a standardized curriculum. Nellie's case is a good example. Before class on the day of Lance's outburst, Nellie had been telling me that this class was behind where they were supposed to be in the curriculum by this date. She really wanted to make up ground that day in class, and planned to get through the homework review as quickly as possible so she could. Lance's joke during the review, which prompted Nellie's action to dismiss him from class, combined with the other students' collective reaction, all but derailed Nellie's plan for a particularly efficient day of coverage in her subject matter. In addition, in a cruel twist of fate for Nellie, another student farted loudly just seconds after Lance was out the door. The entire class heard it, and the laughter was collectively uncontrollable. All told, it took Nellie nearly 10 minutes to deal with Lance (who stalled in actually getting up from his desk, and dragged his feet out the door to go to the principal's office), and then quiet the rest of the class after the fart so they could resume the homework review. In a 50-minute class period, those two back-to-back disruptions ate 20 percent of Nellie's instructional time with that group for the day before she even had a chance to teach new subject matter, and there was no way to anticipate those events before they happened. Nellie thereby had no choice but to adapt her plans for the rest of the week, abandoning some activities she had planned to free more time to catch up on the introduction of new material, something her supervising teacher was pressuring her to do for the sake of curriculum coverage.

Frank completed his student teaching in English/language arts, but in the same middle school where Nellie student taught in math. Again, as a product of the school's grouping practices, Frank had the same group of students in his fourth period that Nellie had in her fifth period, and he faced similar challenges with this class of students in getting them through the subject matter. Much like Nellie's efforts to simply review a homework assignment, Frank had to grind out even the most mundane administrative tasks in the face of this group's ongoing antics:

> Frank [Mr. Keller] calls on another student to write their two truths and a lie on the same board. Students around the room begin to talk again. He says that while he's doing that, he is going to announce the people who will be doing theirs for the next two days. He tells them he needs their "Attention up here" as he stands at the front of the room. He says for those of them "who have your heads facing Dylan, you need to turn here," and then he simply moves to the side of the room where Dylan is and proceeds, saying "Maybe I'll just move over here." (Frank, Secondary English/Language Arts)

The two-truths-and-a-lie activity was one that Frank did over time, intended to help students develop a range of organizational and public-speaking skills prescribed by the curriculum. But just communicating to students the sequence with which they would complete this instructional activity could get bogged down with the incessant distractions this class routinely produced. Frank adapts in the moment, calling for attention authoritatively while also positioning himself differently in the room to keep the task moving in response to student behavior.

Teacher candidates who demonstrate an ability to effectively manage and adapt instruction to the challenging classroom dynamics created by tracking practices, while sufficiently covering their prescribed curriculum standards, received high praise from supervisors. Nicole earned marks of "distinguished" from her supervisors because of the creative ways she adapted instruction to this challenging group of kids. In her final evaluation of the semester, her university supervisor described Nicole's performance in these terms:

> This class consisted of one of the most challenging groups of students I have encountered in more than 30 years as an educator. Ms. Harris [Nicole] embraced this class with compassion, discipline, and commitment to providing a high standard of education to each student.
>
> Possessing a sound knowledge of the relevant state standards governing the third-grade curriculum, Ms. Harris used a wide variety of resources to plan and present lessons that were engaging and challenging . . . Personalizing instruction is a difficult task for any teacher, especially one with little classroom experience. The unique makeup of students in this class made it necessary for Ms. Harris to do this early and often. She started a file of instructional strategies and ideas to help students with various learning and behavioral needs. She also kept a journal to record which of these proved effective with which students. Her lessons were creative and engaging and were presented by using a wide variety of instructional strategies. Despite the many behavioral and emotional issues of her students, Ms. Harris developed a strong and productive learning relationship with each of them. Nicole Harris successfully completed a student teaching assignment that would have scared off many inexperienced teachers. With additional experience, she will become an outstanding teacher. (Excerpt from Nicole's University Supervisor's Final Evaluation)

We see the emphasis on both aligning instruction with "state standards," but doing so in ways that adapt to the "behavioral and emotional issues of her students." Nicole even went so far as to keep a running record of the effectiveness of different techniques with particular students, something for which she was praised in this final review and which reflected her most significant achievement of developing "a strong and productive learning relationship" with each of her students. Weekly observations of my own confirmed that Nicole's student teaching assignment was indeed one "that would have scared off many inexperienced teachers." Much of Nicole's success hinged on her own ingenuity and fortitude, however. The "file of instructional strategies" and the "journal" of "effective" strategies Nicole employed were practices she developed herself to adapt to the "unique makeup of students in this class." In this sense, she complied with, and enacted, the injunction to adapt that structured her training at State University, but in her own creative ways. Because it worked in moving a challenging group of kids through the state standards, she received some of the most effusively positive evaluations among the teacher candidates in this study at the conclusion of her student teaching.

Gender, Authority, and Classroom Management

Evaluations like the one Nicole received in the previous section, along with the evaluation rubrics I discussed in Chapter 3, are the types of organizational job performance descriptions and measures that Joan Acker theorizes are normally, but incorrectly, considered "gender neutral."[3] Indeed, the goals of accountability and other bureaucratic rules of schools make no explicit reference to the gender identities of the people whose jobs are to meet these goals and follow these rules. When people actually perform jobs in organizational settings, however, they necessarily bring their own gender identities to bear on the social interactions through which they perform their jobs. Through local interactions, gender performances become entwined with overall job performances. As such, rationalized meanings about femininity and masculinity inform the ways teacher candidates carry out the classroom management techniques through which they adapt to the dilemmas of coverage and control endemic to teaching.

Femininity, Enhancing the Well-Being of Others, and Authority

Here's the analysis missing in the previous chapters

Femininity as an institutional myth includes the expectation that women will be kind, outwardly pleasant, and enthusiastically supportive in their demeanor. The common (yet offensive) colloquial criticism often leveled at women for having "resting bitch face" reflects the rationalized ideals that women's default countenance should be amiable and friendly. Such expectations for women's behavior are especially forceful in the context of their interaction with children, as feminine ideals assume that women are caring and nurturing "by nature." To be successfully feminine as a teacher in a classroom context, then, means to be kind, outwardly pleasant, and enthusiastically supportive ad infinitum. When performing work roles that require managing people's attitudes and behaviors, women are often expected to engage in a type of "emotion work," as Arlie Hochschild calls it, that involves "affirming, enhancing, and celebrating the well-being and status of others."[4] Women are called upon to "adapt more to the needs of others" more routinely than men, and, consistent with the rationalized ideals of masculinity, men are often given much greater license to exert authority more explicitly and forcefully than women.[5]

These gendered expectations become particularly relevant to teacher candidates in contexts where they must attempt to wield authority over student behavior and manage control of their classrooms.[6] An observation from Nicole's (Ms. Harris to her students) third-grade classroom offers an illustration of how some women inhabit femininity as they perform routine instructional tasks that require concomitantly managing student behavior and covering the curriculum:

> The next example gets the students' attention, as Nicole reads, "There was no school because it snowed." Before asking for the cause and effect,

she asks them, "Do you think that's going to happen?" [It's been wintry, and there is snow in the forecast for the next few days.] Several students say "Yes!" excitedly while others say "no." One student says, "I hope so." They address the cause/effect issue, and move on. "The referee called a penalty on a player for traveling." As she reads this one, there is some noise coming from students in another room; it goes away quickly though. Nicole does something differently this time, and asks them to "hold up your card if you think you have what it is" [meaning cause or effect]. Several students raise their cards, and there is a mix of cause papers and effect papers. Nicole calls on one of the students who is holding up the wrong card in answer to the question, and asks why they think that's the right answer. They are quiet, and other students raise hands to explain the correct answer. [Meanwhile, the girl who moved earlier has her head down on her desk.] They negotiate the right answer through questions and answers from Nicole, and Nicole praises them all again, saying, "You all are so good, I can't get over it!" She gives them another statement, and has them hold the cards up again to see if theirs matches the correct answer. This time, they all get it correct, and Nicole exclaims "Good job!" while clapping her hands softly in front of her chest. The third repetition of this activity addresses a statement describing a boy doing poorly on a test because he didn't do his homework. Nicole asks for the cards, and quickly asks for the cause. They answer in unison, "Because he didn't do his homework." Again, she praises them enthusiastically, repeating "Good job!" and clapping.

Nicole has them transition from this activity to a reading and writing activity which elaborates the lesson on the cause/effect relationship. They are to use their books, and specific pages that Nicole gives them. She also hands out new sheets of paper for them to write more examples of cause and effect from their books. She is mobile around the room as they make this transition in activities. A student asks her, "How many more minutes till lunch?" She asks him, "What time is it now?" He turns to look at the clock and pauses for a few seconds before answering, "A lot." She walks him through telling the time, discussing which numbers the large and small hands on the clock are pointing to. She then moves on throughout the room. She walks to the back, and goes to G. and says, "Give me what you just had." He says "That's it," after handing something to her that I can't see. She asks him, "Nothing else?" He insists not, and she warns as she walks away that future things he plays with will "go in the trash."

(Field notes, Nicole's Student Teaching, Elementary Education)

I observed Nicole's classroom every week during her student teaching, and this exchange is emblematic of her modus operandi in terms of teaching style and the emotion work it entails. Nicole relies upon emotive praise and enthusiasm in providing ongoing feedback to students as they learn new knowledge and skills. While she is genuinely happy for students when they perform well, the emotional display is exaggerated strategically to reward students for their performance and likely encourage others to similar performance (indeed, the praise is often collective, as in "you all," not just individual).

Her emotional displays are closely aligned with traditional gender performances of femininity as well. The mannerisms through which she claps her hands in celebratory praise are clearly feminine displays, and she feigns swooning along with the statement "You all are so good, I can't get over it!" In addition, Nicole was routinely affectionate with her third-grade students (these children were eight and nine years old); hugs were fairly common in her classroom. Indeed, Nicole cultivates such a caring demeanor with her students that on one occasion a student addressed her as "Mom" instead of Ms. Harris:

> Students begin to finish their poems, and Ms. Harris tells them to put them "in the language cubby." Students begin to get up and circulate, and one approaches her saying, "Mom—I mean, Ms. Harris." They both smile at her mistake. (Nicole, Elementary Education, Student Teaching Classroom)

To be sure, Nicole feels authentic affection for her students, but not to the degree or of the same type a mother feels for her own children. Rather, she deploys affection that resembles a mothering relationship as a technical means of managing her students' behavior and motivating them in the context of instruction. She weaves behavior management together with ongoing emotive praise in the ways she conducts instruction in her class. As she carries on whole-class instruction, she moves around the room occasionally correcting individual student's behavior. While supervising the whole class, she confiscates an object one student is playing with, warns of consequences for similar behavior in the future, and immediately moves on with supervision of the class's ongoing activities.

Other teacher candidates engage in similar combinations of motivating positive behavior while concurrently correcting disruptive behavior, and other women aligned these instructional strategies with traditionally feminine performances.

> Ms. Underwood works out the problems as she leads the class through question-and-answering. Her voice is pleasant and enthusiastic as she speaks, providing effusively positive feedback for correct answers. More students are answering questions now, especially a girl sitting in the back. Ms. Underwood encourages that they ask questions as they go. She moves on to another problem, writing it on the board. She calls on one of the girls off to the side to answer a question, turning toward that side of the

classroom as she does. She asks this student, "What are you gonna get?" [when doing the next step]. She answers correctly with some help from her peers. As they go through the problems like this, several students ask questions of each other regarding the math problems.

Ms. Underwood continues asking questions, now drafting responses from a boy, Ian, in the front of my row who struggles with the answer. The girl in the back blurts out the answers a couple of times along with another boy in the group who offers lots of answers. Ian stammers through the answer. Ms. Underwood asks Ian the next question, and as he pauses to think, the girl in the back talks again saying the answer is one. Ms. Underwood says softly to the girl in the back, "Keep your mouth shut." A couple of students quietly say "Oooh" in response. Ms. Underwood asks again, "Ian, what is this?" he says, "Apparently, it's one."

(Field notes, Nellie's Student Teaching, Secondary Math)

Nellie (Ms. Underwood to her students) is similarly emotive in her overall praise of her eighth graders as Nicole is with her third graders, and she solicits positive classroom interaction from a number of students. She also cuts off one student who attempts to answer a question that Nellie wanted to use to engage another student in class participation. As she helps one student who is struggling with the material, she has to manage the behavior of others causing potential disruptions to that effort, all in the context of the overall ethos of enthusiasm and engagement she tries to sustain.

To be sure, both women and men seek to enhance the well-being of their students, academically as well as emotionally, and both must maintain authority in the classroom. But for women to successfully accomplish traditional feminine performances complicates their capacity to exert authority as teachers in ways men rarely experience, since femininity and authority are often defined as incompatible by traditional gender norms. Nonetheless, wielding authority is an essential component of classroom management, and women must work to reconcile these competing expectations in their work. Many of the strategies teacher candidates are exposed to, both in their coursework and in the supervisors they observe, rely on indirect forms of behavior management rather than forceful interventions in student behavior. In one instructional methods course, a required text devoted an entire chapter to cultivating a skill in "ignoring" relatively minor offenses in language and behavior among students, reserving explicit reprimands for highly disruptive behavior. A teacher candidate, Deborah, comments on her course's online discussion forum that she also observes her supervising teacher employ this tactic:

In regard to Whitaker's chapter on ignoring, I have seen this method used in one of my field placements this semester. After a student has said something off-color or disrespectful, she tends to look at me and say "I have to choose my battles." She doesn't say anything to the student unless it's terribly inappropriate or directed at another student. Perhaps she should address the disrespect issue (it's directed at her), but I think she feels it would just cause a bigger problem within the environment, and eventually involve more of the students who feel the need to side with the problem student. (Deborah, Secondary English/Language Arts)

Deborah's ambivalence about this strategy is apparent, as she questions this teacher's tolerance for disrespectful behavior among students. Nonetheless, she rationalizes potential needs for engaging in this strategy, and one she raises is that efforts to act more authoritatively might motivate students to "side with the problem student" and more collectively challenge the teacher's authority. Deborah is sensitive to the perspective that a lighter touch may be appropriate when managing student behavior, even though she does not like the behavior she observed or the way her supervising teacher let it go unaddressed.

Other teacher candidates, especially women, employ behavior management strategies that are similarly subtle in the ways they display their authority. Nicole, whom as I noted previously had a challenging group of third graders for her student teaching placement, discusses one of her own strategies when I asked her how she developed her approach to managing these students:

No, I've learned all of that just this semester [Nicole laughs]. I was thinking too—like, we were talking about two kids in particular—one thing that, for me, is the easiest and most effective [. . . .] It's funny because it's from Harry Wong—But, it's really the repetition, so if you tell them to do something, regardless of what they say, you just say it again in the exact same words and you keep repeating yourself even if you have to do it 100 times. No matter what they say, no matter what response they give back. "No, sit down. No, sit down. No, sit down. No, sit down." For me, that, even with those two kids, even with the different responses that they elicit from me, and my emotions and stuff, that's really the easiest and most effective way for me. So that's kind of how they are like the same. But it kind of took awhile for me to realize [. . . .] Because I'd heard that and thought, "That's so silly." But it really does work. But it took me awhile to pull that out and use that. So I guess there's some things that you learn in school. But I don't know how you'd have a class to prepare you for these kids. (Interview with Nicole, Elementary Education)

One of Nicole's preferred management techniques is effective in two ways for her. First, it works by influencing her students' behavior, and second, it helps her control her own emotional responses to her students' behavior. Again, however, the technique itself is not an assertive use of authority; rather, it is a repetition of an instruction while remaining calm and awaiting student compliance, "no

matter what response they give back" in the exchange. She notes her initial exposure to this technique as part of her UBTE training,[7] but reaffirms the need for
teacher candidates to figure this out via their own experience. What this means
for Nicole and other women teacher candidates is that to be "effective," they
must manage their own emotions in ways responsive to the behaviors of different students, and they must solicit student obedience rather than demand it.

Masculinity, Directives, and "Respect"

Men in this study approach the exercise of authority quite differently. Many
men teacher candidates bring this perspective with them to their training, and
draw upon past relationships with their own teachers to inform this more traditionally masculine approach to forging relationships with students. One teacher
candidate's post to the discussion forum for his course in math instructional
methods captures this set of meanings:

> I feel that the syllabus of any class has to be intimidating. The syllabus
> is usually the first thing the students receive by entering your class, and
> I feel like they need to know you mean business. By no means do I think
> I will be a very hard-nosed teacher, that's why I feel this syllabus has
> to be meaningful. If I start class by being a laid-back, gentle teacher I
> think I could lose control of my class from the beginning. However, if
> the students understand what the first priority of my classroom is, now
> we can begin to build a healthy, respecting relationship as teacher and
> student. (This will also help with classroom management.) When I think
> back to all the teachers that have really made a difference in my life, it
> was the ones that I had a good relationship with out of respect, and if
> I can remember correctly I didn't like a one of them on the first day of
> school. I don't mean to sound extreme and uncompassionate towards my
> students, I just feel like laying down the law and getting it said the first
> day is the best way to start. (Secondary Math Discussion Forum)

Men more routinely feel that students "need to know you mean business," to
the point that intimidation, especially in the way a class is structured, is a useful management technique. By comparison, this teacher candidate views effort
to be a "gentle teacher" as a recipe for losing "control of my class from the
beginning."

Maintaining control of the classroom is ongoing work for all teacher candidates, but in many cases, men relied more on directives to students and less
on the kind of emotive praise we saw with teacher candidates like Nicole. An
example comes from Frank's (Mr. Keller to his students) student teaching:

> Mr. Keller raises his voice at two students, calling them by name and
> saying, "in your seats!" Then he addresses the class, and yells over them,

"Alright!" They quiet a bit, but several still talk. He says, "This is not Mr. Keller's circus; this is Mr. Keller's English class." He says they will get started, "but before we do, I need you to be quiet." Students continue talking, but more quietly. Mr. Keller tells them that "fourth period had some bad experiences" and he doesn't want that for them. The students quiet down.

Mr. Keller's first order of business is to address the books they have recently read for class (novel). He says they "need to return your books to me," and if they don't "I'm going to give your name to the office, and you'll be charged for it." He then reads the names of students who have yet to turn in their books from a list. The students are quiet, but conversation grows as he reads. As Mr. Keller reads, a student, Isaac, walks up to him and stands close; Mr. Keller says, "Isaac, get out of my face; if you have a question raise your hand." The student sits down, saying he wanted to check if his name was on the list. Mr. Keller tells him to simply listen. Some students are surprised they are on the list, and Mr. Keller crosses one off who has apparently turned in the book. Students are beginning to talk among themselves again, and Mr. Keller says, "The chitter-chatter, stop it now."

[handwritten margin note: that's rather mean]

(Field notes, Frank's Student Teaching, Secondary English/Language Arts)

To be sure, all teacher candidates issue directives to students, but the frequency is usually greater and the tone more stern among men. Moreover, men often relied less on appeals to policy or rules when disciplining students, such as Nellie's implementation of a new referral policy for her fifth-period class or Nicole's frequent reference of "classroom procedures" for her third-grade class. Here, Frank warns vaguely of "bad experiences" to these students if they do not quiet down, and it works, albeit temporarily. He flatly orders a student to "get out of my face," followed shortly by a blanket statement to the whole class to "stop it now" when the noise level rises again. As such, Frank tries to assert authority through his own modes of expression and interaction with students.

While men bring these ideas about discipline to their training, they enact them and elaborate their meaning via ongoing interaction, especially interaction with students. Oscar (Mr. Horace to his students) discusses the need to command respect as part of his classroom management, and the emotion work this entails, as he relays a specific interaction he had with a student and his supervising teacher during his student teaching:

I go, "Scott, you stay put." I had stayed by the door. I was like, "You're not going anywhere; we need to talk." So we have him for a sit-down. So me, Scott, and Mr. Clayborn. And before I can get a word in Mr. Clayborn is like, "Scott, what's the problem?" And I'm glad that he took it because at this point I'm upset. I'm trying to gather what I'm going to say to this kid. And it was the weirdest thing because once I started talking, and in retrospect I look back and think, "Who was that talking?!" I guess it was just one of those teacher moments. Something possesses you to say the things that you do.

Mr. Clayborn goes, "Scott, you have given me a hard time, you've been giving Mr. Horace a hard time. So what's the deal?" Scott goes, "I haven't given anyone a hard time!" Mr. Clayborn goes, "That's bullshit, Scott." Which, I found in this setting at the school, cursing is a valuable tool with these kids. Because one, you let them know how serious you are about it, and two, they understand those words as well as anything.

So he kept going on that he's not doing anything wrong. And then I took over, and I was like,

"Scott, you know, you're a smart kid. You're not giving Mr. Clayborn and I the respect that we deserve. You look like a physical, athletic kid. Do you play sports?"

"Yes."

"Well, what sports do you play?"

"Football and track."

"Okay, well do you have coaches?"

"Yeah, I got coaches."

"Well, do you give them respect?"

"Yeah."

"Well, why don't you give Mr. Clayborn and I the same respect? We're not trying to make you a better athlete, but we're trying to make you a better student, educated about some things. I know I'm a student teacher, you know I'm a student teacher, but just because I'm a student teacher doesn't mean you don't give me the same respect. I'm trying to help you out. My goal for you is that you learn something, and I realize that world geography's not the most important thing you're ever going to learn. But, through world geography I'm also trying to teach you how to become a more respectful, disciplined kid and you have to respect that. And, obviously we care about you or we would just let you go and let you act the way that you did."

So, all these words are just pouring from my mouth, and it's like, "Who is that person?!" It was amazing. It was like, did I just say that?

(Interview with Oscar, Secondary Social Studies)

Scott is one of Oscar's most routinely disruptive students. Oscar described earlier in the interview his efforts to pick his battles with Scott at different points in the semester, but on this occasion he hit his breaking point and forced a sit-down with the student after class. As Oscar describes it, on this day in class, Scott's behavior[8] made Oscar, "visibly frustrated, and when I am visibly frustrated it's more like I'm visibly pissed off and I'm fuming." Oscar manages to keep his cool long enough to confront Scott after class with Mr. Clayborn present, but he has to suppress his anger until after class and while "trying to gather what I'm going to say to this kid." The ensuing reprimand is almost entirely concerning "respect," specifically respect for Oscar's and Mr. Clayborn's authority. To be sure, women also seek, and expect, respect from students. But the way in which Oscar and his supervising teacher communicate that expectation to Scott is freighted with rationalized meanings about masculinity. First, Oscar's directives are confrontationally authoritative ("You stay put" and "You're not going anywhere"). Second, Mr. Clayborn models a similar style, rhetorically asking Scott "what's the problem," and using profanity, which Oscar defines as a means of letting students "know how serious you are about it." Third, Oscar uses sports and invokes the very patriarchal imagery of "coaches" as the penultimate authority figure in this boy's life, arguing that Scott should treat his teachers with the same respect he would his coaches. Lastly, Oscar still expresses concern for the student's well-being ("obviously, we care about you"), but that effort to promote Scott's well-being is communicated through traditionally masculine expressions of authority.

Again, Oscar certainly brings these meanings with him to his training, but his own reflection on the process through which be begins activating these meanings while managing student behavior is telling. He emphasizes more than once his dismay at his own statements, wondering "who is that person?" as "all these words are just pouring from my mouth." He relies upon meanings aligned with traditionally masculine gender performances that he takes for granted as legitimate models for boys' behavior, and deploys them with the expectation that Scott defines them as legitimate as well. While Oscar does this purposefully during this interaction with Scott and Mr. Clayborn, he also recognizes the taken-for-grantedness of his ideas about legitimate authority and how they provide a guide for his actions in this context where he confronts a new dilemma inherent to teaching. As he thinks about it, it was "the weirdest thing" and "something possesses you to say the things that you do." Indeed, that "something" includes institutional myths about masculinity Oscar has already learned quite thoroughly in other parts of his life. He actively applies them to this situation for his own purposes in attempting to manage the behavior of this student.

Orientations to Curriculum and Planning

Despite the variety of ways teacher candidates go about the work of classroom management, that work necessarily involves building relationships with students with the goal of promoting their well-being.[9] This central goal was widely shared among teacher candidates, even though they may differ in how they go about the interpersonal work of reaching this goal through managing and motivating student behavior in ways that often align with traditional gender performances. These related elements of daily work routines—the primary interest in supporting students as well as the very dynamic and unpredictable nature of managing student behavior in classroom settings—inform teacher candidates' perspectives about accountability. In an interview, Faye reflected on the day in class when her students began coming to her for help and advice:

> You know, that was like [. . . .] I don't know, she just burst into tears, and then she felt better. And, you know, that's what I'm there for. Regardless of what they, I mean, in the big scheme of things, I don't really care if they know what a charter is or not. I care that they're interested in education, and that they know there are people in education interested in them. That's why, that's what it comes down to. (Interview with Faye, Secondary Social Studies)

Reference to "a charter" is a specific example Faye is citing from the curriculum she was required to teach. While she does not dismiss her responsibility to teach to accountability standards, it is, "in the big scheme of things," secondary to her concern for her students' well-being and her goal of supporting it. Curriculum is a necessary responsibility, but if certain pieces of it get lost for some students, from Faye's perspective, "I really don't care," as long as she can help students develop some attachment to school.[10]

Similarly, other teacher candidates define their curriculum much more broadly than do their state standards. Frank discusses his reasons for earning certification in English/language arts:

> English just includes so many things. That's why, that's what attracted me to it. It's not like books and writing; it's communicating, it's talking to people, it's learning a language, and there's so many different areas like politics, religion. Like, everything kind of flows through that because English is so many things. So I feel like, with English you can actually, I don't know, just touch people's lives. (Interview with Frank, Secondary English/Language Arts)

Frank selected his area of certification with the hope that it would position him to "touch people's lives." Moreover, he views English as a uniquely comprehensive subject matter through which he can do that precisely because it "is so many things." None of this is antithetical to teaching the "books and writing" that would specifically align with the state curriculum, but he neither limits his subject matter to accomplishing that goal nor does he rank compliance with accountability very high in his list of priorities for teaching.

In addition, teacher candidates factor the contingencies of their work environment into the concrete decisions they make in terms of planning. Oscar describes the approach to lesson planning he developed over the course of his student teaching experience:

> You know, the whole lesson planning thing, it's more like at the beginning of the week I have my vocab, I know about the era, I'll pick a topic of which that I want to cover in depth and I just tried to pull all those vocab words together and ideas together and try to link it up to what's gonna happen next. That type of thing. So that's my idea. And really it's not improv, but it's pretty close. And I don't want to go home and spend two hours a night working out some lesson plan that's going to be botched to hell because they're [students] totally despondent. I'm just going in there with ideas, and wherever the class takes me, I'm gonna go with it. So that is my lesson planning. They're not gonna listen to every single thing that I say. So, try to get a bigger idea that you can stick things to. (Interview with Oscar, Secondary Social Studies)

Oscar preferred much less structure to his lessons, and this was his way of adapting to the unpredictable elements of student behavior. In his view, intricate plans run too high a risk of becoming wasted work if students do not respond positively to them. Rather, he consistently relies on some basic features (e.g., "vocab") that capture main concepts in history he wants to teach, and then "wherever the class takes me, I'm gonna go with it."

Teacher candidates come to define the injunction to adapt as a legitimate set of routines for making sense of, and responding to, the demands of accountability in the context of classroom dynamics. In an interview I did with Deborah, she was telling me of a lesson she tried to teach a group of high school students as part of her field experience in a public school just prior to her student teaching. It did not go well, as she experienced the dilemma of managing student behavior. Her topic was linguistics, and the students essentially ignored her. She was upset by this experience, and I asked:

Judson: When you think about next semester, what kind of plans of action do you have for dealing with those types of situations?

Deborah: [Pauses] See, I knew you'd freak me out at some point! [Deborah laughs.]

Judson: Why did that freak you out?

Deborah: I don't have a plan of action! I don't really [. . . .] I kind of don't think you can have a plan, because each situation is going to be different. Part of teaching is thinking on your feet a lot. So, I'm not really thinking of plans, thank you very much!

(Interview with Deborah, Secondary English/Language Arts)

Deborah's emotional response to my question is very telling into her prospective sense-making about teaching. First, the need to adapt is clear in her perspective, but not just because different students have different needs. It is also because students do unpredictable things that require teachers to think on their feet and adapt in the moment. She actively developed this meaning through specific interactions such as this attempted lesson. At the same time, though, she has come to view adaptation as an essential and routine component of teaching, and is in fact resistant—hostile, even—to prescriptive plans for how to handle potential instructional situations before they actually occur. As she defines it, "part of teaching is thinking on your feet a lot."

Conclusion

Through the ways they contend with the dilemmas of coverage and control, teacher candidates inhabit the institutions of education and gender concomitantly. Rationalized ideals of both institutions structure the organizational environments where they work, and they modify these ideals in different ways as they enact the injunction to adapt and traditional gender performances to fit the needs of particular situations they encounter. The challenge of curriculum coverage is inextricably linked to the challenge of classroom control; teacher candidates learn this through the social interactions that comprise classroom life in schools. The expectations of traditional gender performances motivate women and men to employ different means of wielding authority to maintain classroom control and manage student behavior. Whether relying on emotive praise and appeals to rules to solicit student compliance, or relying on forceful directives and appeals to respect to command student compliance, teacher candidates work toward similar goals through different, often gender-conforming, interactional strategies. As teacher candidates develop their own strategies, the ongoing challenge of managing student behavior remains ubiquitous for all of them. All teacher candidates, therefore, must cope with the reality that some of their efforts will work with some students, and some efforts will not work. A very rational response to these conditions is to embrace a degree of ambivalence, and accept that not all plans will go according to plan.

Teacher candidates do embrace these conditions, and this shapes their orientation to accountability. Specifically, teacher candidates come to terms with the fact that from day to day, they simply will not get to it all, at least not in the manner they plan ahead of time. Routinely falling short of full compliance is not because of teacher candidates' own dereliction of duty, but rather to the disruptions structured into their daily work activities by organizational contingencies and classroom dynamics. Teacher candidates do not abandon all hope of effectively aligning their instruction with curriculum standards. Instead, they define state standards as elements of their work that they must continually *try* to address, even though they take for granted that their efforts will be imperfect due to factors beyond their control. A small degree of failure to fully comply with accountability standards becomes normative for teacher candidates in everyday teaching routines, and this quantum of failure itself becomes something to which teacher candidates must learn to adapt as they move ahead each day, trying to adjust their plans as they go and cover their curriculum. Finally, while teacher candidates define standards-based curriculum requirements as legitimate guides for their instruction, they do not define compliance with them as their most central responsibility. Accountability is an aspect of education they incorporate into their broader goals of positively influencing students both academically and socially. They are coached to address state standards in this way, as we saw in Chapter 3, and they express this larger priority in a variety of ways throughout this chapter as they confront the challenge of curriculum coverage in the context of working to manage and motivate student behavior.

5

The Injunction to Adapt, Autonomy, and Diversity of Practice

In prior scholarship examining the teaching career, I found that teachers develop their own preferred approaches to instruction over time, something I call their "arsenals of practice."[1] As they accumulate experience in the classroom, attempting different instructional activities and seeing how students respond to them, teachers forge their arsenal of practices that have proven successful in their view. This process takes time, and as teachers identify instructional activities that appear to be effective, they continually make minor modifications and adjustments to those instructional practices as different situations call for them. Teachers develop these arsenals as they engage in the daily task of addressing accountability standards. While novice teachers often feel they are unable to cover everything when having to plan new lessons from scratch, more experienced teachers become confident in both the effectiveness of their practices as well as their ability to align their arsenal of practices with state standards selectively. Over time, teachers accept that accountability legitimately prescribes *what* they teach, but they define their unique arsenal of practices as essential to their capacity to determine *how* they teach to accountability standards. Additional scholarship finds that such a perspective is widely held by teachers in the accountability era: instructional content should be closely (but not perfectly) aligned with curriculum standards, and instructional methods should be left for teachers to determine and execute largely at their own discretion.[2] This type of sense-making among teachers tends to reproduce combinations of tight- and loose-coupling between curriculum and instruction that have persisted in the accountability era.

The prevailing wisdom in the UBTE program at State University expressed through the injunction to adapt primes teacher candidates to begin the process of developing their own arsenals of practice. We have seen certain elements of such priming in the preceding chapters. Adapting to the unique needs of diverse learners is a tenet of constructivist pedagogy and creatively connecting instruction to state standards is the approach to addressing accountability endorsed by the program. Moreover, as we saw in the last chapter, teacher candidates learn they are largely on their own to resolve dilemmas of coverage and control in their classrooms. But the injunction to adapt also legitimizes a diversity of teaching practice among teacher candidates, and invites them to begin the initial steps of developing their own arsenal of practices. Absent the resource of classroom experience that more veteran teachers use to define their arsenal, teacher candidates draw upon their own backgrounds, experiences, and identities, including their gender identities, to inform the process of trial and error through which they test their ideas for instructional activities.

Beginning to Develop an Arsenal of Practices

As we saw in teacher candidates' evaluation criteria, they are expected to align their instruction "creatively to state standards," which invites innovation and variation among teachers. Supervising teachers frequently pushed teacher candidates to cover the prescribed material, especially if they got behind schedule, but strongly supported teacher candidates' autonomy to determine how they teach the required subject matter. Different teacher candidates embraced this autonomy in different ways and to varying degrees. One way in which we see this type of variation is in how teacher candidates often diverged in their practices from their supervisors and mentor teachers. In this interview with Sara, who was in elementary education, she describes a situation where she had to adapt her practices relative to her supervising teacher:

Sara: The only thing that I really changed was, she doesn't use basal readers. She has book clubs. And I, personally, didn't feel comfortable because I don't have all the standards at the top of my head like she does to do the book clubs . . .

Judson: So what specifically about the basal reader did you find easier to do?

Sara: Well, aside from the fact that it says what the kids need to learn, I'm able to follow a structure, and follow something that works. I could try doing something like a literacy group, but at this point in my career, I don't think I would be fully prepared to do it. She was okay with it. She was happy I told her I didn't feel comfortable because she didn't want me to teach something that I couldn't teach.

(Interview with Sara, Elementary Education)

Sara must address standards, but to do so, she feels she needs a technique different from her supervising teacher because she does not feel as comfortable with her command of the standards at this point. Sara observed her supervisor's practices, concluded a different technique would work better for her, and adopted the basal reader as part of her new arsenal for teaching literacy. She recognizes both techniques as effective ways of meeting the same curricular goal, but at this stage, one technique is more comfortable for her. Moreover, she is praised for making this decision. Both she and her supervising teacher agree there is more than one effective way for how they can teach literacy, and not only is it okay for her to adapt her instructional strategies based on what is most comfortable for her, she should make these types of decisions if she is going to be an effective teacher.

Some teacher candidates, like Sara quoted above, felt more comfortable with practices that offered "a structure" to follow, like the basal readers for teaching literacy. Many teacher candidates relied on similar resources, following texts closely. Even those relying on curriculum guides and textbooks sometimes needed support in figuring out how to adapt the presentation of new material so students would understand. In the following field notes excerpt, Dennis receives such support from his supervising teacher while he is attempting to teach his class of fifth graders about decimals in their math lesson.

> Dennis then says that he wants to go over the "worksheets from yesterday" as it is "pretty evident that you guys need some help with decimals." He gets the stack of worksheets, and asks for the "paper rangers" to pass them out for him. Two students get up, and each one takes half the stack that Dennis has. . . . Dennis calls their attention to go over the worksheet, beginning with number one. Dennis continues to stand at the front in the same place. He calls on a student who gives an answer that Dennis says is incorrect. The student says that this is what he put on the sheet. Dennis walks over and nods, saying "that's marked wrong; one is wrong." Another student answers, "0.123?" Dennis replies with, "Why do you say 0.123?" The student answers, "Because the other one has a zero in the tenths place." [The student is describing one of the options which is the smallest because of this; therefore able to rule it out.] Dennis replies, "Okay; good! . . . All the others have something in the tenths place." Several students look confused, and continue to look at their worksheets. Dennis begins to write another example on the board, and he pauses for a few seconds. After the silence, he turns back toward the class and says, "I'm trying to think how to explain . . ." and trails off as he stares out the window.
>
> Ms. Evans speaks for the first time. She says from the back of the room, "Dictionary skills . . ." She says, "When you look at two words [to rank in alphabetical order], if the first letter is the same, what do you do?" A couple of students say they look at the second letter. Ms. Evans repeats this, and says, "and what do you do if the second letter is the same? Look at the next one." A couple of students say, "Ohhh!" Ms. Evans then tells

them that this is exactly what they have been doing with these problems, and to "listen to what Mr. Ingles is saying because he's doing exactly what he should be."

(Field notes, Dennis's Student Teaching, Elementary Education)

Dennis planned this lesson meticulously prior to class, as he did all of his lessons, and he relied entirely on his curriculum guide for content, as he did here with decimals. Following his curriculum guide, Dennis had tried to explain to students how to compare the magnitude of the digits in tenths, hundredths, and thousandths placeholders in each number. But most of the students in the class struggled to understand how to compare numbers with decimals based on this explanation. Dennis tried to modify his instructional technique in this review session so students understand, but he struggles to come up with an alternative way of explaining the topic after his first effort failed. He literally stopped mid-sentence when "trying to think how to explain," and there was an awkward silence in the room as Dennis tried to come up with a new approach in the moment. Ms. Evans, his supervising teacher, chimes in at this point, and shows how more veteran teachers can draw upon experience to solve instructional problems[3] while also providing valuable mentoring support to Dennis. Ms. Evans knows these students understand "dictionary skills," and how to alphabetize different words because she taught them this earlier in the school year. She also knows these skills are readily applicable to comparing decimals as they involve the same sequential process of comparing placeholders, just with numbers instead of letters.[4] When she invokes this set of skills, the light bulb turns on for many of the students in the class ("Ohhh!"). She also supports Dennis in front of the students, telling them he is "doing exactly what he should be," even if he did not draw the same connections she did in teaching the material. The message to students is that they are capable of understanding what Dennis is teaching if they pay close attention.

Not all teacher candidates receive this kind of practical and supportive mentoring from supervising teachers. Yet there was consensus among supervising teachers that teacher candidates had to adapt different techniques to what suits them best. Ms. Evans echoed this sentiment in a subsequent interview when she described what she thought was the best way that Dennis could improve his teaching:

How can he take some of his knowledge and interests, and I said, "You know, you shouldn't be me. You have to be you, and take your experiences, your loves and passions, and bring them into the classroom."

(Interview with Ms. Evans, Dennis's Supervising Teacher)

Emphasizing that teacher candidates must draw upon their own interests to inform their instruction promotes diversity of practice. While Ms. Evans was a

more involved mentor to Dennis than many supervising teachers, she shares
the view held by many supervisors that teacher candidates must develop their
own sets of practices that they feel work for them. In addition, Dennis's experience in class on this day reflects the trial-and-error process through which novice teachers develop their own arsenal of practices. Experimentation does not
always work; attempting things that do not work well, revising, and in this case
getting some guidance, is the process through which teacher candidates start
identifying preferred practices.

While some teacher candidates preferred structured techniques and guidance from supervising teachers, others were more inventive in their relative
autonomy to experiment with instructional practices. Frank (or Mr. Keller in
class) was one of the more free-wheeling teacher candidates in the study. He
routinely brought in resources and activities from outside the conventions
of his classroom environment or the example set by his supervising teacher.
One day in class, he invited three musicians to come in and help him teach his
eighth graders about the historical and cultural context of one of the novels his
students were reading for class:

Frank introduces each of his guests; they sit with their instruments. One
is playing an electric guitar, another an acoustic bass, and the third a
bass guitar. He says that they are going to play some music, and talk
about "jazz and how it relates to the literature of the times." They begin
discussing a general introduction to jazz and the blues; they say that it is
"made in America." The one with the bass takes the lead on addressing
the students; he says it's "part of African American history and culture."
He says that the blues are linked to the "slave trade" in U.S. history. He
talks about "jazz cities," citing New Orleans. In discussing "instruments
associated with jazz," he cites one of the first instruments as the "diddley
bow." He gets up to draw an illustration, and depicts a string tied across
two "bows" along a wall. He also shows how someone could use a bow
as a slide to change the sound. He emphasizes how African Americans
"improvised" both musically and in terms of resources given they were so
limited in what they could do in a state of slavery. Musically, he describes
how "12-bar blues" included a series of notes that people "repeated over
and over again." Then, the lead guitarist demonstrates this, first with his
electric guitar, then with an acoustic guitar. The guitar is amped, so it's
loud enough to fill the room, but not oppressively loud. I sweep the room;
the students are silent and attentive to both the talk and the demonstra-
tions. Several students are smiling as the music plays. After his demon-
strations (with some accompaniment) the students applaud.

The lead musician asks the class, "Do you know what we mean by
improvisation?" A student raises his hand, and answers, "means you

*Innovative
methods* [handwritten marginal note]

make it up as you go?" He replies, "Right," and he describes this aspect of the music as "sovereign to blues and jazz." He links this again back to the conditions of poverty and oppression through which African Americans created this music, and they "figured it out by talking about it." They had little other option, as under slavery, they were systemically denied "education." Hence, he explains, they developed music they could play on the spot and without having to write it down.

Frank interjects here, and tells the class, "These guys are not a band; they're just three guys I know, but they can play together" because they understand the basics of the blues. . . . The group plays another fairly traditional acoustic blues song, and the teachers in the adjoining room applaud when they finish. The guys ask the class, "How many of you play instruments in here?" About two-thirds of the class raise their hands. The bass player asks if they "understand why the reason they came in is relevant" to their class. There is brief silence. The lead guitarist says, "Many years from now, you know, after the bombs drop [. . . .]" Another says, "That's kind of pessimistic." They laugh, and the lead guitarist goes on, "Whatever, there will be three things that people look back on as unique contributions of American culture: the constitution, baseball, and jazz . . . I didn't make that up." He says others have cited this as well. He notes again that this art form emerged from misery of African American experience such as "horrible prisons" which Blacks experienced in the South, terrible work/slave conditions on "the levees" in the Mississippi Delta and New Orleans, and work on "railroads." The bass player picks up on this idea, and says, "The harsh conditions that the blues grew out of . . . this rich cultural tradition grew out of harsh conditions . . . and was how people could cope with it . . ."

A student asks Frank if he plays, and he says yes, he plays guitar. Several students ask him to play, some pleading, "Please Mr. Keller?" He declines, but says he should have brought his saxophone. Frank then tells the guys to "Play us out" as there are only a few minutes left. Before they begin the last tune, the men tell the class, "For everyone who plays, keep playin', and for those who are not, think about . . ." The bass player says if they take two points away from today, it should be that 1) this music is a simple art form, and in response to things that weren't allowed, and 2) it came from a sad point in time, and was the only form of expression available. With regard to the art and history they've been discussing, "it's not just words on a page"; these are things that came from real people in real conditions. Right before they begin playing, Frank says, "If you play an instrument, and you want to play something for your project, I'm open to that."

(Field notes, Frank's student teaching, Secondary English/Language Arts)

As part of the state curriculum in middle-school English/language arts, Frank's class was reading the novel, *The Contender*. The guest musicians' visit to class was to provide additional background on the art, music, and culture rooted in African American history as exemplified in 1960s Harlem, the setting for the novel. Throughout his student teaching, Frank was keen to develop creative ways of engaging his students' interests; this was especially true with the novels he was teaching, but he strived to come up with engaging practices across his curriculum. For instance, he devised a set of class activities using emoticons and acronyms commonly used in social media and text messaging (e.g., lol, smh) to teach his students about linguistics. In this sense, Frank embraced and endorsed the tenets of constructivist pedagogy that inform the injunction to adapt as he was strongly committed to student engagement as active learners.

He also embraces adaptation in this lesson by inviting his students who play musical instruments to fulfill their project assessment requirements by giving a performance. By allowing students options for how they demonstrate their knowledge of the subject, he differentiates his instruction to accommodate multiple learning styles and abilities. But Frank also modifies the injunction to adapt to fit his needs through the ways he creates his own arsenal of practices and experiments with them via the interactions that comprise his classroom instruction. As such, he subscribes to the prevailing wisdom of the UBTE program, but no other teacher candidate's teaching style or arsenal of practices looks exactly like Frank's—a product of the unique ways he inhabits the injunction to adapt.

Teaching Styles and Gender Performances

In Chapter 4, I discussed the ways teacher candidates conduct the emotion work of classroom management and wielding authority in ways that often align with traditional gender performances. Managing and motivating student behavior is one aspect of emotion work, but developing rapport with students is another aspect, one that adds another element to the diversity in teacher candidates' arsenals of practice and interpersonal "style" of interacting with students. Emotion work, like any other form of work, is something people learn to do.[5] Like other instructional techniques, however, teacher candidates are encouraged to draw from a wide array of individual experiences and elements of their background to learn how to do emotion work in the context of teaching. Teacher candidates activate techniques they have experienced or observed in other facets of their lives that they see as relevant to working with children. Parental relationships, past experiences as students with their own teachers, and prior work experience in other fields become important sources of interpersonal skills that teacher candidates appropriate and modify to fit particular instructional situations. Since teacher candidates vary in these sets of prior experiences, and draw from them as they see fit to craft their own arsenal of practices, the ways that teacher candidates conduct this aspect of their work promotes both creativity and diversity in practice. Moreover, the collective sense that diversity of practice, including the emotion work of instruction, is legitimate for teachers adds another element to teacher candidates' culture of ambivalence: there is more than one effective way to do this job.

None of this is to say that there are not patterns to how teacher candidates learn to perform this element of teaching. Especially given the sources of experience teacher candidates rely upon, the ways in which teacher candidates have learned to successfully enact traditional gender performances throughout their life course inform how they perform emotion work with students. In this sense, people "do gender" as they do the work of teaching.[6] However, women and men modify institutional myths of femininity and masculinity in ways that coordinate the injunction to adapt with different gender performances. In other words, women and men engage in different forms of emotion work with students in ways that align with gendered expectations for their behavior, while at the same time defining their emotion work as a key means of crafting their own approaches to instruction. Nellie's supervising teacher was a man in his mid- to late-thirties, and he describes some key differences between his and Nellie's teaching styles that align with the differences in their everyday gender performances:

> The only thing I would say I do better than Nellie is the discipline. I take control of the classroom probably a little better than she did. But at the same time, to give her credit, she was probably a little more patient with the kids than I am. She had the patience to work with them and wanted to spend that one-on-one time with them, where I want them to be more independent. So that was the only thing we had to work through was she liked to coddle kids, which is okay! Which is fine! She likes to pull them back to her desk and let them hover around her and she'll work through stuff with them, which is probably great for their education. But I don't do that because I want them to be more independent. So that's a difference in our philosophies, but there's nothing wrong with either one.
>
> (Interview with Mr. Bower, Nellie's Supervising Teacher)

While Mr. Bower emphasizes the merit of both his and Nellie's approaches, the language he uses to describe the differences is infused with gendered meanings. According to Mr. Bower, the individual attention Nellie structures into her practices is a form of "coddling," and she "let them hover around her." Conversely, he wants students "to be more independent." These meanings align with distinctions between femininity and masculinity as institutional myths, the rationalized ideals that women are more nurturing and likely to coddle children, and men are well suited to model the rugged autonomy that independence implies.

Mr. Bower is quick to emphasize the legitimacy of both styles, however. While "coddling" does not promote the independence Mr. Bower wants to instill in his students, he still defines it as a legitimate practice that is "probably great for their education." Indeed, the notion that a variety of teaching styles is both good for students and appropriate for teachers is woven into how Mr. Bower mentors Nellie, and their differences in style are informed by the differences in gender norms with which their respective styles conform. Moreover, these gendered meanings are woven into the ways Nellie inhabits the injunction to adapt by developing an arsenal of practices. The routine individual meetings Nellie structured into her classes was a distinct way of differentiating instruction to meet the unique needs of her students, even though her supervisor defined the practices in ways that align with gender performances.

Inhabiting the injunction to adapt by differentiating how one deals with different students often elicits emotional responses from teacher candidates as well, both positive and negative. In an interview near the end of her student teaching, Nicole discusses how two of her students—both of whom required ongoing behavior management—pushed her buttons in different ways.

> You know, that's really hard for me. I am such an emotional person, and she elicits [. . . .] I can feel it, she gets my adrenaline pumping more, whereas he doesn't. Sometimes with her, it's like, I have to go sit down and it's like, "Don't talk to me, don't look at me, don't move, don't even breathe in my direction!" You know, it's hard for me to hold that in and not just let loose and really say what I want to say. (Interview with Nicole, Elementary Education)

Both students Nicole discusses here were routinely disruptive in class, but the behavior of one of them was much more bothersome to Nicole than that of the other. She views the more severe—and individually targeted—anger she feels toward a particular student as something she must suppress, in part because it is so severe. To "let loose and really say what I want to say," in her view, would do more harm than good because it would be too harsh. Precisely because her genuine emotions are so intense, Nicole must find ways of removing herself from interaction with the student to regain control over her anger. As such, her emotion work involves methods of managing her own emotions in different ways in response to different students and how they interact with her.

Adapting to student needs also elicits positive emotions for teacher candidates, and provides opportunities for cultivating rapport with students. Faye described to me in an interview what she defined as her most positive experiences in the context of her student teaching:

> The best things have happened the past two days. Yesterday after third period [three words inaudible], this girl came in. And she's one of the

sweetest girls, and she's done a lot of extra credit, taken like a definite interest in the class. Anyway, she's like the last one to go, and she's like, "Can I . . . can I . . ." and she just burst into tears. And so we sat and talked, and she just had like so many things going on. And, um, that was just [. . . .] I don't know. I felt [. . . .] You know, at the end she's like, "I feel so much better" and "I couldn't tell my mom these things because my mom gets too worried and worked up, and then she watches me all the time. I didn't know; I didn't want to tell any of the people at school because, like, then they would, like, think things of me. And I know, you know, you're going away, so [we both laugh]. So it's fine."

And then, like, um, and then I had lunch. At the end of lunch, I had a girl come in, and I had been telling them to come in if they don't under-stand something, "Come in, come in, come in." I don't think they do that often. And so, I finally had a girl come in at lunch and say, "I don't understand what we're doing. I don't understand it; I don't." And so, like, we sat down, and then she [. . . .] And another boy came in after school to review for the test, and then another girl came in during lunch today, and we reviewed for the test tomorrow. And it was just like, "They're finally getting it!"

(Interview with Faye, Secondary Social Studies)

Standing in as a confidant when a student did not feel she could talk to her own mother about a stressful personal problem is the moment that Faye describes as one of the most rewarding experiences of her student teaching. She feels greater reward in successfully counseling a student through their own emo-tionally charged problems than she does in successfully performing academic instruction.[7] In fact, she views the two elements of her job as interconnected. Faye cites several examples of students finally taking her up on her offer for individual tutoring after class as evidence of her success. Cultivating sufficient rapport with students so they feel comfortable seeking her help—whether to talk through a personal problem or review academic material—is of central importance to Faye's work. In the particular example she describes, Faye deploys a traditionally feminine gender performance to carry out this instance of emo-tion work. The student who confides in Faye no doubt feels comfortable discuss-ing this personal problem with Faye in ways she would not with male teachers, and Faye uses that comfort level to her advantage in helping this student. In this sense, Faye's competence at "girl talk," so to speak, equips her for this central aspect of the work of teaching. Likewise, her existing skill set at "girl talk" also equips her to adapt to needs of this student in the moment. This interaction was unanticipated and Faye adapted her activities of the day in effort to enhance the well-being of this student. As such, Faye enacts the injunction to adapt in how she performs certain elements of femininity via interaction with students.

Rapport building through interpersonal interaction strategies and gender-conforming performances plays out in the mundane routines of classroom life. I include the following two excerpts from field notes, one from Frank's (Mr. Keller to his students) middle-school English class and one from Nellie's (Ms. Underwood to her students) middle-school math class, and discuss the elements of their respective styles in the classroom.

> Mr. Keller then says, "What we're going to do now is two truths and a lie." This is a routine they have done in at least one prior class. He asks what this activity is about since some students missed it the first day. He calls on a student who raises his hand, and the student explains that it's when someone makes three statements, two of which are true and one of which is false. The class must try to figure out which statement is a lie. Mr. Keller says this is correct, and says that "We'll have two people go every day . . . two of them are true, and one of them is false." He says there are two reasons for doing this: "First, it helps everyone get to know each other better; and second, you get to practice speaking in front of the class," which is in preparation for a new assignment coming up. One student, who has been writing his two truths and a lie on the side board, is standing next to the board, and Mr. Keller asks him to read his statements. The first one reads: "My sister is missing two toes." He explains this one by saying she was "wearing sandals" one day, and he was swinging an axe, and he accidentally cut off two of her toes—he smiles as he tells the story. Almost all of the students immediately identify this one as the false statement. Mr. Keller asks them why, and calls on students who raise their hands. As a couple of students explain their positions, Mr. Keller summarizes, saying that they are "comparing what he has done before." Then he says they will "vote as a class" with a show of hands which they think is the false statement. Overwhelmingly, they agree that the first statement is false. The student admits this is correct, and Mr. Keller says, smiling, "So your sister's not missing two toes; you didn't cut them off, good." The students laugh at this. (Frank, Secondary English/ Language Arts)

The "two truths and a lie" activity is one that Frank employed multiple times. As he tells the class, this was in part to prep the students for more elaborate public-speaking tasks that were to come later in the semester. Frank engages the students playfully in this activity, and invites them to engage in a similar tone. Though no one bought the story, everyone had fun with the "My sister's missing two toes" response, including Frank, who jokingly praises the student ("So your sister's not missing two toes; you didn't cut them off, good."). Frank strikes a convivial tone with the class that he sustains with a laid-back demeanor and deadpan sarcasm.

Keeping students engaged in instructional activity is in no way a simple task. Rather, it involves complex combinations of subject-matter knowledge, activity planning, affective interaction and feedback, and discretion with authority. Frank, like all teachers, is in the process of developing his own "teaching style" of accomplishing these interrelated and ongoing skills in managing his classroom. Nellie (again, Ms. Underwood to her students) has a teaching style of her own, and comparing close observation of her classroom practice with Frank's helps reveal that much of what constitutes "style" can be examined as emotion work.

> Ms. Underwood continues, at this point ignoring Maggie who has her hand up waving. On the next problem, Ms. Underwood has them check their work by substituting a number for the variable "x" and doing the computation. They work through the problem, and she asks the class, "Is the circle open or closed?" They answer correctly, with Ms. Underwood reminding them that if the inequality has an equal-to, then it is closed. They begin another problem, and at the point of division, she asks, "Are we flipping the sign?" The class says "Yep!" in unison. They work through the steps, and get to a point where the inequality is incorrect; she asks if it's correct. They say no, and Ms. Underwood says, "No, this is bad . . . We want to make sure we're telling the truth with inequalities. We want to make sure we're not lying with our math . . ."
>
> As they fix the problem, I sweep the room; the students are all engaged in the lesson with occasional discussion among themselves. There are three girls on the side of the room next to the Calculator Caddie who are quiet, never commenting unless called upon. Three other girls are active in the lesson, offering answers and talking with their classmates. Ms. Underwood continues giving positive feedback as they go, at one point commenting, "I *love* that answer!" Throughout the lesson, nine of the students offer answers, Ms. Underwood calls on students seven times, and only twice do students not know the answer when called upon. (Field notes from Nellie's student teaching, Secondary Math)

Frank and Nellie conducted their student teaching in the same school, a happenstance of placement by their UBTE program. As such, they had many of the same students even though they taught different subjects, and they were similarly competent as student teachers, each receiving high marks and routine praise from their supervisors. Both Frank and Nellie keep their students engaged in their instructional activities. Nevertheless, their respective approaches are decidedly distinct. Frank routinely used sarcastic forms of humor whereas Nellie rarely did. Conversely, Nellie routinely gushed praise to students for good performance whereas Frank was much more sparing in praising students. Nellie weaved abundant individual attention for students into her instructional routines, both in the ways she conducted whole-class instruction and in the blocks of time she scheduled for individual conferences, whereas Frank relied primarily on whole-class instructional activities and some small-group work. Comments like "I *love* that answer!" and "We want to make sure we're telling the truth with inequalities" are her way of making students comfortable affectively in ongoing instruction, whereas Frank relies more on dry humor. These elements of emotion work enable each of them to develop rapport with their students and serve as a technical means, rooted in social skill, through which they engage their students as active learners in instructional activities. The differences between them align with traditional gender performances, which serve as sources of their respective skill sets in emotion work. Frank is less emotionally demonstrative than Nellie, consistent with the emotional detachment associated with masculinity; Nellie is enthusiastically emotive in her praise for students, consistent with the supportive "perkiness" often expected of women (especially young women). Both types of gender displays, as uniquely performed by each of them, get the job done, so to speak, and satisfy the range of professional expectations bound up in the injunction to adapt.

In some cases, though, traditional gender performances render teacher candidates ill-equipped to successfully enact the injunction to adapt, and this hinders their ability to adapt to student needs in ways that enhance student performance. Such challenges emerge not due to gender performances per se, but in the ways particular teacher candidates inhabit them in the context of instruction with students in classrooms. A number of instances from Dennis's student teaching experience in a fifth-grade classroom highlight the incongruence that can emerge between the ways people inhabit gender conformity, in this case masculinity, and attempt to carry out the emotion work of instruction with young kids.

Dennis circulates around the room as students take the social studies test. Students have periodic questions, and Dennis goes to them when they raise their hands. Ms. Evans (supervising teacher) turns on some soft music (a recording of an acoustic guitar) on her CD player in the back as they take their test and then quietly leaves the room. One boy finishes first and turns in his test after about five to seven minutes. A second student turns it in shortly thereafter. All others keep working. A girl, Whitney, sitting near the front of the room looks worried as she reads the test questions, and frowns as she writes answers periodically. Several students write some, then stare off into space, and there are several with furrowed brows. After a couple more minutes, Whitney, who appears to be struggling, raises her hand and Dennis goes over to consult with her. I can't hear their exchange, but Dennis kneels next to her desk and listens as she begins to cry quietly. He speaks to her, pointing at the exam. She wipes tears from each eye as Dennis speaks; she responds a couple of times. Dennis says something else and she nods as he gets up to walk away and she begins writing again.

Dennis announces to the class that he will "give you until 11:05 to get the test finished up. Be sure you check your answers." Students keep working as individuals turn them in one at a time. Whitney stops writing and turns her test over on her desk; she looks at one of her friends next to her and mouths the words, "I don't know!" She looks at another classmate and mouths the words "I don't know any of this," as tears well up again. Her peers look away without responding, returning attention to their own tests. She raises her hand again, and Dennis returns to her. They have a similar exchange as before, with Dennis pointing and talking to her softly. She shields her eyes from the rest of the class with her hand as she looks and listens. Dennis leaves again, circulating around the room. Whitney writes periodically, crying and appearing confused. Dennis stops by two more times at her desk to check on her, but the exchanges are brief. At 11:07, he announces to the class, "Okay, check any final answers . . . If you're not finished, you'll have to work on it at recess and finish it then. We need to move on to science, but we'll take a restroom break first."

Students turn in their tests and line up in standard procedure at the front of the room to go to the restroom. Whitney lines up with her friends, crying unabashedly now and covering her eyes with both hands as she faces the dry-erase board away from the rest of the class. I can't hear what she says, but her friend pats her on the back and says, "I know." Dennis then leads them to the restroom and they file out of the classroom.

(Field notes, Dennis's student teaching, Elementary Education)

Dennis was as unprepared to manage Whitney's emotions on this day in class as Whitney was unprepared to take this test. She melts down as she takes it, and the emotional distress further inhibited her ability to perform the tasks the exam required of her. Whitney was a strong student academically, and her emotions were no doubt driven by the anxiety induced by her unpreparedness, something that was unusual for her. Dennis made several visits to her side to counsel her, but to no avail. By the time Dennis had them line up to leave the room, Whitney was sobbing and inconsolable.

In a subsequent interview, I asked Dennis about this day in class, and for him to elaborate on the exchanges he had with Whitney at her desk:

Dennis: Well, I just kind of read through the questions with her, and asked her, "Well, what do you know about this? We went over this in class; just think back to what we did." And I gave examples of some of the things that we did that dealt with the question. You know, "Think back to the stuff we did. Just calm down, think through it, and do your best. Give your best answer." The second time I went through it, I actually had to give her some clues because she was not getting anything. And . . . Yeah, that test ended up not going well for most of the kids.

Judson: And you were surprised at how little they took upon themselves?

Dennis: [. . .] Yeah, and I looked at some of the multiple-choice questions and was like, "Okay, they might get a little confused on this, so I'll give them a break on those." But then the essay questions, we went through the essay questions exactly word for word in class before the test was given. Like, the study guide *was* the essay questions. So . . . [Dennis chuckles.] And she didn't know the essay questions. I'm like, "You know, I can't help you."

Judson: After that, what did you do with her and the other students?

Dennis: She ended up coming back during recess and finished the test. That helped calm her nerves, and she got a second chance and she was in there by herself working on it. But, um . . . I didn't really know what to say [Dennis chuckles.] I helped her as much as I could. I can't give you the answers to the test . . . It was a textbook test, so they had seen the format. I don't know . . . Maybe it was in the way I prepared them, I made them nervous. I don't know. Before the test, they got frazzled, I don't know . . .

(Interview with Dennis, Elementary Education)

Dennis was at a complete loss as to what to do with Whitney as she took the test, either regarding how to help her with the material or how to ease her anxiety. Dennis's efforts at emotion work are informed by traditional gender performances as well. Dennis displays an emotional aloofness often linked with masculinity throughout his interaction with Whitney, never expressing either empathy or sympathy in the course of their exchange. Moreover, his blunt directives to her suggest he views her emotional reaction as inappropriate ("just calm down, think through it"), and his description of the retake that "helped calm her nerves" characterizes her behavior in a way that aligns with common stereotypes of innate female hysteria. In this sense, Dennis accomplishes a traditional gender performance that is successfully masculine, and he does what makes sense to him as appropriate in this context. Yet such a gender performance renders him ineffective in the emotion work required to successfully adapt to this student's needs in the moment and enhance her performance. Dennis was keenly aware of his failure at the appropriate emotion work ("maybe I made them nervous"), but completely unsure how to correct it (he repeats the phrase "I don't know" three times in this exchange).

This day in class with Whitney was just one instance in which Dennis struggled to relate to his students, their maturity levels, or their intellectual capacities. Neither Dennis nor his supervisors, though, subscribed to gender stereotypes to make sense of his difficulties in this regard. In other words, they did not conclude that this was evidence of his innate incapacity—or by default, men's innate incapacity—to work effectively with children in a caring or nurturing way. Rather, they cited his lack of prior experience working with children, experience that many of his women peers regularly obtained prior to student teaching, and gender structures' differential access to these ancillary experiences:

Dennis: It probably, I wish I would've worked with kids more, volunteered at Boys and Girls Club or [local children's museum], or something like that. My experience with kids is nonexistent except for my field experiences, so . . . That would've helped a lot I think in just dealing with them and knowing how to talk to them. That's probably the biggest thing, a little more experience with kids.

Judson: Did you feel like you had a lot of opportunities to do that?

Dennis: Um . . . Yeah, I could've gone to the [children's museum] and volunteered there. At the same time, this year I was so busy, you know. And like, a lot of girls, they go to summer camps and stuff like that, and my summers, I'm working trying to make money and summer camps don't pay squat [Dennis laughs]. So . . .

Judson: What kind of summer jobs did you work?

Dennis: Landscaping mostly. Manual labor; pays well, but it sucks . . . And we talked about that a lot with Ms. Evans [supervising teacher] and Heather [Dennis's university supervisor] as something that would've helped in the classroom . . .

I'm big on them [students] thinking on their own, and that didn't translate well into her classroom because she tells them all how to think [Dennis laughs]. It's not all bad, it's just how she is. But . . . But, I'm big on, you know, think for yourself. And then, I have to keep on telling myself sometimes they don't know how to think, so that's something I have to teach them also.

(Interview with Dennis, Elementary Education)

Much like Mr. Bower (Nellie's supervising teacher) emphasized teaching his students "independence," Dennis envisioned similar goals for his students prior to his student teaching. Also like Mr. Bower, Dennis acknowledges that a variety of approaches among teachers is legitimate; while he emphasizes his differences with Ms. Evans, he also adds that her approach, "it's not all bad, it's just the way she is."

Once he began working with fifth graders on a daily basis, though, he concluded that his expectations were unrealistic, in no small part because the way he tried to communicate to students to "think on their own" did not work with them or what they were used to. He and his supervisors attributed this wholly to his lack of experience working with children prior to his student teaching, which he describes as "nonexistent." He notes that "a lot of girls" (referring to women teacher candidates) obtain more experience working with children, as gender-conforming types of jobs for adolescent girls involve child care (e.g., "summer camps" or babysitting) more routinely than gender-conforming types of jobs for adolescent boys (e.g., "landscaping" or other forms of "manual labor"). In this sense, his prior gender conformity in other facets of his life limited his access to an important form of preparation for teaching that many women completing UBTE programs often receive via their own initiative. Other men in the cohort sample preparing for elementary education also obtained more experience working with young children than Dennis did prior to student teaching (e.g., work as camp counselors, volunteer with Big Brothers, Big Sisters). But Dennis's pathway to student teaching, through which his only prior work with children came from the completion of his formal UBTE field experience requirements, was shared by other men in the study and reflects broadly persistent gender segregation in the labor market[8] that steers men away from paid work with children.[9] This proved to be more problematic for Dennis than men preparing for secondary education (Oscar or Frank, for instance), as their closeness in age to high-school teenagers, compared to Dennis's distance in age from fifth graders (these kids are 10–11 years old), enabled them to relate to their students more than Dennis was able to do.

We see in Dennis's case another example of how institutional myths intertwine in the ways different people inhabit them. The relatively minimal training UBTE provides teacher candidates specific to classroom management fosters their reliance on other parts of their biographies—biographies enabled and constrained by other institutions—to inform the strategies they develop in performing the emotion work of teaching and their arsenals of practice. Dennis was at a particular disadvantage in that neither his UBTE experience nor his prior gendered experience provided him much to draw upon when confronted with a situation like that day in class when Whitney became so upset. Dennis's gender-conforming behavior does little to help him relate to his students or respond to their emotions. Nicole's gender-conforming behavior in an elementary classroom and Oscar's gender-conforming behavior in a high-school classroom were real assets for them in their ability to relate to different students in different contexts. But gendered meanings only become assets or liabilities in the performance of instructional practice by virtue of the ways people enact them in interaction and adapt to the different situations in which they are called upon to act.

Ambivalence in Autonomy

Teacher candidates inhabit the injunction to adapt that comprises their formal training at State University through the diverse arsenals of practice they begin developing in their coursework, and subsequently in their student teaching. Like other institutional myths, they largely define the injunction to adapt as legitimate and embrace the expectation that they will need to develop their own preferred practices that equip them for ongoing adaptation as they accumulate experience. Yet they also modify the meaning of the injunction to adapt as they make it relevant to their own experience, sometimes in ways that are not consistent with the meanings their teacher educators link with the injunction to adapt. An example comes from a discussion in the elementary methods class I observed on a day when Todd, the faculty instructor, invited teacher candidates' critique of the constructivist strategies he had been teaching them throughout the semester.

Todd says that today we will "reflect and discuss to critically assess what kind of teacher we're training you to be, and whether you agree or disagree with that." Todd says there is "a specific kind of dogma underlying here, and before you go into [teaching] you want to really think about that."

One teacher candidate says she feels the approach they've been learning forces "the student to come up with" their own understanding with the "teacher as an aide" in that process. Todd writes these characteristics on the board, "student-centered, facilitator." Todd asks what else is fundamental about the type of teachers they're preparing them to be, saying, "You've been swallowing this for two years." Another student says the "anticipation guide is something you could use every day." Todd says ok, and writes "flexibility" on the board.

Denise raises her hand at this point, and says, "I feel like for two years, I've been taught to be the perfect teacher, get the perfect job, and it's not going to work out that way. It's almost like I know I'm going to fail."

Todd sympathizes with this, and lists things that can arise in or around real classrooms, such as "parents' work" and issues with homework. Kevin raises his hand and says he thinks "these four lessons are not ideal or very realistic for first grade." He says he spent "most of our time" on management and other activities. Another student seconds that it almost takes "an ideal class for this to work." Kevin says, though, he thinks it "could work for fourth and fifth grade." Another teacher candidate follows by saying, "It's too scripted." Todd listens and writes on the board as they talk, "integration; ideal; scripted."

A teacher candidate adds that she felt like she "had to be *so* prepared for these lessons," and questions whether she could continue like this indefinitely. Todd responds, "I used to joke that I didn't have a life my first year of teaching, but if you have a conscience at all, you'll sacrifice a social life to do that." The same teacher candidate says she feels like "we'll really be students for the rest of our lives or careers" to keep

coming up with new material. Todd confirms this, saying teachers need
to become "a jack of all trades."
(Field notes, Methods Course in Elementary Education)

In this exchange, we see complex combinations of endorsement and critique,
as well as compliance and resistance, among teacher candidates. In many
ways, teacher candidates actively support many of the central features of the
injunction to adapt and the constructivist pedagogy that informs their methods
training, and feel that the concrete strategies they have learned in this class
practically facilitate its accomplishment. They appreciate that the strategies are
"student-centered," and that they offer "flexibility" for adaptation. At the same
time, they are keenly aware of prospective realities in their future classrooms
that motivate them to question the practicality of these strategies. The preparation requires a lot of work, and they question if they can practically expect
"to be so prepared" day in and day out. In addition, teacher candidates express
a commitment to the injunction to adapt that even supersedes the degree of
ongoing modification these strategies require, in one case arguing the strategies are "too scripted," and almost require "an ideal class for this to work." One
teacher candidate argues that they are not practical for particular students (first
grade), but might be adaptable for others (fourth and fifth grades). Finally, one
teacher candidate, Denise, feels the strategies they have been taught expect and
assume a degree of perfection that is so impractical, she has been set up to fail.
Even though Todd sympathizes with some of the critiques, he still pushes back
at some points, appealing to "conscience" and "sacrifice."

Modifying the meanings of prevailing institutional myths—or in this case,
the "dogma" of the injunction to adapt, as Todd calls it—is a process Tim Hallett
shows us is key for how people inhabit institutions.[10] Sometimes myth modifications are outright rejections of institutional legitimacy, but in many cases, as
Lisa Nunn shows us,[11] they are nuanced revisions and reaffirmations of institutional legitimacy. The latter are more akin to what we see among these teacher
candidates. In many ways, they embrace and commit to the responsibilities of
engaging students and adapting to their needs. At the same time, their interactions and accumulated experience inside classrooms, where they have observed
routine practice and classroom realities, show them that translating the strategies they have learned in UBTE is unlikely to be easy, practical, or even appropriate in some cases. When they view such disconnections between their training
and prospective work environments, they modify their definitions of appropriate action to reconcile competing institutional realities. We see this sense of
ambivalence emerge among teacher candidates, and it is rooted in the routines
of their training. As Denise puts it, to be the teacher she has been trained to
be in UBTE is to be "perfect," and fully embodying the injunction to adapt is to
continually achieve that perfection. But her experience tells her that perfection

is unattainable, and she and her peers must make sense of how to reconcile that "failure" as they prepare to enter the daily grind of classroom teaching.

The same set of issues arose on another day in this methods class, and the ensuing discussion took place:

> A teacher candidate mentions the principal who came to talk with them in their field experience course and something this person said which suggested they wouldn't be encouraged to do things like this type of lesson they have been learning; in other words, it would not be "easy to carry out." Todd says there were several things on which he "disagrees with that principal." He gives the example of a statement the principal made, which was as Todd puts it, "You can tell by third grade who's going to fail." He characterizes the principal's attitude as "that's it; it's their [students] problem." He says he questions whether "as a principal," it is appropriate to espouse that type of philosophy.
>
> But he asks them if they "think there is time for this [lessons like the democracy project]?" A teacher candidate answers that they as teachers have to "battle for what you want to do most." Todd confirms this, saying it "goes into your passion," and he tells them they don't have to "passively do what you're told from above" when working in schools. Rather, "you have the power and authority to do this in your classroom . . . That's what I want you to connect. Think back on this semester, and try to find time for this. It can be very useful, and think about justification for doing it. You want to be able to tell them what standards it hits [when asked by administrators]."
>
> (Field notes, Methods Course in Elementary Education)

Here we see Todd, the teacher educator, and teacher candidates expressing somewhat different perspectives on the prospective classroom autonomy teacher candidates can expect in future work. Todd implores them to adopt the particular practice he has taught them, and to take advantage of their future classroom autonomy, emphasizing that "you have the power and authority to do this in your classroom." This does not square with what teacher candidates have been told by a principal who currently runs a school, and they were collectively uncertain that adopting the lesson would be "easy to carry out" and feared they "wouldn't be encouraged to do things like this type of lesson." One teacher candidate does acknowledge that teachers have to "battle for what you want to do most," an endorsement of teacher autonomy and diversity of practice as legitimate. But it is unclear if this statement signals his endorsement of the lesson itself or his broader belief in the legitimacy of teachers' autonomy to select their own practices. Todd doubles-down on the practices he has taught them and appeals to their prospective autonomy to engage in the practices. Teacher candidates retain a degree of skepticism, however, about the degree to which

Todd's perspective is realistic for them in future classrooms, even though they expect a degree of autonomy.

Prospective autonomy was indeed a double-edged sword for teacher candidates. In one sense, they defined it as a necessary resource of discretion to develop their own arsenal of practices. On the other hand, it was at times also a source of anxiety, and they were often uncertain they would be capable of successfully complying with all of the expectations bound up in the injunction to adapt in relative isolation. One teacher candidate appealed to her peers in a discussion to rely on each other as a way to cope with these prospective challenges in their student teaching:

> In order to get over the fears that we have, we need to use each other. Over the past year, our class has become very close and has grown through this scary, yet rewarding process. We need to make our lesson plans available to each other as well as be a contact to talk to when things get tough. I think the most important thing to know is that we are not going through this alone. Everyone feels the same way . . . lost and scared, excited, nervous, etc. We need to share this with each other and encourage each other on when things get overwhelming. This is how we can conquer our fear about teaching. (Leslie, Online Discussion Forum, Secondary Mathematics)

Despite this particular teacher candidate's efforts to mobilize support among her peers as they transition into student teaching, for most teacher candidates it was a very isolating experience. Most of them were scattered across the region by their student teaching placements, and that combined with the workload most of them faced rendered them all but cut off from the kind of contact Leslie calls for among her peers. Even when teacher candidates were placed in the same school, the "structural looseness"[12] or "egg-crate model" of schools' organization sequestered individual teacher candidates in their classrooms. As such, many teacher candidates were left alone to feel the conflicting emotions of student teaching—"lost and scared, excited, nervous"—as they confronted the challenges of teaching for the first time.

Hillary's student teaching experience illustrates how autonomy creates competing tensions for teacher candidates as they inhabit the injunction to adapt and confront the daunting challenges of fulfilling it on their own. First, Hillary (high school math) talks about how "lucky" she was with the overall makeup of the classes she was assigned to student teach:

> It was good. I got really lucky. My students were awesome. I mean, they were just fun, I had a great time with them. I had two classes of Algebra II that I taught every day, and then I saw Algebra I every other day because we were on block scheduling. And so normally, most classes you see every

other day, you have four classes a day, but Algebra II was an everyday class because there's so much material.

My supervising teacher, he was there like the first two times I taught Algebra I, which is what I started with. And then the first maybe half of a class I taught Algebra II and then he was outta there. And so I was like, "Okay . . ." It was a struggle in that aspect, but for actually teaching in the classroom was easy for me. I had fun, and I just got really lucky. (Interview with Hillary, Secondary Math)

Especially given her supervising teacher's absenteeism, Hillary's positive experience with her students was fortunate for her sense of the overall quality of her student teaching. It also afforded her autonomy to develop her own arsenal of practices that she enjoyed using, and that were well received by students. Later in the interview she described how she developed her own system for providing her students with guidelines for writing their own class notes and how to use them as a study guide. Her students loved this, and many saw real improvement in their grades relative to their performance with Hillary's supervisor, their regular classroom teacher. As Hillary put it, several students pleaded with her, "please don't go," when it was time for her to end her student teaching and transition them back to their regular teacher's instruction.

It did not go off without a hitch, however. Hillary did have a particularly troubling situation emerge with one student:

Hillary: I had one student, about three weeks before I was done, who threatened to kill me. And he had done it before to another teacher. And that was why he was in my classroom.

Judson: Wait, he was in your classroom because [. . . .]

Hillary: He threatened another teacher, and other students. He'd drawn pictures of it, and all that. Well they found them [. . . .] The administration at [high school] doesn't do anything. So, anyway, one thing led to another one day in class, and he was sleeping, and another girl bumped into him, and he was just like, "Fuck you!" going on and on, and of course I stepped in, and I was like, "That's not acceptable. Calm down." Well, then he got mad at me, and goes, "You better watch it! You don't know what I could do to you!" and goes on and on. And so, that got messy. And at that point, I was like, I'm done. I'm done doing this, I'm ready to have my own classroom, have control, and all that.

Judson: So, when that happened? I mean, what did you do?

Hillary: I didn't really know what to do. I just told him to calm down. I didn't want to make a big deal out of it, and I didn't want the other students to catch on to me panicking. Immediately, I was like, "Oh crap, he's going to come to school tomorrow with a gun!" Luckily it was toward the end of the period, he went back to sleep, and I just let him sleep. I just was like, "Do whatever you want." Then I went and told the department chair, and then I called my supervising teacher, and he was at home sitting on the couch. And I was like, "Okay . . ."

Judson: What was his [the student] background?

Hillary: He was home-schooled up until freshmen year. And he has a slight bit of autism. He was always a really nice kid, he just didn't want my help. Whenever I said, "Let's sit down, and let's work on this" he'd be like, "No! I don't need your help." And eventually I gave up, I'm like, "I don't know what else to say to this kid." He wasn't mentally stable whatsoever.

Judson: Did he have an IEP? Did they consider him special needs?

Hillary: No . . . I mean, I never saw his IEP. And, I saw everybody else's, his was not in there. He was in the LD/BD classroom, but he had to leave because of the threats he put against those students and that teacher. And it was just a mess. At that point, I'm like, "I'm done. I give up. Get me outta here." And it just got to be overwhelming, and I didn't have much help, so . . .

(Interview with Hillary, Secondary Math)

Rightfully so, Hillary took the student's threat seriously. We see in this episode Hillary's effort to fulfill the injunction to adapt and each element of the institutional environment that informs it. She tried to work effectively with this student. She tried to help him understand curriculum with which he struggled and work with him individually to accommodate his needs, efforts that the student continually resisted combatively. She tried to adapt calmly in the moment to manage his threatening behavior, and he responded by going back to sleep. Add her supervising teacher's chronic absence (he was not even in the building when the student threatened Hillary), and Hillary was largely on her own to deal with a troubling situation for which no one in the school had prepared her.

Indeed, in some cases, adaptation and responsiveness do not work, or at least do not appear to work. Nearing the end of her student teaching, after repeated efforts to reach out to the student, and then the ensuing threat on her life, Hillary had had it ("I'm done. I give up. Get me outta here."). She quite literally gives up on the injunction to adapt in this particular case, and all of the related rationalized ideals of accountability and compulsory education the injunction to adapt exemplifies. It is important to note, however, that her reaction to this situation is to immediately look ahead and envision how the situation will be better as a new teacher: "I'm done doing this. I'm ready to have my own classroom, have control, and all that." For Hillary, much of the source of this problem was handed to her when she took over someone else's classroom in the middle of the school year. She views having "my own classroom" as a mechanism for securing more "control" over her work conditions with students. Even if such control might not give her more influence over classroom placements for students, it would likely at least provide her more background information to help handle such situations in the future. From her perspective, exercising greater control over her own prospective classroom will equip her to better execute her arsenal of practices through which she can fulfill the injunction to adapt. As such, she only gives up partially, and only in relation to this particular student. Nonetheless, she defines the experience as one in which she exhausted all possible avenues for effectively adapting to this student's needs, and at that point, "I don't know what else to say to this kid." Moreover, she "didn't have much help, so . . ." For Hillary, cases such as this one represent instances where a degree of failure is all but inevitable for teachers.

Conclusion

It has long been lamented by teacher educators that teacher candidates tend to tune them out, and frequently ignore or eschew the content of their training in favor of their pre-existing affinities for teaching and the practices of their favorite teachers from their pasts.[13] An inhabited view of the institutions that structure teaching and teacher education reveals a different process unfolding. In many ways, teacher candidates in this study strive to fulfill the injunction to adapt that constitutes the prevailing wisdom at State University's UBTE program. But the ways they are trained invite and reward a diversity of teaching practice, and teacher candidates, like their supervisors, are sympathetic to the idea that there is more than one legitimate way to skin a cat instructionally. In addition, while teacher candidates buy into the injunction to adapt and often strive to fulfill it in their teaching, they define actually performing it ad infinitum in day-to-day teaching interactions as representing a type of ideal perfection that is unrealistic to achieve in every case. Ambivalence emerges among them, as they strive to develop their own sets of practices that equip them to live up to an unachievable standard, defining a degree of failure as inevitable.

6

The Demands of Becoming a Teacher

Teacher candidates make sense of the injunction to adapt in ways that form the foundation of a professional culture of ambivalence. They develop a shared sense that ambiguity, contingency, individuality, and responsiveness are inherent to the work, and this culture is robust among new teachers. Teacher candidates leave UBTE profoundly unsure about their instructional impact, or the range of possible effects, if any, their instruction may have on different students. While they have the vague sense they will improve with experience, they expect a long road of trial and error ahead of them, they expect adaptation to always be a defining feature of their work, and they expect a great deal of diversity in teaching styles among each other. This culture of ambivalence is not defined by new teachers as simply a training deficiency. It is an interpretive production driven by social interaction through which teacher candidates define ambivalence as an inevitable dynamic of teachers' work, born out of the perpetual need for adaptation. In other words, they are not trained or told explicitly to be ambivalent as teachers. Rather, ambivalence emerges as *they* modify the meaning of the injunction to adapt and the wider institutional myths that inform it. Because these cultural meanings emerge out of the ways teacher candidates inhabit institutions, they are infused with legitimacy. In other words, for new teachers, ambivalence is a rational professional norm.

A culture of ambivalence among teacher candidates has broader implications for how they define the appropriate role of the teaching profession in addressing a range of educational problems. These wider problems manifest in teachers' daily lives in a number of ways: the wide range of ability levels to which they must differentiate instruction, along with the unpredictable and sometimes volatile behaviors they must manage, all while attempting to cover a standardized curriculum in organizational and cultural contexts they do not control. Teacher candidates become keenly aware of their responsibility to engage with inequalities and differences among students in their work; indeed, they are indoctrinated into an ethic of adaptation. But the ways teacher candidates inhabit their professional socialization into this institutional environment often link ambiguity, contingency, and individuality with adaptation. Some techniques will be more engaging for certain students than others; different teachers have different approaches to teaching the same topics; some students just "click" with certain teachers more than others; interruptions could come at any point without warning; students could have something externally affecting their capacity to perform in school, the source of which teachers may or may not be aware. From teacher candidates' perspective, teachers continually adapt, but what plays out with different students is anybody's guess, and that's just the way it is. As Deborah put it in Chapter 4: "I don't have a plan of action! And I don't think you can have a plan, because every situation is different." Ironically, then, the very training in adaptation intended to equip teacher candidates to effectively address the heterogeneity among students instead makes them ambivalent about their capacity to do so.

Teachers, Education Policy, and a Culture of Ambivalence

Holding Teachers Accountable

A culture of ambivalence among teachers poses a problem for educational institutions, even though this culture emerges as a response to how educational institutions are structured. Under accountability in a compulsory system, there should be no ambivalence among teachers about what they are supposed to accomplish or whether they have accomplished it. As originally ratified into law by the No Child Left Behind Act (NCLB), 100% of the nation's students were to reach proficient levels in math and literacy by 2014. It did not work out that way, and the federal government has since undone that mandate through the law's reauthorization as the Every Student Succeeds Act (ESSA). Extensive scholarship on teachers during the NCLB era foreshadowed its failure in this regard. James Spillane shows how teachers filter the mandates of standards-based curriculum through their pre-existing beliefs and practices in instruction, at times misinterpreting the intent of accountability policies and at other times privileging their own preferred techniques.[1] Other scholars find similar patterns, documenting the varied ways in which teachers comply with accountability policies in piecemeal fashion, nearly always retaining a large proportion of their existing practices and modifying them minimally to align with externally imposed requirements.[2] Through these types of responses to accountability among teachers, it appeared that a modified version of loose coupling between policy and classroom practice was undermining the goals of accountability to promote more consistent results from schools in making sure all students reach academic proficiency.

Accountability did not go away, however. Policymakers have instead shifted its focus from schools to teachers, primarily as a condition for states to obtain waivers from the United States Department of Education, sparing them the NCLB sanctions for missing the 2014 goal. Many states have also retained teacher evaluation policies since the passage of ESSA. Such initiatives were intended to increase the clarity with which we could see the "value added" by individual teachers to student performance on standardized tests and thereby better monitor their instructional practice. It has only marginally done so, in many ways creating new ambiguities in the effort to distinguish the "good" teachers from the "bad" ones.[3] Nonetheless, measures of student performance on standardized tests have become part of the reality for evaluating teachers' job performance: all but seven states in the country have teacher evaluation systems that include such measures as of the 2016–2017 school year.[4]

One thing these policies did accomplish was to increase anxiety, frustration, and disillusionment among many teachers across the country. In some districts, like Chicago, teachers have worked through their unions to try to limit the degree to which measures of teacher influence on student test scores impact their compensation and evaluations.[5] Despite these types of local efforts, as I noted, standardized testing is the new normal in public education, and it is seen as a tool for everything from evaluating teachers to rating schools to closing student achievement gaps. The frequency of testing, and the time in the school year devoted to testing, have increased precipitously, also to the chagrin of teachers as well as parents.[6] As I discussed briefly in Chapter 1, the growing dissatisfaction with these new realities among teachers is implicated by many observers as one of the forces contributing to growing teacher shortages and declines in UBTE enrollments in recent years.[7] In an open letter that went viral online and was later reposted by *The Washington Post*, a former teacher articulates some of this dissatisfaction as she explains why she "just can't work in public education anymore":

> I am tired of having to perform what I consider to be educational malpractice, in the name of "accountability." The amount of time lost to standardized tests that are of no use to me as a classroom teacher is mind-boggling. And when you add in mandatory quarterly district-wide tests, which are used to collect data that is ignored, you get a situation that is beyond ridiculous. Sometimes I feel like I live in a Kafka novel. This is No. 1 on my district's list of how to close the achievement gap and increase learning: Making sure that all teachers have their learning goals posted every day in the form of an "I Can" statement. I don't know how we ever got to be successful adults when we had no "I Can" statements on the wall.[8]

"Standardized tests" are foregrounded in this former teacher's critique, but it is the oppressive way in which her work is prescribed and micromanaged

("I feel like I live in a Kafka novel")—and the role testing plays in this regime—
that she finds so offensive. Indeed, it violates her professional sense of how the
job should be done, characterizing the expectations of current work environments as "educational malpractice."

Where does such vitriolic opposition to existing policy among teachers
come from? Much has been said and researched about the ways in which the era
of accountability has infringed upon teacher autonomy, creating anxiety and
antipathy among teachers.[9] To be sure, the stress and resentment felt among
teachers due to the loss of autonomy is very real and well documented. But there
is likely more behind the "epistemic distress" Tim Hallett shows us that teachers can feel so bitterly when they are authoritatively forced out of established
routines.[10] Teachers' distress over their work is growing in its scope, visibility,
and impact on people's willingness to remain in the profession, and likely contributing to the growing perception that teaching is an undesirable line of work
to enter. Close attention to the culture of ambivalence I identify in this book
can deepen our understanding of the social sources of teachers' growing disillusionment with public education. Relative loss of autonomy is certainly part
of the explanation, but there are other elements of the professional culture of
ambivalence that shape new teachers' sense-making about their work in ways
that foster certain hostilities to trends in education policy over the last 10 years.

Accountability in a Compulsory System

Teacher candidates are primed to mediate between the competing institutional pressures of accountability and compulsory education. Indeed, teacher
candidates in the middle of the NCLB era (2006–2007) clearly understood and
anticipated the realities of accountability. Moreover, I found little evidence of
aversion to accountability as a rationalized ideal among teacher candidates.
They viewed "state standards" as the core of the subject matter they were
responsible for teaching, and largely defined as legitimate the task of explicitly linking the content of their lessons with state curriculum standards. While
they were coached by education faculty to creatively appropriate the standards
and make them their own for the purposes of instruction ("You can play the
interpretation game," as Todd said in one methods class), teacher candidates
rarely resisted a standardized curriculum or defined it as overly constraining.
A uniform, prescribed curriculum itself is not something teacher candidates
necessarily define as antithetical to their professional enterprise.

How they go about teaching said curriculum is where the injunction to
adapt becomes central for teacher candidates. Differences in ability levels
among students is the primary institutional force that drives this perspective,
an inevitable product of compulsory public education. Simply put, inequality and heterogeneity in student ability is legally mandated into public school
classrooms, and the institutional myth that free education is a right guaranteed

to all is the rational basis for this structured condition of public education. This rationalized ideal finds expression among the faculty and training protocols of the UBTE program at State University, but teacher candidates inhabit this ideal themselves. Many teacher candidates embrace the challenge of teaching a uniform curriculum to a range of ability levels, like Betsy: "I like the challenge of keeping the kids that are ahead ahead, taking the kids that are behind and get them caught up, and somewhere in the middle of trying to keep sanity."

It is a challenge indeed, but embracing that challenge is distinct from defining it as universally attainable to consistently bring all students to a minimum level of academic proficiency. The ways that teacher candidates inhabit the institutional myths of accountability in a compulsory system promote a culture of ambivalence. From their perspective, we do the best we can to differentiate instruction and help all of our students, and then see what happens. Moreover, students must meet teachers halfway, and if for some reason they do not, teachers are limited in their impact. As Oscar put it, "There's some that just don't want to learn. I want to teach all kids, but if they don't want to learn, there's only so much I can do. I want to reach every kid that I can, but there are some kids that don't want to be reached." Other teacher candidates come to similar conclusions about the behaviors and abilities students bring with them to the classroom. Recall Hillary's experience with the student who threatened her. Her sentiment was, "I'm done. Get me out of here," and "I don't know what else to say to this kid." Compare that student, though, with Hillary's overall student teaching experience and how "lucky" she was to have such positive relationships with the majority of her students who saw improvement in their grades with her as their teacher. Hillary continually "adapts" so "they will be successful," as she says in an earlier chapter, but she accepts there are individual students she is unable to reach.

Teacher candidates' ambivalence about meeting the goals of accountability also emerges as a response to the troubles that students may bring with them to school. When one of her students "just really needed to talk" about personal problems, Faye emphasized, "That's what I'm there for. I mean, at the end of the day, I really don't care if they know what a charter is or not. I care that they're interested in education and they know there are people in education interested in them." Teacher candidates often prioritize their role in helping students with the various social problems they bring with them from outside the classroom over their role in helping them achieve academic success. Nicole felt similarly about many of her third graders dealing with family problems at home: "Sometimes I just want to hug them." Nicole worked hard to improve her students' academic skills, but her primary concern was their social and emotional needs in the face of hardships she knew many of them faced at home. Obviously, their academic performances were affected by their home lives, but her concern for their well-being went beyond enhancing their literacy or math skills. She was much more focused on creating what her supervisor called a "productive learning relationship" with her students.

Sustaining such relationships with students is often, but not always, complementary to the goals of accountability, and requires student effort as well, effort that may be impeded by factors external to the classroom. Balancing these competing ideals of public education constitutes a key element of the culture of ambivalence. Teacher candidates learn to address accountability standards, but other goals are equally, if not more, important to them. As such, teacher candidates are primed to comply with accountability, but only to a degree. If they perceive that mechanisms of accountability (i.e., incessant standardized testing) overwhelm their capacity to perform other aspects of their work that contribute to a "productive learning relationship" with diverse students, they are likely to resist in the ways we have seen more teachers do in recent years. Moreover, increased effort to link student test performance to the value added by individual teachers runs counter to the ambivalence many teacher candidates feel due to the impact of various factors in students' backgrounds and motivation that may negatively affect their performance and which are beyond teachers' control.[11] Given the ample research showing how profoundly family social class background influences student performance in school,[12] teacher candidates' ambivalence about their capacity to overcome existing inequalities in student ability levels and academic performance is not unfounded.

Contingencies beyond one's control are key ingredients of ambivalence. Recall the routine contingencies woven into the training sequence, as well as the workday in student teaching, to which teacher candidates are primed to adapt. Indeed, a key reason I use the term "injunction" to conceptualize the role of adaptation in this analysis is simply that teacher candidates have no choice but to adapt as they are powerless in many situations to predict or prevent contingencies that arise. The bureaucratic conditions that structure such contingency into their training and work routines add another element to teacher candidates' collective ambivalence concerning their approach to meeting instructional goals. Despite the best-laid plans, unforeseen things can and do arise, both in the schedule of school activities and among the different groupings of students with whom teacher candidates work. As such, supervisors often advise teacher candidates that "whatever you don't get to today, there's always tomorrow," and "you just have to work around it." Teacher candidates come to define this element of their work as a legitimate response to bureaucratic realities, but not before going through a frustrating learning process in which they initially confront routine interruptions (remember Nicole's rhetorical question to her supervising teacher, "How am I supposed to do this?!").

In ways similar to what Richard Ingersoll documents in his research on power and control in teachers' work,[13] teacher candidates respond to their profound lack of control over school-level policies by retreating to their classrooms and the elements of their work they are able to control. However, teacher candidates retreat prospectively. In other words, they look forward to the point in time when they will "have my own classroom," a phrase that came up often among teacher candidates in this study. We see here why autonomy comes to matter so much to teachers. It is not necessarily because of some self-serving preference for privacy or secrecy. It is to protect the degree of autonomy necessary to engage in ongoing instructional adaptation to different contingencies arising within an organizational environment that can routinely intrude, or even structure, one's classes in ways that require adapting instruction to different groups of students. Nellie's tailor-made discipline policy for her fifth-period class is a good example. The administration grouped her classes in ways that required her to alter her instructional strategies across different classes. Even though she was teaching the same curriculum to several classes, her fifth-period class was routinely behind the others due to their frequent behavioral disruptions. Teacher candidates also learn to adjust their plans from day to day to account for unexpected, administratively imposed interruptions (e.g., fire drills, student referrals, and testing days); such adjustments also require autonomy in making judgement calls as to how to proceed on a given day and normalize uncertainty in how each day will play out. Such bureaucratic conditions in schools render the following types of questions daily realities for teachers: Will I get through everything I have planned for today for all of my classes/subjects, and if not, how will I adjust?

Seen from this perspective, it is not surprising that teachers who have learned to operate in such environments, and who have defined their primary work responsibilities as adapting to contingency, would react negatively when schools enforce overly prescriptive mandates for either instructional practice or evaluative measures. Policies requiring all "learning goals" be posted and written in the same language, like the disgruntled teacher cited in her open letter quoted earlier in the chapter, amount to a type of predetermined instructional script that teacher candidates learn to eschew. Such policies intrude upon teacher instructional autonomy, but they offend the sensibilities teacher candidates develop about working in schools in other ways too. School-level policies that constrain teachers' capacity to adapt to day-to-day contingencies are particularly bitter pills to swallow for teachers when it is often school-level policies that contributed to many of those contingencies in the first place. Policies that constrain or potentially sanction adaptation violate teacher candidates' commitment to the injunction to adapt. In addition, these policies run against the grain of teacher candidates' culture of ambivalence: we adapt as best we can to a preponderance of contingencies we cannot control.

Gender Conformity, Diversity of Practice, and the Emotion Work of Engaging Students

Wider cultural norms are likewise beyond teacher candidates' control. Yet cultural norms such as traditional gender performances are forcefully brought to bear on the very minutiae of teacher candidates' practices and definitions of teacher professionalism. Teacher candidates take for granted that rationalized ideals of femininity and masculinity are largely innate qualities of women and men. Because they define gender in these traditional ways, they view elements of traditional gender performances as legitimate guidelines for behavior for both teachers and students in educational institutions. In particular, teacher candidates define elements of masculinity as innate in ways that foster a "boys will be boys" attitude concerning sexualized behavior. Related meanings concerning femininity prescribe appropriate behavior for women teacher candidates, and monitoring one's physical appearance becomes a professional responsibility for women to deflect the sexual urges of boys that they define as "natural," though they are in fact rationalized heteronormative assumptions. As Faye explains, "High school boys are high school boys, you can't ignore that," and Frank reiterates, "You're dealing with a bunch of boys going through puberty, so they're going to be looking for anything!"

For women as well as men teacher candidates, defining linkages between gender conformity and teaching in this way adds another element to the injunction to adapt. In sum, there are sources of student behavior, such as masculinity, that simply are what they are, and teachers must accommodate these aspects of students' lives in how they carry out their professional responsibilities, even those as intimate as managing one's body through "professional" appearance. Another quality of the culture of ambivalence emerges in these meanings surrounding the interconnections between gender conformity and managing student behavior. Boys' behavior in this regard is defined as something to contain and deflect rather than alter. Teacher candidates confront this type of ambivalence both directly and indirectly. Recall Sara's fixation on how "awkward" it must have been for her classmate when a sixth-grade boy told her "Damn, you're fine!" rather than express offense at the boy's sexually objectifying comments to his teacher. In addition, Dave was genuinely fearful that he would be assumed by others to have initiated a romance with a student when it was the student who asked him out. In such experiences, teacher candidates define traditional gender performances of masculinity and femininity as constantly in tension with expectations of teacher professionalism. No matter what women wear, there will always be a degree to which students objectify them; no matter how men behave, there will always be a degree of suspicion that they may be acting upon their sexual impulses. Ambivalence becomes woven into the meanings teacher candidates develop about the role gender plays in their professional enterprise. Though they try to embody teacher professionalism in the course of enacting their own gender conformity, they define as inevitable a perpetual risk of failing to some small degree.

How teacher candidates inhabit gender conformity in the context of teaching reaches into their personhood in ways other than the management of their professional appearance. In Chapter 5, I showed how emotion work is central to how teacher candidates construct their initial arsenals of practice, and these exercises in emotion work are often, though not always, gender-conforming performances as well. Both women and men try to cultivate what they would call "productive learning relationships" with their students, but how they cultivate those relationships, build rapport, motivate, and engage students all involve the use of their affective and other interpersonal skills. Such interactions are the everyday media for gender performances as well,[14] and gendered displays become constitutive elements of each teacher candidate's style. A key way in which Nicole maintained the "productive learning relationship" with her third graders was the emotive and affectionate ways she expressed praise for their successful performance and good behavior. While this was only one element of her successful style, it was an important one, and it very clearly conformed to rationalized ideals of traditionally feminine behavior. Other teacher candidates blended both gender-conforming and nonconforming behaviors in their style. Frank commonly used directives and sarcasm to manage student behavior, strategies that align with masculine displays of authority. He also modeled an alternative to hyper-masculine displays to his students when he performed music with his friends whom he invited to class to teach his eighth graders about the socio-cultural roots of blues music relevant to a novel they were reading.[15] In other cases, men teacher candidates, such as Oscar, strategically drew upon sports as a means to identify with boys specifically, both to build rapport and manage behavior.

For all teacher candidates, drawing upon their gendered familiarities, interests, and interpersonal skills aligns with the injunction to adapt. Not only should they adapt to their students, but they should adapt their strategies to their own personalities. Supervisors actively encourage them to incorporate their personalities into their instructional planning, techniques, and decision-making. Recall from Chapter 5 Ms. Evans's strongest ongoing advice to Dennis: "You have to be you, and take your experiences, your loves and passions, and bring them into the classroom." People's identities include their gendered biographies, and the active ways they are encouraged to personalize their instruction invites them to inhabit gender in the teaching styles they cultivate.

Attention to the processes through which teacher candidates inhabit wider cultural ideals in the ways they develop their craft sheds additional light on the social sources of resentment among teachers when they perceive policies and administrators to be overly intrusive and prescriptive in evaluating their instructional practices. In short, it's personal. If teachers learn that the basis for their teaching practices should grow out of their social identities, their personalities, and their biographies—their "experiences, loves, and passions," as Ms. Evans puts it—then efforts to externally monitor, modify, or judge those styles and practices can easily be interpreted as personal affronts rather than neutral interventions. Moreover, these dynamics of teachers' professional socialization indoctrinate them into a culture of ambivalence by reinforcing the shared idea that, when it comes to teaching style and practice, there is no one right way. There is a multiplicity of creative and effective instructional styles, emergent and sustained out of the personal ways in which different people inhabit aspects of their culture that have behind them the weight of institutional legitimacy.

A multiplicity of teaching styles and practices are the tools teachers use to engage students in their own learning process. Connecting with students, piquing their interests, and stimulating their curiosity by tailoring instruction to their particular needs are the essence of constructivist pedagogy. As I discussed in Chapter 1, this instructional philosophy is rooted in long-standing scholarship in teaching and learning informed by the childhood development branch of psychology. These disciplinary foundations are certainly institutionalized in teacher education, as one would be hard-pressed to find a UBTE program in the United States that did not have course requirements in educational psychology. From day one, teacher candidates are taught about the merits of "constructivist" pedagogy, an instructional approach that is responsive to the unique learning capacities and predispositions of individual students through constant effort to "differentiate" instruction to best motivate them to take ownership over their own education. Education faculty implore teacher candidates to privilege instruction that make students "active learners" through "problem-solving," "inquiry," and "discourse," as opposed to "teacher-directed" instruction (e.g., lecturing) in which students are more "passive" receivers of information.

Not only do such foundations in pedagogy root the injunction to adapt in a discipline-based ontological worldview about the nature of learning and development, they are also antithetical to a one-size-fits-all approach to education that many teachers and teacher educators believe standardized testing regimes incentivize. One of the most common complaints among teachers about testing is that it stifles their creativity to engage students in meaningful lessons.[16] Part of the creativity required to engage students who are diverse in their capacities and interests lies in the process of continually trying to "adapt," "modify," and "differentiate"—terms that education faculty emphasized, teacher candidates adopted, and student teaching evaluation forms codified as scoring rubrics— all instructional activities to accommodate and interest as many students as possible. Many teachers, however, feel compelled to respond to the parameters of standardized testing by coaching students in the narrowly defined ways of expressing content knowledge that increase the odds of higher scores.[17] Doing so would hardly permit teacher candidates to follow the advice of one education faculty member, Beth, who advised that they "pretend every student has an IEP (individualized education plan)."

Striving to engage as many students as possible by continually adapting to the seemingly limitless range and diversity of student interests is a daunting proposition, to be sure. Especially as novices to teaching, it is little surprise that teacher candidates' prospective sense-making about their capacity to perform constructivist pedagogy day in and day out would entail ambivalence. Recall from Chapter 5 the day in Todd's elementary methods class when this came up in discussion. As one teacher candidate put it: "I feel like for two years, I've been taught to be the perfect teacher, and it's not going to work out that way. It's almost like I know I'm going to fail." Indeed, teacher candidates retained a degree of skepticism in their ability to engage and motivate all of their students through differentiated instruction and adaptation, due in part to the practical constraints to the time needed to prepare stellar, differentiated lessons every day as well as the many factors external to the classroom that affect student motivation. While teacher candidates do feel they will improve with experience, experience does not eliminate ambivalence in this regard. In an interview from my own prior research on teacher careers, one veteran teacher who was quite confident in her effectiveness expressed this sentiment when I asked her if she felt her arsenal of teaching practices was successful with her students: "with most of them most of the time."[18] Indeed, teachers come to terms with the notion that a quantum of failure is endemic to the job, and this is not due to their proclivity for dereliction in duty. It is an interpretive response to an institutional environment that can create unrealistic expectations.

Institutional Persistence and Change in Teacher Education

A New Take on "Turmoil"

In many ways, Tim Hallett anticipated key sources of NCLB's demise (or at least its revision) in his research on the "turmoil" that emerged at an urban elementary school when administrators vigorously enforced accountability on teachers' practice.[19] According to Hallett, the new local regime created "epistemic distress" for teachers, "that is, a displacement of meaning, certainty, and expectations," that "stripped [teachers] of the routines that organized their universe."[20] As teachers in schools around the country began experiencing similar epistemic distress in their work as accountability was more widely enforced, it contributed to a broader policy environment where this version of accountability's "legitimacy is no longer taken for granted, but is negotiable."[21] Indeed, many factors precipitated NCLB's reauthorization in late 2015, but without question, the turmoil its implementation created for teachers, and how that ratcheted up in patterned ways beyond local contexts, certainly played an important role.

The turmoil of accountability did not end for teachers in fall 2015, however. Again to quote Hallett, "accountability lives"[22] in many persistent ways for teachers. Accountability lives on in the policies of the majority of states. Even though ESSA does not itself require that teacher evaluations be tied to student performance, as I noted earlier, most states do have such requirements on the books.[23] For the majority of U.S. teachers, accountability lives indeed, albeit via policy mechanisms modified from past ones.

My study builds upon Hallett's insights into these social problems in public education by elaborating in further detail the potential sources of teachers' epistemic distress. To be sure, when accountability came to town in the form of new policy and enforcement, it was a confusing experience for many teachers that jarred them out of existing routines they relied upon to make sense of their daily work. But it also runs counter to the ways teacher candidates make sense of the ontological assumptions, practical realities, and personal investments of becoming a teacher. Policies that attempt to micromanage practice, require uniformity, and emphasize particular measurements of learning outcomes are not defined by teachers as just disorienting intrusions. For many teachers, they are dismissive challenges to their knowledge base about teaching and learning; they are unrealistic expectations made impractical by organizational routines as well as influences on students' lives external to schools and classrooms; they are callous insults to the elements of teachers' personalities and identities that inform their teaching styles and practices. In addition, such policies communicate to teachers that creative adaptation to diverse students and unpredictable contingencies is not their greatest professional strength, but rather, it is a liability to be minimized as much as possible. Many teachers would have great difficulty reconciling the ways they define their work with something so hostile to those definitions.

The degree of epistemic distress will vary, of course, among teachers and teacher candidates. Some will take greater offense at accountability policies than others and find different degrees of consistency with their definitions of their work. Among many factors informing this variation is timing. Cynthia Coburn shows in her research how the timing of policy change within a teacher's career partially influences how they make sense of and respond to it.[24] We see similar evidence with the teacher candidates in my study concerning the timing of their transitions through training. Keep in mind these teacher candidates completed their teacher education in spring of 2007, prior to much of the shift in the focus of accountability policies from schools and standards to individual teachers and their impact on student outcomes. These policy changes became more mainstream after these teacher candidates completed their training and were in the early years of their teaching careers. In other words, the teacher candidates in my study were not trained for the realities of the value-added world. Many of the ways schools and districts have implemented value-added measures and related policies concerning instruction would likely run counter to the injunction to adapt and the culture of ambivalence to which these teacher candidates subscribe. Micromanaging instruction impinges upon ongoing adaptation, and efforts to tightly couple student outcomes to teacher instruction undermines a professional culture of ambivalence. Consequently, the teacher candidates in this study are at high risk for epistemic distress in their early careers and are likely to view value-added policies as creating turmoil.

Teachers who are currently so bitterly resentful of the policy environment in public education are people like the teacher candidates in this study. Trained 10 or more years ago, they view current versions of accountability as an assault on the core meanings they developed as the very foundation of their professional culture and identities. For some, like the teacher whose open letter was posted in *The Washington Post*, they "just can't work in public education anymore." For others, they continue to do the work, but are "dismayed" at the conditions under which they must do it.[25] Potential recruits to teaching likely see and hear current teachers' turmoil in public education, and it may well contribute to their motivation to consider other career paths. Indeed, since Hallett's study, turmoil appears to have taken a broader toll among teachers.

The Embedded Structure of Inhabited Institutions

The shared sense among many teachers that accountability causes turmoil is itself evidence that, despite the many things they do not control, teachers do control how they make sense of their environment. Despite the intent of accountability to increase standardization and transparency in education, teachers have the power to redefine its effects as causing more chaos than clarity. In fact, this is a broader human condition known as phenomenology: the process by which people develop understandings about their world based on the meanings their experiences have for them. No matter how powerless we may feel in our world, we always exert agency over how we understand it.

That is not to say that our understandings are void of context. On the contrary, as I have argued throughout this book, people's sense-making is enabled and constrained by the social institutions that structure their world, but people actively interpret what these institutional conditions mean in the everyday interactions they have in specific local settings. It is the close attention inhabited institutionalism pays to these local settings, and the social interactions that happen there, that sets it apart from other contemporary institutional theories that emphasize the role of human agency in constituting institutional environments.[26] Organizational settings represent crucial meso-level contexts within which macro-level institutional myths are made relevant to people's everyday lives through the micro-level meaning-making they carry out in social interaction with others.[27] In other words, the organizations where people go to work or go to school are the places where they have things to do with other people, and those places are also embedded within wider institutions. Lisa Nunn's analysis shows persuasively how students' definitions of what it means to be successful are embedded within and shaped by the distinct organizational culture of their high schools, which are embedded within and shaped by wider cultural ideals of the "American Dream." As she explains, "people who operate within a school refine cultural schemas to fit the circumstances and sensibilities of that particular environment."[28]

We see similar embeddedness in the ways teacher candidates in this study inhabit wider institutional myths. Accountability, compulsory education, masculinity, and femininity are all made relevant to their professional socialization via the local interactions teacher candidates have with others in the UBTE program at State University and the public schools where they student teach. Yet these specific organizations are by no means the only settings where you would find people inhabiting these rationalized ideals. In this sense, they are "extra-local,"[29] despite the notably local flavor they are given by the people who enact them in particular places. These factors are important for understanding professional socialization generally, and teacher education specifically, as dynamic reproductive forces. Only by immersing ourselves in organizational settings can we see the ways multiple actors are actively defining situations vis-à-vis others' definitions. Faculty, administrators, and supervising teachers make sense of institutional myths themselves, and they also serve as mouthpieces for the organization's formal definitions as well. Teacher candidates are receivers of these formal meanings, but they are not passive receivers. Indeed, we know from the sociology of childhood that socialization processes are not one-way flows of information that children absorb, and thereby become more like adults. Rather, William Corsaro shows us how children take ideas and ideals they learn from the adult world and tinker with them to make them relevant to their own interests that emerge out of their own peer cultures.[30] If five year olds are active meaning-makers, then older children, and certainly adults, are as well.

The adolescent high school students in Nunn's study do not simply internalize their school's culture by downloading the messages they hear from teachers and principals. They forge their own "success identities" in ways that largely reproduce, but also subtly challenge, elements of their school's culture.[31] Likewise, as they become teachers themselves, teacher candidates do not blindly comply with the injunction to adapt. Instead (and ironically) they adapt it to "fit the circumstances and sensibilities" of the situations and settings that, over time, comprise their professional socialization. Since teacher candidates take versions of the injunction to adapt that faculty and supervising teachers offer them and make them their own, they necessarily reproduce ethics and practices

of adaptation, and the preference for autonomy such adaptation engenders, that
have long been common to the teaching profession.[32] But the ways they reproduce these elements of teaching are creative, dynamic, and varied interpretive
processes. Frank, for instance, came up with using common text message acronyms as a means of teaching his students about dialect and the social context
of language development in a way that was very different from his supervising
teacher. That was his way of adapting his instruction to engage the interests of
his students to teach them a prescribed curriculum in a way that was comfortable for him. Sara, on the other hand, followed a much more scripted technique
for teaching literacy to her students than her supervising teacher modeled to
her, which was her way of adapting her instruction to engage the ability level of
her students to teach them a prescribed curriculum in a way that was comfortable for her. These are two very different approaches to teaching language arts
that emerge out of the interpretive processes through which Frank and Sara
enact their own commitment to the injunction to adapt.

Examining teacher education as inhabited in this way, in which rationalized meanings linked with institutional myths are modified and manipulated
in diverse ways among people positioned within organizational settings, sheds
light on a perplexing pattern in the existing research on teacher education, as
well as a pernicious problem for teacher educators. As I discussed briefly at the
end of Chapter 5, there is a common concern that teacher candidates shut out
the content of their training, and rely on what they think they already know
about teaching.[33] My findings offer an alternative storyline. Teacher candidates
do not roundly eschew the practices and philosophies of UBTE. On the contrary, they earnestly commit to the injunction to adapt that UBTE faculty issue
them. But they inhabit the injunction to adapt, and a professional culture of
ambivalence is their modification of the institutional myths that structure their
worlds. They modify and rationalize meanings to make them relevant to present
situations; they draw upon their prior life experiences as resources for developing practice; they express their personalities and social identities in how they
interact with their students. As such, what it means to adapt in the performance
of instruction can be very different from one teacher candidate to another, and
it also means something very different among teacher candidates compared
to education faculty. And yet, teacher candidates who may be operating very
differently—and therefore may appear to be ignoring their training and going it
alone—are, in fact, acting in the name of the injunction to adapt and defining
it as legitimate.

That teacher candidates commit to the ideals espoused by faculty, but enact
strategies for fulfilling them that diverge from faculty expectations, actually
makes them similar to other professionals in training, such as medical students,
who enter a profession with even higher prestige than teaching.[34] Moreover, faculty and supervising teachers alike advise teacher candidates to creatively draw

upon their own backgrounds as they figure out how to execute instructional strategies. Indeed, teachers across career stages make sense of their work in ways that are embedded within both their institutional environment and their respective biographies.[35] This necessarily cultivates diversity in meaning and practice among teachers, even as they subscribe to many of the same ideals. Many researchers, policymakers, and observers of teacher education lament how "relativism is the rule" in UBTE, as Arthur Levine[36] characterizes it. My findings show that this apparent "relativism" is better understood as the cultural reproduction of institutionalized structures in education, rather than simply an outcome of a derelict field of training programs collectively unwilling or unable to effectively equip new teachers with sufficient skill sets to teach.

An Interconnected Institutional Environment

The nuance and diversity with which people make sense of their institutional environment is amplified by the fact that they are often making sense of multiple institutional myths at a time. As I have discussed throughout the book, institutions, and the ideals that are their structure, interconnect with each other as people enact them concomitantly in daily life. Such interconnections are especially relevant to the analysis in which I show how teacher candidates infuse definitions of teacher professionalism and teaching practice with gendered meanings. Certainly, gender scholars show us that gender shapes the ways we make sense of, and carry out, all other roles in our lives, a key element of how it functions as an institution.[37] In other words, teacher candidates' gender performances are not independent of their teaching performances; they are one performance comprised of intertwined meanings about what is appropriate in particular social settings and interactions.

The interconnections of institutional myths, however, are not limited to those between gender and professionalism. All of the institutional myths subject to examination in this book intertwine with each other in the ways they inform teacher professional socialization, and their nexus is the injunction to adapt.[38] Schools are populated with students who are diverse learners with unique and varied interests, motivation, ability levels, and family backgrounds (i.e., compulsory education), so you must adapt to engage the range of your students' proclivities and pre-existing conditions. Administrative authority supersedes your authority and creates routine contingencies beyond your control (i.e., bureaucracy), so you must adapt to an unpredictable work environment. All students regardless of their prior skills or behaviors must reach proficiency in a standardized curriculum (i.e., accountability), so you must adapt to the behavior and skills students bring into your classroom while covering all subject matter in time. Students benefit from different teaching styles, including those that nurture and support their personal growth (i.e., femininity), as well as those that discipline them to be respectful and independent (i.e., masculinity), so you must adapt to students' emotional needs in ways that fit the strengths of your style. Men and boys are innately and heteronormatively sexually aggressive (i.e., masculinity), and as women teachers your responsibility is to deflect these natural urges, so you must adapt how you display your body accordingly.

Of course, not all teacher candidates experience or inhabit these institutional myths in the same ways; indeed, a collective ethic of individual adaptation breeds heterogeneity in meaning and practice. But they are all enabled and constrained by this same constellation of rationalized ideals that structure the injunction to adapt into their professional socialization, and this coalesces into a professional culture of ambivalence. In this sense, the interconnected institutional myths in my analysis are tantamount to what Clifford Geertz conceptualized as the "webs of significance" that comprise culture.[39] But since they are institutionalized meanings that teacher candidates have woven together, they imbue their professional culture with interlocking sources of legitimacy in the ways they define it. Put another way, teacher candidates do not only draw upon one set of rationalized meanings to legitimize their definitions of the work of teaching, they draw upon several sets of rationalized meanings that mutually reinforce each other to legitimize their definitions of the work of teaching. It is little surprise, then, that they would become so wedded to the ideas that adaptation and ambivalence are inherent to the job. To echo my refrain throughout the book concerning how people make sense of social institutions in their daily lives: that's just the way it is.

These institutional interconnections make for a powerful reproductive force, and shed light on the durable nature of educational institutions. The ways that teacher candidates reproduce some elements of the teaching profession reinforce and sustain the ways they reproduce other elements of the institutional environment. The rationalized idea that "boys will be boys," which is the basis for gender conformity in teacher candidates' definitions of professionalism, also resonates with rationalized meanings of constructivist pedagogy which emphasize that students possess different aptitudes and predispositions. In both sets of meanings, these are "natural" elements of childhood development to which teachers must adapt. Moreover, that these characteristics among students are external to teachers' control resonates with how teacher candidates make sense of bureaucracy in a compulsory system of education. There are many conditions of their work environment and their students' lives that are beyond their control, and they must adapt as best they can. In addition, developing their own teaching style as the chief means of coping with conditions beyond their control, as well as creatively addressing curriculum standards, primes teacher candidates to reproduce patterns of tight coupling among teachers in the content they teach and loose coupling among teachers in how they teach it. The coherence teacher candidates construct in the ways they invoke different institutional myths to inform their professional culture bolsters the legitimacy they attribute to their definitions of teacher practices and responsibilities, and thereby buttresses the reproduction of multiple institutional arrangements in education.

The power of teacher education as a reproductive force notwithstanding, a culture of ambivalence can act as an avenue of change. I have noted the heterogeneity in practice the injunction to adapt promotes, and a key feature of teacher candidates' culture of ambivalence lies in the shared belief that there is more than one way to skin a cat instructionally. Such a professional culture invites classroom innovation, even though it is often in the form of modifying existing practices in modest ways. Especially during the spring semester of my field work observing student teaching placements, I frequently saw teacher candidates execute their own creative lesson plans. Frank, for instance, was particularly inventive in his daily instruction, as was Nicole. Almost daily, Frank brought in different resources and examples to teach his students the middle-school language arts curriculum, including live music, games, current events, popular culture, and technology. Nicole brought as many resources as she could into her classroom for her third graders to use,[40] and always gave her students lots of different examples of stories to sustain ongoing dialogue as a means of teaching literacy and comprehension. Other teacher candidates engaged in similar practices, just with less frequency and for different teaching purposes. Oscar used popular music as part of his classroom environment to build rapport with students; Dennis used as many experiments to teach science as he could with his fifth graders; Hillary developed her own unique way of crafting review notes and study guides for her high school algebra students. At least once every week, I left a teacher candidate's classroom impressed with the imaginative way in which they taught a particular topic or handled a particular classroom dynamic.

On those occasions, however, I also marveled at the fact that, other than teacher candidates' students, I was the only person who had seen it. Teacher candidates would bring into the classroom their own "experiences, loves, and passions," drawing upon a range of sources from wider culture, only to have the techniques they developed sequestered there in that room with those students. In many cases, even teacher candidates' direct supervisors were unaware of their trainee's instructional innovation, and teacher candidates had few opportunities to discuss their techniques with others. Indeed, while the "structural looseness" of schools that is so well documented in the literature affords teacher candidates a degree of classroom autonomy to innovate, it also renders that innovation a largely private and secluded enterprise.

The Limits and Possibilities of Teacher Education[41]

All parties with a meaningful stake in UBTE (and even some without one) have always had high expectations for what it, and the new teachers it produces, can accomplish. As I discussed in the introductory chapter, improving UBTE is chief among the policy initiatives intended to improve public education overall. If we can just find a way of producing better teachers, then we can produce better educational outcomes. I do not disagree with the idea that great teachers have great impact on their students. But I also hope the analysis in this book will help deepen the prevailing discourse about both the limits and possibilities of teacher education. First and foremost, neither UBTE programs nor the teachers they produce exist in a vacuum. They are embedded in the very same institutional environment we often expect them to improve. Second and moreover, they often reproduce and reaffirm elements of that institutional environment as much as they modify elements of that institutional environment. We tend to view prospective teachers as potential agents of the positive change we want to see in education; we should instead view them as responsive reflections of the way things are in education.

The last 15 years have been tumultuous for teachers, and teacher education programs are confronting declines in enrollments. Accountability, without question, brought about abrupt institutional change to which teachers and teacher educators had to adapt. Yet there is evidence that education policy is undergoing revisions in ways that may realign it more closely with the institutional myths at the core of teacher candidates' culture of ambivalence. We started to see this evidence during the reform process leading up to the passage of the Every Student Succeeds Act in late 2015. Tim Hallett and Emily Meanwell show how the seeds of this law were sown during congressional hearings concerning the reauthorization of NCLB in 2007.[42] During those hearings, a range of policy stakeholders in accountability gave testimony arguing that NCLB actually "leaves children behind" in a variety of ways. The particulars of the law, many argued, motivated teachers and administrators to devote more attention to some student populations than others, in effect leaving some students behind. In this sense, people inhabited accountability by modifying its meaning as antithetical to its stated goals. The one-size-fits-all approach of accountability, they argued, does not alleviate existing inequalities among students—it aggravates them.

We can hear echoes of the injunction to adapt and culture of ambivalence in these types of arguments that have brought about revisions to accountability. From the standpoint of many educators, different kids need different things, and different teachers go about addressing those needs in different ways. Moreover, this ambivalence about effective processes and outcomes in education can quickly turn to resistance when narrower definitions are externally, and authoritatively, imposed.[43] We have seen teachers modify, mediate, and at times challenge the various iterations of accountability that have been brought to bear on public education over the last two decades, but the scaling back of accountability represented by ESSA indicates that policymakers are bending toward closer alignment with meanings about instruction central to teacher candidates' professional culture of ambivalence. Make no mistake, accountability is here to stay, at least in some form. While ESSA was a scaling-down of accountability, it was by no means a wholesale rejection or departure from accountability. But accountability is an inhabited institution, and its meaning, implementation, and compliance are all negotiated among people contending with local realities. It may be that going forward, accountability in practice is softened with a degree of ambivalence, and there will be renewed appreciation for a multiplicity of approaches to instruction and definitions of successful outcomes. If so, then UBTE programs and the recent cohorts of teachers they have trained will have played a salient role in reshaping the policy landscape to be more inclusive of their definitions of teacher professionalism.

Ambivalence is not apathy. The fact that teacher candidates interpret constructivist pedagogy and a system of compulsory education as requiring diversity in practice among teachers, as well as constraining their impact on student outcomes, does not mean they do not care about educational inequalities or view them as immutable. I was in the field for more than 15 months studying almost 50 teacher candidates. I never observed any actions nor heard any expressions indicating that teacher candidates were indifferent to educational inequities—perhaps complacent in some instances, but not apathetic. It is also important to note that neither of these elements of teacher candidates' professional culture make them different from other, more prestigious professions. Physicians, for instance, vary in their practices and widely accept that unequal health outcomes among their patients are beyond their immediate control.

This ambivalence, though, and the rationalized meanings that undergird it, can inform decisions and actions among teachers that have the potential to aggravate existing inequalities. In her seminal work on the relationship between families and schools, Annette Lareau shows how middle-class parents secure educational advantages for their children by requesting individual accommodations for them in their day-to-day schooling activities, accommodations that working- and lower-class parents are much less likely to seek or request from educators.[44] Paired with the findings of this book, we see that when middle-class parents approach teachers to plead their case that their child's needs are unique and require individual accommodation (i.e., "differentiated instruction adapted to the unique needs of diverse learners"), they are speaking the language of constructivist pedagogy that is deeply embedded in teachers' shared understandings of effective teaching. Moreover, working- and lower-class parents do not tend to speak this language due to differences in their cultural capital. Even though they may not intend for the accommodations they routinely allow for middle-class students to exacerbate inequalities, when they act on rationalized meanings that inform their work in this way, they can contribute to the educational advantages some students receive and others do not. There is a growing body of research examining the interrelationships between parents, schooling practices, and inequality across levels of education,[45] scholarship that could usefully inform UBTE curriculum as well as professional development for teachers.

Other ways in which the rationalized meanings can serve to reaffirm existing inequalities are more obvious with regard to gender. Heteronormative institutional myths of femininity and masculinity inform teacher candidates' culture of ambivalence in ways that define sexual aggression and objectification as natural, almost inevitable, elements of social life. Such sense-making increases the likelihood that prospective teachers will support and enforce schooling practices, such as dress codes, that reify the sexual objectification of girls and women.[46] I argue this is an element of teacher professional socialization, both in UBTE programs and in public schools, that warrants closer scrutiny and more forceful intervention. We know from a range of scholarship in the sociology of education the harmful effects schools have on students when they legitimate and tacitly support various forms of discrimination based on gender and sexuality.[47] Teacher educators, veteran teachers, and school administrators alike need to be more willing to challenge traditional assumptions about gender and sexuality, as well as subject their local practices to closer examination concerning how they are informed by these traditional assumptions.

The good news is that many teacher candidates show an openness to the fluidity of gender norms in the ways they inhabit traditional gender performances, even as they practice gender conformity overall. Moreover, they are alive to inconsistencies between certain school-level policies and wider institutional change in gender norms (e.g., Deborah's sense that "dressing professionally has changed"). As such, future cohorts of teacher candidates will likely be responsive to efforts to challenge the harmful effects of traditional gender performances as part of their training, especially as they observe other institutional forces endorsing greater equality along lines of gender, sexuality, and gender identity (i.e., the recent United States Supreme Court decision, *Obergefell v. Hodges*, supporting marriage equality). Given the overall ways in which teacher candidates inhabit gender conformity, however, while they are likely to be responsive to societal change in gender relations, teacher candidates are unlikely to be forceful agents of it themselves. As most people do when challenging the influence of social institutions, they will need broader support in any effort to alter the ways that taken-for-granted assumptions about gender shape their daily practices as teachers.

Ultimately, making sense of taken-for-granted assumptions is how we all inhabit institutions in everyday life. Professional socialization processes are certainly windows of time when institutional myths are more malleable to modification, as newcomers think about and discuss how to act appropriately in routine situations more explicitly than more experienced practitioners.[48] But this should not be interpreted to mean that newcomers to a profession, in this case teacher candidates, are somehow "blank slates" that can be molded into whatever idyllic prototype of teacher we might envision. Teacher candidates, the people and programs who train them, as well as the schools and communities that receive them, are all enabled and constrained by interconnected social institutions that are simultaneously stable and in flux, persistent and changing. While teacher candidates certainly exert their own agency in how they define the work of teaching, we must remember that most of the conditions informing the ways they do so are institutional. Since institutions are both durable and dynamic, new teachers' definitions of teaching mirror the tension between stability and change in our broader cultural and social priorities. In this sense, their ambivalence reflects societal ambivalence, a societal ambivalence born out of the competing views among us concerning "the right way" to raise children, "the right way" to run organizations, "the right way" to address inequalities, "the right way" to handle gender issues in school or the workplace, and "the right way" to implement policy. New teachers will grapple with these tensions as long as such tensions are bound up in our social institutions. In the meantime, we can be confident that among all of the things we expect new teachers to do, there is one thing they will *try* to do in the face of all the competing pressures endemic to their institutional environment. They will try to adapt.

APPENDIX:
SITE, CONTEXT, AND MY ROLE
AS AN ETHNOGRAPHER

Today's Teacher Education and Its Historical Background

UBTE in Its Current Form

According to the United States Department of Education, there were approximately 730,000 teacher candidates enrolled in teacher education programs in the United States during the academic year 2009–2010.[1] Among that population of teacher candidates, 88% were enrolled in "traditional teacher education programs," which are undergraduate university-based teacher education programs housed within four-year colleges and universities. In addition, 80% of teacher education program completers came out of these UBTE programs in that year as well. Alternative teacher education programs do offer pathways into teaching for a non-trivial proportion of total incoming teachers (12%). Enrollments in these alternative programs are fairly evenly split between those housed within colleges and universities (e.g., post-graduate training programs) and those housed outside higher education (e.g., Teach for America). Even among alternative pathways into teaching, roughly half of those prospective teachers who obtain their training in this way do so through university-based programs. As such, higher education is the institutional environment through which approximately 94% of all incoming teachers earn their credentials. Clearly, UBTE represents the type of training and pathway into the teaching profession for the overwhelming majority of incoming teachers.

Undergraduate UBTE programs are similar in their basic content, requirements, and sequence. Many programs require an application process for admission into their university's teacher education program (indeed, this was true at State University). In other words, one does not simply declare education as their major; rather, college freshmen and sophomores apply to their university's teacher education program. Screening is usually based on "minimum grade point average, personal essays, or a minimum basic skills test score."[2] Typically, teacher candidates begin their programs as sophomores, and though specific course requirements vary by program, the majority "generally include courses in how to teach (pedagogy), as well as academic content, and sometimes include courses on working with special populations (such as special education students or English learners)."[3] In conjunction with coursework and academic preparation, teacher candidates are required to accumulate "supervised clinical experience" in K–12 school settings. These supervised clinical hours include observations and tutoring, but without full classroom control, which teacher candidates acquire while completing coursework prior to student teaching (the median number of such hours is 120). Student teaching—supervised classroom teaching during which the teacher candidate takes full responsibility for a classroom—is the last stage of training, and the median number of student teaching hours among teacher candidates nationally is 520.[4]

The demographic characteristics of the teacher candidate population in the United States is remarkably similar now to what it has been historically. Again, during the 2009–2010 academic year, 74% of the population of teacher candidates enrolled in teacher education programs were women.[5] As I alluded to in Chapter 1, the racial and ethnic composition of teacher candidates remains consistent with its past while becoming increasingly inconsistent with that of student populations nationwide. We see this if we compare teacher candidates and students among African American, Hispanic/Latino, and white populations: 68% of teacher candidates identity as white, compared to 53% of K–12 students; 11% of teacher candidates identify as Hispanic/Latino, compared to 23% of K–12 students; 9% of teacher candidates identify as Black or African American, compared to 16% of K–12 students.[6] Moreover, teacher candidate populations tend to be more white and more female than broader undergraduate student populations overall.

A Brief Institutional History

UBTE is indeed the predominant pathway into teaching, and higher education is the dominant institutional force that defines and legitimates this approach to teacher education. It has not always been this way, however, and the historical development of teacher education provides important context for understanding contemporary institutionalized arrangements of UBTE and how they won out, so to speak, over alternative approaches to teacher education in the past.

Prior to the mid-19th century, teacher preparation, and teaching as an occupation itself, was in no way systematized or uniform by any standards. As James Fraser characterizes it in his exhaustive analysis of the history of teacher education in the United States, "the only real requirements for the job were a willingness to declare oneself fit to teach."[7] At the time, men were the people able and willing to make such declarations. It was not until roughly the 1830s that efforts began to more systematically train teachers in the knowledge and skills for instruction, something that unfolded alongside a trend in which teaching became dominated in numbers by women instead of men. Horace Mann and Catherine Beecher were key figures of leadership in these respective and related trends, and they were instrumental in the development and proliferation of "normal schools" for teacher preparation.[8] An instrumental part of Mann's broader political enterprise known as the "common school movement," state normal schools emerged (slowly and ploddingly) as the model training programs for staffing mass public education with teachers who possessed three equally important sets of capacities: academic knowledge in subject matter, proficiency with instructional technique, and a cultivated commitment to public service.[9] From Beecher's perspective, women were uniquely capable relative to men to perform the role of teacher as defined in this way.[10] She became as influential as Mann in crafting and promoting normal schools for teacher education, recruiting women into teaching, and sustaining networks for placing teachers in schools upon training completion.

Normal schools indeed played an important role in the development of teacher education in this country, and persisted for nearly 100 years, experiencing their heyday in the early 20th century. The origins of many key features of contemporary UBTE are traceable to the normal schools of decades—even centuries—past. Student teaching, a practice that remains the most important component of training in the eyes of teacher educators and teacher candidates alike, was conceived and designed in the earliest normal schools. Despite their enduring influence, normal schools were by no means monolithic or uniform in their structure or functioning. In fact, they varied in almost every way possible. Fraser characterizes their dizzying diversity:

> . . . [A] normal school could be a 1, 2, 3, 4, or occasionally a 5-year program . . . It could be the equivalent of high school, or it could require a high school diploma for admission . . . It could limit admission to women or offer coeducational programs . . . It could be limited almost exclusively to students preparing to be elementary-level teachers or it could move its focus to the preparation of high school teachers, principals, and other educational leaders . . . They played many different roles to many different people in their century of existence.[11]

While their flexibility made them attractive to a wide range of potential students as well as the state legislatures for whom they satisfied diverse needs, normal schools' lack of coherence made them vulnerable to criticism, and ultimately to co-optation by more powerful institutions that came to dominate the social arenas of professional training and credentialing. Over time, the normal school model was replaced by the university department, or school, of education as the prevailing site for teacher education.

The ascendancy of the university school of education to virtual monopoly status in teacher education played out over a number of decades. The first models for what education departments would ultimately look like originated at the University of Iowa and the University of Michigan in the late 1800s. In particular, the University of Michigan's School of Education, by the turn of the 20th century, was an early version of what we now know that unit of a university to look like. Committed to a more science-based teacher education rooted in psychology, the required program for prospective teachers in the School of Ed at Michigan included "100 hours of academic work, including 31 hours in psychology and 15 hours in education, including the history of education, principles of teaching, educational psychology, and student teaching."[12] The School of Ed at Michigan also created master's and Ed.D./Ph.D. programs in education, now a mainstay in similarly sized schools of education. Following the lead of places like Michigan and Iowa, private universities also invested in their programs in education and threw the weight of their institutional prestige behind similar models. At Johns Hopkins University, they further solidified psychology as the scientific and disciplinary foundation of teacher education. G. Stanley Hall at Johns Hopkins, and later at Clark University in Massachusetts, was a strong and influential advocate for the proposition that "for education to be a profession . . . then it needed to be anchored in science, in psychology, and in university programs that understood the hard science that was the professional root of schooling."[13]

Hall's ideas diffused with his students who found positions at places like Stanford University, Indiana University, and Ohio State University. This model of teacher education also took hold at Columbia University's Teachers College, which became the standard-bearer of university schools of education and where one of the most notable public figures in education policy, John Dewey, was on the faculty from 1905–1952. It was not just the endorsement of high-profile people or prestigious universities, however, that drove the processes through which teacher education became controlled by schools of education. The increasing demand for high school education in the first half of the 20th century was a key basis upon which university officials argued that teachers' backgrounds needed to be more academically rigorous and discipline-based than what they argued was offered by normal schools. Moreover, school of education and university officials saw a tremendous need for some kind of accreditation system that could bring more order and consistency in what was taught in high schools and colleges, and how teachers were trained and credentialed to work in them. Universities partnered with philanthropic organizations such as the Carnegie Foundation to establish criteria and governing bodies (e.g., North Central Association of Colleges and Secondary Schools) for high schools and colleges to become accredited. Throughout the 1920s and 1930s, it became increasingly common that accreditation for secondary schools was conditional on all of their teachers possessing a four-year college degree.[14]

By the 1960s, UBTE had arrived at its heyday, and it has become increasingly institutionalized over subsequent decades.[15] Other scholarship in sociology traces similar mechanisms and developments through which universities have positioned themselves as the gatekeepers for membership, training, and credentialing of various professional groups. Paul DiMaggio and Walter Powell, for instance, offer a new institutionalist account of the role that universities have played in the development of "managerial professions," whose proliferation constitutes an "isomorphic force" through which organizations in similar fields come to resemble each other closely.[16] In other words, professionals operate similarly in different environments because they subscribe to the same norms, practices, and rationalities learned in professional training. More recent scholarship examines similar phenomena from the perspective of inhabited institutionalism. Tim Hallett and Matthew Gougherty make the compelling call for reinvigorating empirical analysis of professional socialization in professional degree programs.[17] In their research on master's programs in the administrative professions (e.g., public administration, public policy, and public health degrees), they call for increased scrutiny of how people creatively modify, challenge, and reaffirm rationalized meanings about, among other things, accountability and bring them to bear on a wide range of prospective organizational settings that people with these degrees enter for work. Here again, we see higher education emerge as a dominant institutional force for credentialing and rationalization in much the same way it did for the training and certification of teachers in the 20th century.[18]

The School of Education at State University

Size and Structure

The School of Education that served as the chief site for this study is a large, doctoral degree-granting school that is part of a Carnegie Research I University in the Midwestern United States (again, to which I refer as "State University"). The teacher education program is highly nationally for both its secondary and elementary education programs. The School is composed of different academic departments: educational psychology, curriculum and instruction, educational administration and policy, instructional technologies, and language education.[19] Depending on their specialty area, teacher candidates fulfill course requirements across all of these academic departments during their training. The Teacher Education Office is the administrative subunit of the School that controls and coordinates the program requirements for all teacher candidates' coursework, early field experience,[20] student teaching, and licensure. According to the university's official enrollment data, during the academic year of 2006–2007 when I collected my ethnographic data, the School of Education had a total undergraduate enrollment of over 1,000 in the fall semester and just over 800 in the spring semester.

The size of the teacher education program in terms of enrollment is itself an important constraint for teacher candidates, faculty, and university administrators alike. To keep class sizes relatively small (20–30), departments had to rely on many doctoral students and adjunct faculty to help education faculty cover the teaching load. In addition, the Teacher Education Office has the enormously complex job of securing both field experience and student teaching placements in regional schools for hundreds of teacher candidates each semester. This, of course, depends upon the willing and voluntary participation of public school principals and teachers to allow teacher candidates into their schools and classrooms. Every year in the spring semester (which is when most complete their student teaching), the Teacher Education Office is responsible for placing approximately 600–700 teacher candidates in area schools for student teaching placements.[21] Arranging enough student teaching agreements with school principals and teachers for 700 individuals to each have a classroom for a semester is no small task. Some public school figures are unwilling, and others change their minds after a placement has been made. Repeatedly throughout data collection, members of the focal and cohort samples had their placements changed at the last minute, and they along with the teacher education program administrators had to scramble to find a new placement. In Chapter 3, I analyze how these types of bureaucratic functioning necessarily incorporates uncertainty and unpredictability into the training process in ways that inform teacher candidates' sensemaking about their prospective work environments.

Enclaves of Teacher Candidates

The way in which teacher candidates are grouped and distributed within the organization of the School of Education is important for shaping the training process for them. While fulfilling early course requirements, teacher candidates take classes that are inclusive of all possible specialty areas. For example, courses that fulfill requirements for everyone (such as classes on the social and cultural history of education) can include students in both elementary and secondary education as well as all subject matter concentrations. They can also include students training in special education at either the elementary or secondary levels. Additional courses that satisfy requirements for all students are split between elementary and secondary students. For example, all teacher candidates are required to take a course in teaching students with special needs, but there are separate courses on this topic for elementary and secondary education students. Most teacher candidates fulfill these types of course requirements in conjunction with additional requirements in the College of Arts and Sciences during their sophomore and junior years.

Beginning in the spring semester of the junior year, teacher candidates typically begin their courses on teaching methods. At this point, they are divided into groups by grade level and subject matter specialty area, and they take sets of courses in pedagogy in two consecutive semesters. These sets of courses that are taken concurrently are called "clusters" for elementary teacher candidates, and "blocks" for secondary teacher candidates. There are two of these sets that are taken sequentially with the first in the spring semester junior year, and the second in the fall semester senior year. For both elementary and secondary teacher candidates, they typically transition into their student teaching in the spring semester senior year immediately after completing their blocks or clusters. Upon completion of the student teaching component, they graduate with their bachelor's degree and are qualified to apply for their state teacher's license, which the Teacher Education Office helps them do.[22]

During the cluster/block courses, groups of 20–25 teacher candidates take a set of typically three courses in different elements of pedagogy. In most cases, the same group of 20–25 takes the same set of courses together, and the same group also takes both their first and second cluster/block together in two consecutive semesters. These groups spend an entire academic year together leading up to their student teaching. They complete most assignments together, complete their field experience requirements together, and many develop fairly close friendships in the process. Consequently, teacher candidates in the same cluster/block log a great deal of time together and experience much of their formal training collectively. This is an important organizing principle of the teacher education program that fosters the development of peer cultures among teacher candidates, and the collective routines through which they acquire their training are the vehicles for the ways they make sense of, and become primed for, their prospective work roles.

An equally important element of the cluster/block model for training is its division by grade level and subject matter. While it is true that teacher candidates develop rather strong peer cultures, they do it in relatively small enclaves. Moreover, they typically do not even know other teacher candidates in other clusters or blocks. To illustrate how this works, I refer to Table 1 that lists the focal sample for the study. Hillary, Nellie, and Paul, for example, are all in secondary mathematics, took the same block together, and knew each other well. There were also members of the cohort sample who took this block with them, and knew these three. Deborah and Frank, however, took different block courses from each other even though they were both secondary language arts teacher candidates. The same is true for all three teacher candidates in elementary education in the focal sample; Sara and Nicole were in the same cluster, but Dennis was in a different cluster. In my observations, I documented the peer interactions and collective routines for all members of the focal sample and cohort sample, but they were neither the same nor were they overlapping clusters or blocks. Rather, they were rigidly distinct, even though they were completing the same process and requirements.

I emphasize this condition of the sample and their training process because it is important to the interpretation of findings I present in the chapters. The key findings of the ethnography represent patterns in teacher candidates' collective routines, sense-making, and perspectives that were consistent both within and

TABLE 1

School Characteristics—Focal Sample Student Teaching Placements

Name	Grade/Subject	School Size	Region	% F/R Lunch	% Non-White
Dennis	Elementary	529	Rural	30	2
Sara	Elementary	297	City, small	14	14
Nicole	Elementary	352	Rural	24	0
Frank	2nd English	370	Rural	28	1
Deborah	2nd English	745	Rural	24	1
Nellie	2nd Math	370	Rural	28	1
Hillary	2nd Math	1,939	City, small	25	8
Paul	2nd Math	1,417	City, small	25	8
Oscar	2nd S.S.	2,962	City, large	30	45
Faye	2nd S.S.	1,644	Town, fringe	27	1
Betsy	2nd S.S.	250	Rural	28	1

Common Core of Data, Public Schools 2005–2006

across these enclaves of teacher candidates in the overall sample. As such, I am able to document both the ways teacher candidates developed perspectives collectively, but also the ways that patterns in their perspectives were similar and distinct across groups of people who did not know each other and did not interact with each other. For those patterns of similarity in teacher candidates' perspectives and sense-making—of which there are many that I present in the preceding chapters—the design of the study and the nature of the sample lend strong support to the claim that these patterns reflect wider social conditions of the teacher education process, and are not unique to one group of people.

Program Requirements

Specific course requirements vary somewhat depending on grade level and subject matter distinctions. All teacher candidates have courses they must take in the School of Education as well as in other schools within the university, usually the College of Arts and Sciences. The Teacher Education Office provides all teacher candidates with formal course requirements and options for fulfilling those requirements. Teacher candidates also receive their formal university advising through the Teacher Education Office. The range of courses teacher candidates take in the School of Education are distributed and controlled by the different academic departments I listed previously. Multiple departments teach prerequisite courses for the clusters or blocks. For example, faculty and graduate students in the educational psychology department teach required courses on educational psychology; teacher candidates are required to take seven credit hours in educational psychology before they can begin their courses in pedagogy. Likewise, faculty and graduate students in educational administration and policy teach courses on the history of American education and multiculturalism, or "pluralism," in public education. In early coursework, then, teacher candidates see a range of instructors from multiple departments, and they all satisfy the same course requirements rooted, in part, in psychology.

The department of curriculum and instruction teaches most of the courses in pedagogy, but not all. All language education courses, for both elementary and secondary students, are the charge of the language education program. Moreover, within curriculum and instruction, there are subunits of faculty and graduate students who teach different grade levels and subject matters. Mathematics education is its own program, as is social studies education, science education, and elementary education. These departmental and program distinctions within the School of Education create the different enclaves of teacher candidates I described previously, as different courses in pedagogy are the responsibility of different units. In addition to course requirements, teacher candidates must attend orientation meetings conducted by administrators in the Teacher Education Office. There is an elementary orientation meeting for these teacher candidates prior to when they begin their clusters to review their program requirements. In addition, in the fall semester prior to student teaching, there is a mandatory "Pre-Professional Meeting" for all teacher candidates; the administrator who oversees student teaching placements conducts this meeting, and it is designed to review requirements for student teaching. I observed both of these meetings as part of the data collection.

While fulfilling their coursework, teacher candidates also have field experience requirements to complete. Beginning in the sophomore year, they must log a minimum number of hours in a local public school observing a teacher and their classroom. They do this each semester through the fall semester of their senior year, when most of them must log 40 hours observing a teacher in a local school. The Teacher Education Office makes these placements, and in most cases teacher candidates are assigned in pairs to one teacher. They typically observe these classes together, and complete assignments reflecting on their observations together. In many cases, teacher candidates will teach one lesson to the class, and they will often do this with their partner. They are regularly required in their cluster or block courses to discuss their observations with their classmates and instructors, typically reflecting on things they like and did not like about what they saw and how it can inform their future teaching strategies.

Group discussions and projects were another common required routine for teacher candidates in their cluster or block courses. Across grade level and subject matter, group work was ubiquitous. Faculty in the School of Education shared a strong commitment to "cooperative learning," and the majority of course assignments required that teacher candidates work with a group of classmates, or at least a partner, to complete them. Examples include weekly discussion assignments on their field experience, designing unit plans for future use, researching teaching strategies or subject matter topics, designing worksheets and assessments for future use with students, and developing modifications to lessons for students with special needs. As such, not only were teacher candidates taking the same cluster or block of classes with the same people, they were constantly interacting with each other in routine.

Online discussion forums associated with both cluster/block courses were also common practice. With the exception of one cluster I observed, all teacher candidates were required to make at least one post per week to the online discussion forum in which they responded to something of their classmates. This served as an extension of the classroom, and was designed to offer teacher candidates further avenue for exchange about their training experiences and future work. These discussion forums served as yet another interactional routine through which they collectively made sense of their experiences.

Finally, all teacher candidates were at some point during their cluster/block courses required to design and teach a lesson plan to their class of peers, usually with a classmate as a partner. Teacher candidates would select a topic, research it, design a lesson plan, acquire necessary resources, and teach it to their peers. Upon completion of the lesson, they would then receive feedback on their teaching from their faculty instructor as well as their classmates. These "peer-taught lessons" were a part of all teacher candidates' coursework in teaching methods, and were therefore common priming events for future classroom teaching.

Teacher candidates, then, were involved in multiple, ongoing collective routines in their coursework leading up to their student teaching. While the tenor of these interactions varied somewhat depending on the personalities within different subgroups, the routines were the same across clusters and blocks. As such, the contours of the training process were the same for all teacher candidates. Upon the transition into student teaching, these coursework routines were largely replaced by the daily work routines of teaching in public schools. Their peer group interactions were replaced by instructional routines with students and supervising teachers, and for many teacher candidates, they were cut off from the peer ties they had developed through their coursework. Nonetheless, the new instructional routines with students also served as important priming events, as they were teacher candidates' initial experiences with full control over their classrooms and the workday. Instructional routines during student teaching were also extensions of their coursework routines, as the peer-taught lessons, planning, and debriefing about practices were abbreviated versions of the daily work routines teacher candidates performed with students and supervising teachers during their student teaching. Nonetheless, many teacher candidates lamented the loss of contact with their peers that coincided with the beginning of their student teaching. Some were able to maintain informal ties, but not everyone.

Informal Routines and Peer Relationships

Spending so much time together during formal training routines, it is no surprise that many friendships developed within the enclaves of teacher candidates. These informal relationships and routines associated with them were common, though they did vary with regard to the closeness of the relationships different teacher candidates developed. Nonetheless, these relationships served as important sources of social support for teacher candidates, as well as key avenues for sense-making about the work of teaching. Many subgroups of friends emerged within different clusters and blocks, and some clusters/blocks were more cohesive as a whole than others. The elementary cluster that I observed the most throughout the fall semester was one such group that was rather cohesive as an entire group. Almost every day in class, a student brought candy to share with everyone, and for Halloween, they put on a potluck party in class with several students contributing. The teacher candidates in this group took on all of these activities themselves, and the faculty instructor rarely organized them. As such, the ethos within this group was very open and jovial. Class discussion was very open and participatory, and there were rarely any overt personality conflicts. Moreover, they spent a lot of time with each other outside of class, often helping each other with assignments as well as meeting for lunch between classes. In addition, the teacher candidates in this cluster also organized a "Cluster Bar Crawl" in December, both in celebration of the end of the semester and in anticipation of their student teaching. They collectively decided on multiple bars in town to go to together throughout the evening of this event, and they made T-shirts for everyone to wear that night that said "Cluster Bar Crawl."[23]

For this group, the bar crawl was actually an informal priming event for them. They were keenly aware of the transition they would be making in the following semester, and that it would disperse them to different schools for student teaching. It was important to them that they mark this point in time with a celebration. Moreover, in interviews and observations the following semester, it was clear that several of them missed the connection they had with their peers in their cluster. Dennis, a member of the focal sample who was in this cluster, was placed in the same school for student teaching as two other members of his cluster. But he did not get to spend much time with them as they all had individual classrooms within which to teach, and he was completely cut off from the rest of the cluster. Dennis expressed on a couple of occasions a desire for more opportunities to interact with his friends from the cluster to share experiences in the classroom. Yet he, like most teacher candidates, had such opportunities greatly limited upon transitioning into student teaching, and a strong source of social support largely dissolved at this stage of the training.

Some teacher candidates managed to stay in touch during their student teaching more than others, but it was largely dependent upon circumstance. Three teacher candidates from the mathematics block that I observed were very close friends, even though their block as a whole was not quite as cohesive as the elementary cluster described above. These three teacher candidates (all of whom were women) studied together during the fall semester in both their education courses as well as their advanced math courses, and they spent a great deal of social time together as well. Moreover, during their student teaching, all three of them were placed in local high schools that kept them relatively close geographically. While their daily routines in schools kept them isolated from one another, they maintained their close friendship ties through multiple social outings per week. On these occasions, they often discussed their teaching experiences and vented any frustrations they may have had. Another example includes two teacher candidates from my focal sample who, though in different subject matters (Nellie in math and Frank in language arts), were placed in the same school for student teaching. They did not know each other prior to student teaching, but had daily interactions in their school to discuss their experiences and students that they both had in class. While they did not develop a close friendship, the daily opportunities for exchange with a peer about their teaching was welcome for both of them.

Informal ties and friendship routines were important to teacher candidates, even though they were more readily available to them during the coursework phase of their training. Peer networks were largely dispersed upon the transition to student teaching, but some were able to maintain ties with old friends and in some cases develop ties with new ones. Both these types of informal relationships and the formal collective routines associated with their program requirements provided the vehicles for sense-making through which teacher candidates experienced priming events and developed perspectives about teaching.

My Relationships with Teacher Candidates

Obvious but important to note and discuss, one of the people involved in this study was me. Given the ethnographic methodology I employed to conduct this study, it is appropriate to offer some description of my role and relationships with other study participants.[24] One does not typically spend blocks of time with the same people every week for 15 months and not develop some type of relationship with them. Indeed, I was able to build rapport with these teacher candidates, and my relationships with them evolved over time in ways that enabled me to collect the rich, detailed data that form the empirical basis for this book.

First, my own prior experience completing a university-based teacher education program provided an immediate source of common ground that I could draw upon to recruit teacher candidates to participate in the study. When I met them, these teacher candidates were preparing to begin their last year of training, which included their student teaching. Not surprisingly, this was a source of both excitement and anxiety for many of them. My ability to demonstrate my understanding of the sources of these sentiments they were feeling about their training enabled me to make a quick connection with almost all members of the focal sample from the very beginning. Additionally, like prior research shows is a common trend among teacher candidates,[25] many of my teacher candidates had a number of frustrations about their training experience up to this point (e.g., they felt as yet unprepared to handle classroom management, and found little in their required coursework to be practically helpful on this issue). They explicitly cited a desire to share their experiences as the subject of research that might shed light on the sources of these frustrations. Their view of me as an "insider" to teacher education, so to speak, facilitated what ultimately became their ongoing and time-consuming participation in a lengthy study.

Precisely because the research design of the study involved following teacher candidates through the transitions of this window of training, sustaining rapport over time was important as well. My participation in their weekly routines, as well as certain conditions of UBTE itself, proved useful in maintaining the relationships with teacher candidates which promoted the processes through which they candidly shared their perspectives and experiences with me in observations and interviews. Because I actively participated in their classes with them in the fall, completing class activities with them and engaging in discussion day after day, we developed convivial relationships over this period of time. This proved particularly important for the transition into student teaching in the spring semester. As I noted earlier, teacher candidates became extracted from their network of friends in the program as they completed the most taxing part of their training. By coming to their classroom every week and observing them teach, I was in many ways the only person they "knew" with whom they maintained close contact during student teaching. Even for those who maintained contact and communication with friends outside of school, I was the only adult who was not a supervisor that they could talk to about their experiences who also had firsthand knowledge of what they were experiencing day in and day out. These conditions of their training, combined with my ethnographic techniques that kept me in close contact with them in the settings where they were working, went a long way in sustaining positive relationships that made the teacher candidates in this study very open, detailed, and frank in what they shared with me as part of my data collection. As such, I was able to make vivid accounts of what scholars of ethnography emphasize is central to the methodology: "members' meanings—the perspectives, understandings, concerns, and points of view of those studied."[26]

ACKNOWLEDGMENTS

The larger project that forms the basis for this book would not have been possible without the participation and generosity of the teacher candidates, teacher educators, public school teachers, and principals whose perspectives and experiences comprise the data for this study. I am very grateful for their involvement in this research.

Since this is a book about teaching and teachers, it is especially important to thank the teachers and mentors who supported my development as a sociologist. The faculty and graduate students with whom I worked while completing my doctorate in the Department of Sociology at Indiana University played formative roles in shaping both my career as a scholar and the scholarship that ultimately became this book. In particular, I thank Bill Corsaro, who is a profoundly influential figure in my research as well as my career. His expertise in the study of socialization, as well as conducting ethnography, very strongly informs the analysis in the preceding pages. I am also very grateful to Bill for his ongoing advice, support, and friendship over the years. Likewise, Tim Hallett is an invaluable mentor and colleague. Always generous with his insights, Tim has been instrumental in helping me find a theoretical home for my research in inhabited institutionalism, and I thank him heartily. I am also grateful to Pam Walters, Bradley Levinson, Maurice Garnier, Brian Powell, Tom Gieryn, Patricia McManus, and Eliza Pavalko for the advice and support they have provided on this project. In addition, a number of my fellow doctoral students in IU Sociology were helpful in their support and feedback on various elements of this research. I thank Rashawn Ray, Josh Klugman, Emily Bowman, Oren Pizmony-Levy, Emily Meanwell, Jenny Stuber, Emily Fairchild, Azamat Junisbai, and Barbara Junisbai. The early stages of this research were supported by the Stewart Scholarship in the Department of Sociology at Indiana University.

I am also grateful to my colleagues in the Department of Sociology at Loyola University Chicago, who have been wonderfully supportive in my work on this book. I thank Anne Figert, Rhys Williams, Marilyn Krogh, Kelly Moore, Dana Garbarski, Judy Wittner, Peter Rosenblatt, Tal Wright, Quintin Williams, Nathalia Hernández Vidal, and Taylor Tefft. I am also deeply grateful to other colleagues in sociology who have played key roles in this book's development. In particular,

I thank Lisa Nunn and Michael Haedicke for their extensive and insightful feedback on earlier drafts of this project. I am also very grateful to Peter Mickulas, my editor at Rutgers University Press, for all of his hard work and guidance in seeing this book to fruition.

Finally, the successful completion of this book would not have been possible without the unwavering love and support of my family. I thank my parents, Tom Everitt and Sandy Shearer, for instilling in me an enduring interest in education and a respect for its importance. I thank my siblings, Leslie Wininger and Clark Everitt, for always being the support system to me that only brothers and sisters enjoy. Above all, I am most thankful to my wife, Jill Everitt, and our kids. While I am deeply grateful for their love and patience as I worked on the book, I am also thankful for the ways they serve as a limitless source of inspiration and motivation to tell the empirical story within these pages. Educational institutions shape the lives of children—as well as those of the adults in their lives—in ways both intended and unintended. As Jill and I raise our children together, I am reminded daily of the very personal stake we all have in working toward a deeper understanding of public education and how it functions.

NOTES

INTRODUCTION

1. All names of people, places, and organizations have been changed to pseudonyms to protect participants' anonymity and confidentiality.
2. Some of the data presented in this book originally appeared in *Assessing Teacher Quality* (Everitt, "Teacher Education and Accountability").
3. Darling-Hammond et al., "Does Teacher Preparation Matter?"; Goldstein, *The Teacher Wars*; Labaree, *The Trouble with Ed Schools*; Levine, "Educating School Teachers."
4. Jennings and Corcoran, "Beyond High-Stakes Tests"; Kelly, "Understanding Teacher Effects"; Johnson, "Will VAMS Reinforce the Walls of the Egg-Crate School?"; Darling-Hammond, "Can Value Added Add Value to Teacher Evaluation?"
5. Porter, "Grading Teachers by the Test"; Strauss, "Resistance to Standardized Testing Growing Nationwide."
6. Levine, "Educating School Teachers."
7. Common Core State Standards Initiative (http://www.corestandards.org/).
8. Johnson, "Will VAMS Reinforce the Walls of the Egg-Crate School?"
9. United States Department of Education, Preparing and Credentialing the Nation's Teachers.
10. It is common for people to use the words "institution" and "organization" interchangeably, as is often the case when referring to specific colleges and universities, but they are distinct. Organizations are particular settings functioning within broader institutional environments. As such, specific universities (e.g., Harvard) are organizations that operate within the broader social institution of higher education. In other words, organizations are local, whereas institutions are extra-local (Hallett and Ventresca, "Inhabited Institutions"; Hallett, "The Myth Incarnate"; Meyer and Rowan, "Institutionalized Organizations").
11. Binder and Wood, *Becoming Right*.
12. In my characterization of social institutions, I draw heavily from a theoretical tradition in the study of organizations and institutions known as "new institutionalism." For exemplars of this tradition, see DiMaggio and Powell, "The Iron Cage Revisited"; Meyer and Jepperson, "The 'Actors' of Modern Society"; Meyer and Rowan, "Institutionalized Organizations"; Rowan and Meyer, *The New Institutionalism in Education*; Powell and DiMaggio, *The New Institutionalism in Organizational Analysis*. I am particularly influenced by Meyer and Rowan's ("Institutionalized Organizations") seminal work in new institutionalism and its importance in the development of inhabited institutionalism (see Hallett, "The Myth Incarnate"). Meyer and Rowan, as well as Hallett, make clear the distinction between "institutions" and "organizations," a distinction I also emphasize in my discussion here as well as my analysis in the chapters that follow.

13. Meyer and Rowan, "Institutionalized Organizations."

14 In Chapter 1 and the appendix, I elaborate in more detail the history of teacher education and how UBTE emerged as the predominant pathway to becoming a teacher.

15. United States Department of Education, *Preparing and Credentialing the Nation's Teachers.*

16. This alone is a source of great debate about the merits and drawbacks of UBTE, one that I do not enter on any clear side. Rather, my attention is on the ways that higher education structures teacher education and how this shapes teacher candidates' sense-making about teaching.

17. Darling-Hammond et al., "Does Teacher Preparation Matter?"; Labaree, *The Trouble with Ed Schools*; Levine, "Educating School Teachers."

18. Corsaro, *The Sociology of Childhood.*

19. Britzman, *Practice Makes Practice*; Deering and Stanutz, "Preservice Field Experience as a Multicultural Component of a Teacher Education Program"; Labaree, *The Trouble with Ed Schools*; Levine, "Educating School Teachers"; Liston and Zeichner, *Teacher Education and the Social Conditions of Schooling.*

20. Coburn, "Beyond Decoupling"; Diamond, "Where the Rubber Meets the Road"; Goldstein, *The Teacher Wars*; Hallett, "The Myth Incarnate"; Kelly, "Understanding Teacher Effects"; Spillane, *Standards Deviation.*

21. Barr and Dreeben, *How Schools Work*; Entwisle, Alexander, and Olson, *Children, Schools, and Inequality*; Hurn, *The Limits and Possibilities of Schooling*; Schneider, "The Social Organization of Schools."

22. Long-standing debates endure about the professional status of teaching, both in the scholarship of professions and in popular discourse more broadly. By and large, people frequently conclude that teaching falls short of the status of a profession. This tends to be driven by comparing teachers with other professions, especially physicians who have long been considered the standard-bearer of a profession (i.e., sharing a body of expert knowledge, governing their own group membership and ethical standards; see Abbott, *The System of Professions*; Friedson, *Professional Dominance*; Merton et al., *The Student Physician*). As such, teaching has been characterized as a "semi-profession" (Etzioni, *The Semi-Professions and Their Organization*), a "silver-medal profession" (Johnson, "The Prospects for Teaching as a Profession"), and "special, but shadowed" (Lortie, *Schoolteacher*). Recent scholarship, though, challenges this common approach to labeling professions based on pre-established checklists of criteria that medical doctors, among others, exemplify. Hallett and Gougherty ("Professional Education in the University Context") call for revision to these checklist approaches to labeling professions, and cite scholarship that conceptualize professions less narrowly (see Brint, *In an Age of Experts*; MacDonald, *The Sociology of the Professions*; and Owen-Smith, "The Institutionalization of Expertise in University Licensing"). Owen-Smith, for instance, defines professions as "any occupation in which experts draw upon abstract bodies of knowledge to solve problems they might never have encountered before" (65). In their work on professional socialization in managerial degree programs, Hallett and Gougherty argue that such a definition is a better empirical fit than traditional checklist approaches since "the people who work and learn in these programs generally conceive of themselves and the degrees as professional" (8). As I show in the following chapters, the same is true for teacher candidates and teacher educators, and institutionalized meanings of "professionalism" are commonly invoked in defining work-related action for teachers in the contexts of UBTE as well as public schools. As I also show, teacher candidates certainly

grapple with using "abstract bodies of knowledge," such as progressive pedagogy and accountability standards, to "solve problems they might never have encountered before" in the daily decision-making of instruction. Based on both these academic definitions and empirical realities, I use the word profession when referring to teaching as a type of work and teachers as an occupational group. This conceptualization of profession also provides the basis for examining teacher education as a process of professional socialization.

23. As of 2013, 76% of the 3.5 million total teachers in the United States were women (see National Center for Education Statistics, *Digest of Education Statistics, 2013*).

24. Goldstein, *The Teacher Wars*.

25. The "feminization" of occupations tends to be accompanied by lower status and pay relative to occupations dominated in numbers by men (Aulette and Wittner, *Gendered Worlds*; Kimmel, *The Gendered Society*; Padavic and Reskin, *Women and Men at Work*).

26. See Williams, *Gender Difference at Work*, for occupational sex segregation and how the experiences of people working in "non-traditional" jobs reveals the power of traditional gender norms, stereotypes, and expectations to influence people's behavior.

27. See Martin, "Gender as Social Institution," and Risman, "Gender as a Social Structure," for discussion of how gender operates as a social institution. Also, see Acker, "Hierarchies, Jobs, Bodies," Fairchild, "Examining Wedding Rituals through a Multidimensional Gender Lens," Ridgeway, "Framed Before We Know It," and West and Zimmerman, "Doing Gender," for examples of how gender has institutional dimensions that can be observed in face-to-face interaction and everyday routines.

28. *Educational Researcher*, March 2015, vol. 44, n. 2; Kelly, *Assessing Teacher Quality*.

29. Harris, *Value-Added Measurements in Education*; Also, see *Educational Researcher* special issue (March 2015, vol. 44, n. 2) devoted entirely to the effects and implications of the rise in "value-added models" (VAMs) as a means of measuring teacher performance.

30. Levine, "Educating School Teachers"; Sanchez, "A Vision for Teacher Training at MIT"; journals in education research devote a great deal of their pages to the analysis of best practices for teacher training (e.g., *Journal of Teacher Education*).

31. Evidence of the effectiveness of the TFA approach is mixed. The organization and its founders offer a variety of success stories (see Kopp, *One Day, All Children*); others observe that while many TFA teachers are successful, many are not (see Goldstein, *The Teacher Wars*). Research that compares TFA teachers with UBTE-trained teachers finds that TFA teachers are not as effective in the classroom (see Darling-Hammond et al., "Does Teacher Preparation Matter?").

32. Sanchez, "A Vision for Teacher Training at MIT."

33. Levine, "Educating School Teachers"; RAND Corporation, "Teachers Matter"; United States Department of Education, "Improving Teacher Preparation."

34. RAND Corporation, "Teachers Matter." Emphasis on "school-based" factors, though, can be misleading. While teachers are often cited to be the most influential "school-based" factors on student achievement, they are not the most influential factor overall. Decades of research finds family socioeconomic status (SES) to be among the most influential factors in student achievement and attainment; moreover, teachers and schools rarely overcome family SES (see Bourdieu and Passeron, *Reproduction in Education, Society, and Culture*; Jencks et al., *Inequality*; Lareau, *Unequal Childhoods*; Lucas, *Tracking Inequality*; Sewell and Hauser, "The Wisconsin Longitudinal Study of Social and Psychological Factors in Aspirations and Achievements").

35. I am not alone in this overall endeavor concerning the study of teachers' work. For an important example of a collection of studies and scholars who offer an alternative

to "market models" of accountability in the evaluation of teachers' work, see Kelly, *Assessing Teacher Quality*.

36. Rich, "Teacher Shortages Spur a Nationwide Hiring Scramble (Credentials Optional)."
37. Strauss, "Indiana's Got a Problem."
38. E.g., Greene, "Why a Teacher 'Shortage'?"
39. Rich, "Teacher Shortages Spur a Nationwide Hiring Scramble (Credentials Optional)"; Strauss, "Teacher: Why 'I Just Can't Work in Public Education Anymore.'"
40. Giddens, *The Constitution of Society*.
41. Hallett and Ventresca, "Inhabited Institutions," and Hallett, "The Myth Incarnate."
42. Corsaro, *The Sociology of Childhood*.
43. Hallett and Ventresca, "Inhabited Institutions," 229.
44. Everitt, "Teacher Careers and Inhabited Institutions"; Hallett, "The Myth Incarnate"; Nunn, *Defining Student Success*.
45. Aurini, "Patterns of Tight and Loose Coupling in a Competitive Marketplace."
46. Haedicke, "Keeping Our Mission, Changing Our System"; Haedicke, *Organizing Organic*.
47. Binder, "For Love and Money."
48. Dorado, "Small Groups as Context for Institutional Entrepreneurship."
49. McPherson and Sauder, "Logics in Action."
50. Nunn, *Defining Student Success*.
51. Everitt and Levinson, "Inhabited Institutions in New Destinations."
52. Meyer and Rowan, "Institutionalized Organizations," which is widely acknowledged as the founding piece of work in new institutionalism.
53. This is a key reason that organizations within the same institutional field (i.e., higher education) tend to resemble each other in their structure and form (DiMaggio and Powell, "The Iron Cage Revisited"; Strang and Meyer, "Institutional Conditions for Diffusion.")
54. Indeed, Meyer and Rowan's conceptualization of "institutional myths" is that of a widely shared cultural ideal, not necessarily something that is "false" or imaginary. The bipartisan support that the No Child Left Behind Act received at its passage is evidence that the myth of accountability is a deeply entrenched cultural ideal—people take for granted that schools and teachers should be accountable for their performance.
55. Meyer and Rowan, "The Structure of Educational Organizations"; Weick, "Educational Organizations as Loosely Coupled Systems."
56. Hallett, "The Myth Incarnate," 69.
57. Blumer, *Symbolic Interactionism*, 19.
58. Hallett, "The Myth Incarnate," 69.
59. Ibid., 70.
60. Nunn, *Defining Student Success*.
61. Ibid.
62. See Everitt, "Inhabitants Moving In," as well as subsequent chapters.
63. Coburn, "Beyond Decoupling"; Diamond, "Where the Rubber Meets the Road"; Spillane, *Standards Deviation*; Spillane and Burch, "The Institutional Environment and Instructional Practice."
64. See Everitt and Levinson, "Inhabited Institutions in New Destinations," for another empirical example of how institutional stability and reproduction is inhabited. Also, see Lawrence and Suddaby, "Institutions and Institutional Work," for a complementary conceptualization of how people actively maintain, challenge, and disrupt institutions through their own agency and interaction.

65. Cuban, *Inside the Black Box of Classroom Practice*; Spillane, *Standards Deviation*.

66. Goffman, "The Arrangement between the Sexes"; Goffman, *Interaction Ritual*.

67. Ridgeway, "Framed Before We Know It," 147.

68. West and Zimmerman, "Doing Gender."

69. Ibid.,146.

70. Martin, "Gender as Social Institution," 1264.

71. See Fairchild, "Examining Wedding Rituals through a Multidimensional Gender Lens"; Martin, "Gender as Social Institution"; and Risman, "Gender as a Social Structure."

72. Ridgeway, "Framed Before We Know It," 152.

73. Pascoe, *Dude, You're a Fag*.

74. Eder, Evans, and Parker, *School Talk*.

75. Adler, Kless, and Adler, "Socialization to Gender Roles"; Fine, *With the Boys*; Thorne and Luria, "Sexuality and Gender in Children's Daily Worlds."

76. Armstrong and Hamilton, *Paying for the Party*; Ray and Rosow, "Getting Off and Getting Intimate."

77. Adler et al. "Socialization to Gender Roles"; Eder, *School Talk*; Fields, *Risky Lessons*; Pascoe, *Dude, You're a Fag*; Trudell, *Doing Sex Education*.

78. Martin ("Gender as Social Institution"), as well as Risman ("Gender as Social Structure"), make the compelling argument that gender operates as a social institution and should be conceptualized as such. However, neither theoretical argument invokes the concepts or perspectives of new institutionalism (NI) in much detail. As I will argue, drawing upon the insights of NI, especially as it informs inhabited institutionalism, is useful in bringing conceptual coherence to the ways we examine gender along with other social institutions.

79. Meyer and Rowan, "Institutionalized Organizations."

80. Though theorizing gender more broadly, Acker ("Jobs, Hierarchies, Bodies") argues that organizational practices "assume a heterosexual male body" in routine operating procedures such as job evaluations. Also theorizing gender more broadly, Ridgeway ("Framed Before We Know It") emphasizes the unreflective ways in which people make sense of gender via interaction by drawing upon meanings that "we all assume we all know."

81. Pascoe, *Dude, You're a Fag*.

82. Understanding these sets of gender norms as "myths" is useful for challenging a false gender dichotomy, as these meanings about gender are institutionalized social constructions rather than obdurate realities or innate qualities (see Berger and Luckmann, *The Social Construction of Reality*. Moreover, they are relational to each other as well as other social identities (Ispa-Landa, "Gender, Race, and Justifications for Group Exclusion"). As institutional myths, however, they are not inconsequential falsehoods; on the contrary, they are decidedly impactful in the ways they enable and constrain all people's behavior, even those who eschew, disrupt, or challenge them. Their impact, though, is driven by the same social phenomena through which all institutions affect daily life: in the ways people inhabit them.

83. Merton et al., *The Student Physician*.

84. Cahill, "Emotional Capital and Professional Socialization"; Davis, "Professional Socialization as Subjective Experience"; Haas and Shaffir, "The Professionalization of Medical Students," Lortie, "Shared Ordeal and Induction to Work"; Smith and Kleinman, "Managing Emotions in Medical School."

85. Becker et al., *Boys in White*, 435.

86. Corsaro, *Friendship and Peer Culture in the Early Years*; Corsaro, *The Sociology of Childhood*.

87. Corsaro and Molinari, *I Compagni.*
88. Everitt, "Inhabitants Moving In."
89. Emirbayer and Mische, "What Is Agency?"
90. Corsaro and Molinari, "Priming Events and Italian Children's Transition from Pre-school to Elementary School"; Corsaro and Molinari, *I Compagni.*
91. Merton, *Social Theory and Social Structure*, 438.
92. See Weick, *Sensemaking in Organizations*, for discussion of the "retrospective" nature of people's sense-making.
93. Becker et al., *Boys in White.*
94. Corsaro, "Interpretive Reproduction in Children's Peer Cultures," 162.
95. Hallett and Ventresca, "Inhabited Institutions."
96. In particular, the lack of any people of color is a limitation of the sample. While this limits the possibility to examine race and ethnicity as mechanisms that shape the professional socialization process, it reflects the dearth of racial and ethnic diversity in this School of Education at the time of data collection. This is one way in which the School of Education at State University is somewhat distinct from other, though not all, UBTE programs in other locales. Nonetheless, the overall teaching workforce itself is dominated in numbers by white teachers as well.
97. For more detail on the site, context, sample, and analysis, please see the methodological appendix.

CHAPTER 1. COMPULSORY EDUCATION AND CONSTRUCTIVIST PEDAGOGY

1. See Labaree, *The Trouble with Ed Schools*, for a review of the extant literature on teacher education and its bitterly critical tone.
2. Dreeben, "Teaching and the Competence of Occupations"; Johnson, "The Prospects for Teaching as a Profession"; Levine, "Educating School Teachers"; Liston and Zeichner, *Teacher Education and the Social Conditions of Schooling*; Strauss, "Researchers Urge Arne Duncan to Drop Proposed Teacher Prep Regulations."
3. Levine, "Educating School Teachers," 35.
4. Meyer, Ramirez, and Soysal, "World Expansion of Mass Education."
5. Dewey, *The Child and the Curriculum.*
6. Dewey received his doctorate from Johns Hopkins University, and was no doubt influenced by G. Stanley Hall's insistence on establishing psychology as the scientific foundation of university-based programs in the study and practice of education.
7. James, *The Principles of Psychology.*
8. Dewey, *Democracy and Education.*
9. Piaget and Inhelder, *The Psychology of the Child.*
10. Vygotsky, *Mind in Society.*
11. Ormrod's book was the primary text for multiple sections of required courses in educational psychology in the program at State University, and it is a widely popular text for such courses.
12. Gardner, *Frames of Mind.* Gardner labels his eight modalities of intelligence as "musical-rhythmic," "visual-spatial," "verbal-linguistic," "logical-mathematical," "bodily-kinesthetic," "interpersonal," "intrapersonal," "naturalistic," and later "existential."
13. See Dewey, *The School and Society*; Dewey, *Democracy and Education.*
14. Gardner, *Frames of Mind*; Ormrod, *Educational Psychology.*
15. For examples of this literature, see the James A. Banks *Multicultural Education Series* published by Teachers College Press, as well as Dillar and Moule, *Cultural Competence.*

16. Hallett and Gougherty, "Professional Education in the University Context," 14.

17. Corsaro and Molinari, *I Compagni*.

18. Corsaro and Molinari, "Priming Events and Italian Children's Transition from Pre-school to Elementary School," 17.

19. This is one of six "guiding principles" that serve as the basis for evaluation, so there are six such scoring rubrics, all of which factor into teacher candidates' overall evaluation. Teacher candidates are keenly aware of these assessment standards as copies of these scoring rubrics are included in the "Student Teaching Handbook" that is standard issue for all teacher candidates prior to entering their student teaching semester.

20. It is important to note here what I observed to be an ongoing conflation of cognitive ability and learned skill level among students, both in the evaluation protocols and course content of instructional methods classes. This evaluation rubric, for example, references "learning styles" and "ability levels," and tends to treat them similarly as pre-existing conditions that students bring with them to teachers' classrooms and which must be accommodated. Neither the rubrics nor discussions of these student characteristics in methods courses tended to distinguish between these sources of student heterogeneity. In other words, there was rarely distinction made between actual cognitive proclivities and more social sources of difference in prior student skills (not the least of which, family socioeconomic background). Both were routinely treated as pre-existing conditions, so to speak, that students brought with them, and to which teacher candidates must adapt their instruction to accommodate. As I show in the following chapter, teacher candidates also tend to conflate these different elements of student heterogeneity, but not always.

21. Ridgeway, "Framed Before We Know It," 147.

22. My own gender identity and performance is likely another important factor here, as Nicole would likely feel more comfortable discussing the management of female bodies in the context of teaching (and by implication, the management of her own body) with another woman than she did discussing it with a man.

23. In this class for secondary mathematics, the gender composition was pretty evenly split between women and men.

24. Acker, "Hierarchies, Jobs, Bodies."

25. They scheduled several of these orientation meetings on different days and times late in the fall semester to enable all of the several hundred teacher candidates in the program to attend. Each meeting was held in a large auditorium with stadium seating. I estimate at this particular meeting that I attended there were over 100 teacher candidates in attendance, including 3 members of the focal sample and 12 members of the cohort sample. All of the teacher candidates involved in this study attended one of these meetings.

26. West and Zimmerman, "Doing Gender."

27. Such findings echo Walkerdine's (*Schoolgirl Fictions*) analysis, in which she shows how the institutionalized discourses and practices of "progressive pedagogy" serve to normalize meanings about the "naturalness" of male students' aggressive sexuality, and according to such discourses "it is the female teacher who is to *contain* this" (24).

28. "Constructivist pedagogy" is a later iteration of "progressive pedagogy," especially when viewed from an institutional perspective. Both are, at their core, "child-centered" approaches to instruction. The term "constructivist" emerged as a way of more explicitly incorporating the insights of developmental psychology, a term used by Piaget. Earlier versions of progressive pedagogy espoused by Dewey and others were also rooted firmly in the field of psychology, and the widespread adoption of the term "constructivism" reflects the ties between UBTE and the ongoing development of the field of psychology.

29. Walkerdine, *Schoolgirl Fictions*, 24.
30. Ridgeway, "Framed Before We Know It," 152.

CHAPTER 2. THE CHALLENGES AND ASSUMPTIONS OF ADAPTING TO ALL STUDENTS

1. Wolf, *The Beauty Myth*.
2. Though an ironic choice of words, it was not my sense during this interview that Hillary was literally referring to someone actually being groped. Rather, she was simply referring to suffering disciplinary consequences by saying "nabbed in the ass."
3. Marsiglio, *Men on a Mission*; Pruit, "Preschool Teachers and the Discourse of Suspicion."
4. Corsaro, "Interpretive Reproduction in Children's Peer Culture," 162.
5. Corsaro, *The Sociology of Childhood*.
6. Kelly, "Understanding Teacher Effects."
7. Martin, "Gender as Social Institution"; Ridgeway, "Framed Before We Know It"; West and Zimmerman, "Doing Gender."
8. To be clear, managing professional appearance and techniques of differentiated instruction are not equivalent phenomena, but they are given coherence in the ways they respectively align with the rationale of adaptation to student characteristics. They are sets of practices along with professional ethics that, taken together, comprise the injunction to adapt that teacher candidates are indoctrinated into through their training and that they place at the core of their definitions of effective teaching.

CHAPTER 3. ACCOUNTABILITY AND BUREAUCRACY

1. Lortie, *Schoolteacher*.
2. Teachers are becoming increasingly joined by other professions in this regard. As bureaucracy has become the dominant organizational form of political economy, both here and elsewhere around the world, the majority of workers spend their entire work lives employed by bureaucratic organizations, including the traditional professions. As such, this tension between the autonomy and discretion afforded professions and the standardization of outcomes that is often the central goal of bureaucracy has become a more widespread characteristic of work life for people across sectors of the labor market (Brint, *In an Age of Experts*; MacDonald, *The Sociology of the Professions*). This has long been a subject of study in sociology, spanning both time and theoretical traditions, from Weber's (*Theory of Social and Economic Organization*) notion of the "iron cage" of bureaucracy, through the ongoing development of theory and research on "coupling" in organizations (Bidwell, "The School as a Formal Organization"; Meyer and Rowan, "The Structure of Educational Organizations"; Aurini, "Patterns of Tight and Loose Coupling in a Competitive Marketplace"), to decades of research on the professions (Abbott, *The System of Professions*; Brint, *In an Age of Experts*; MacDonald, *The Sociology of the Professions*), to some of the foundational works in inhabited institutionalism (Hallett and Ventresca, "Inhabited Institutions"; Hallett and Ventresca, "How Institutions Form").
3. Bidwell, "The School as a Formal Organization."
4. See Weick, "Educational Organizations as Loosely Coupled Systems" for the first conceptualization of loose-coupling and its organizational features; see Meyer and Rowan, "Institutionalized Organizations" for discussion of the role that a "logic of good faith"

plays in minimizing organizational uncertainty and thereby preserving schools' legitimacy in the field of public education.

5. Barr and Dreeben, *How Schools Work*; Bidwell, "Analyzing Schools as Organizations"; Cuban, *How Teachers Taught*; Datnow and Castellano, "Teachers' Responses to Success for All"; Rosenholtz, *Teachers' Workplace*; Waller, *The Sociology of Teaching*.

6. Coburn, "Beyond Decoupling"; Diamond, "Where the Rubber Meets the Road"; Everitt, "Teacher Careers and Inhabited Institutions"; Spillane, *Standards Deviation*.

7. Hallett, "The Myth Incarnate."

8. At least in the case of NCLB, this did not work. Under the original law, schools were required to bring 100% of their students to "proficient" levels of performance in reading and math by 2014. The overwhelming majority of schools in the United States did not meet this goal. The U.S. Department of Education began issuing waivers to individual states so they could avoid sanction under this component of the law, contingent upon adopting other policies, most notably policies that tied student performance measures to individual teacher evaluations.

9. While many might point to the notable political influence of teacher unions, their influence on accountability policies has been mixed. Despite opposition to various elements of accountability, teacher unions have certainly not prevented the passage or dissemination of accountability policies (indeed, NCLB had strong bi-partisan support at the time it was passed in 2001). In more recent years, even the most successful efforts of local unions to limit the influence of accountability on teacher evaluations still incorporated elements of accountability in labor contracts (see McCune, "Chicago Teacher Union ratifies contract that ended strike"). Finally, like unions in other sectors of the economy, membership in teacher unions is declining (see Toppo and Overberg, "Fewer Than Half of Teachers Now Covered by Unions"; United States Department of Labor, "Union Membership (Annual) News Release").

10. Ingersoll, *Who Controls Teachers' Work?*

11. As I will discuss in more detail in the concluding chapter, most states now include measures of student performance in teacher job evaluations. This was largely incentivized by Race to the Top, and remains in place at the level of these state governments under ESSA.

12. This is a pseudonym, but there was a commonly used and recognized nickname for this office, which is itself a reflection of the way people referenced the ubiquity of bureaucracy in the daily life of the UBTE program. The hub of bureaucratic decision-making and information was the "Admin Suite," and everybody knew what that meant.

13. Frank's case is actually a success story by comparison. He ultimately received the course credits he needed, graduated, and became certified. Other teacher candidates were not always as successful in navigating the maze of course requirements, especially when the slate of required courses spanned across academic units of the university, which was common for secondary education majors who had to take subject matter courses in the College of Arts and Sciences as well as courses in the School of Education. Teacher candidates preparing for secondary education in language arts/English, math, and social studies frequently ran into scheduling problems which often lengthened their time to degree. Oscar, for instance, had to take summer school and still took longer than the traditional four years to graduate. Many teacher candidates in the focal and cohort samples knew of classmates who faced similar situations, and time to degree was a nagging concern for many teacher candidates, as well as the lingering anxiety that there may be some obscure requirement of which they were

unaware until the last minute that could delay their student teaching and/or their graduation.

14. Everitt, "Teacher Careers and Inhabited Institutions."

15. NCLB explicitly mandated that 100% of students reach levels of proficiency in reading and math by 2014. As noted earlier, while the federal government has backed away from this requirement through waivers to states and ESSA, most states continue to tie student performance outcomes to evaluations of teacher and school performance.

16. While manifestations of accountability policy varied by state, standards-based assessment for evaluating school performance and "Adequate Yearly Progress" was the central form that accountability took at this time. As I discuss in the concluding chapter, accountability has evolved since then to zero-in more directly on individual teachers and their instructional practices in ways antithetical to the injunction to adapt that provided the core principles of my teacher candidates' training experience.

CHAPTER 4. DILEMMAS OF COVERAGE AND CONTROL

1. Lucas, *Tracking Inequality*; Oakes, *Keeping Track.*

2. Eder, "Ability Grouping as a Self-Fulfilling Prophecy."

3. Acker, "Hierarchies, Jobs, Bodies."

4. Hochschild, *The Managed Heart.*

5. Ibid.

6. The UBTE program at State University offered little formalized training in classroom management per se. Most of the techniques for managing student behavior were incorporated into instructional methods courses rather than entire courses on behavior management itself. Such treatment of classroom management techniques in the curriculum, however, is not unique to State U; it is in fact quite common in UBTE broadly.

7. Harry K. Wong Publications, Inc., is a widely known source of instructional techniques, especially with respect to classroom and behavior management. Their online source of materials can be accessed at www.effectiveteaching.com.

8. Scott slept at his desk with his head down, and in prior classes routinely ignored Oscar's effort to maintain authority over when exactly class was dismissed. This particular occasion was only a week or two into Oscar's student teaching, and Scott had lied when Oscar asked him his name. It was this lie that made Oscar so angry.

9. Everitt, "Teacher Education and Accountability."

10. Empirical research supports Faye's perspective here. Increased attachment to school does indeed translate into more positive academic performance, including better attendance, lower dropout rates, and higher graduation rates (Hallinan, "Teacher Influences on Students' Attachment to School"; Muller, "The Role of Caring in the Teacher-Student Relationship for At-Risk Students").

CHAPTER 5. THE INJUNCTION TO ADAPT, AUTONOMY, AND DIVERSITY OF PRACTICE

1. Everitt, "Teacher Careers and Inhabited Institutions."

2. Coburn, "Beyond Decoupling"; Diamond, "Where the Rubber Meets the Road"; Everitt, "Teacher Careers and Inhabited Institutions"; Spillane, *Standards Deviation.*

3. Everitt, "Teacher Careers and Inhabited Institutions."

4. Ms. Evans is using an instructional technique known as "scaffolding" here and modeling it for Dennis. Scaffolding is a process by which an instructor uses students'

existing knowledge as the basis or starting point for introducing new knowledge to them in a way that draws upon ideas, concepts, or knowledge with which students are already familiar. In other words, you use what students already know as the scaffold upon which to build their understanding of what they do not already know. This is a very common, and very useful, technique that is consistent with the injunction to adapt because it can be employed in a wide variety of ways to teach a wide variety of topics. It also has its roots in constructivist theories of psychology and childhood development, most notably in the work of Lev Vygotsky and his concept of the "zone of proximal development."

5. Though not always emphasized as such, Hochschild's *The Managed Heart* is primarily a study of professional socialization. She shows with very candid data how corporations in the airline industry actively train flight attendants in mental techniques for managing their own emotions so as to guide interactions with customers that solicit positive emotional responses from them. Flight attendants are trained both prior to beginning paid work and in ongoing ways, required to complete extended training throughout the time they work for the company. Indeed, emotion work is a set of learned and cultivated practices; it is not an innate quality.

6. West and Zimmerman, "Doing Gender"; Ridgeway, "Framed Before We Know It."

7. Everitt, "Teacher Education and Accountability."

8. Aulette and Wittner, *Gendered Worlds*; Padavic and Reskin, *Women and Men at Work*; Williams, *Gender Differences at Work*.

9. Allan, "Male Elementary Teachers"; Marsiglio, *Men on a Mission*.

10. Hallett, "The Myth Incarnate."

11. Nunn, *Defining Student Success*.

12. Bidwell, "The School as a Formal Organization "; Johnson, "Will VAMs Reinforce the Walls of the Egg-Crate School?"

13. Herbst, *And Sadly Teach*; Labaree, *The Trouble with Ed Schools*; Liston and Zeichner, *Teacher Education and the Social Conditions of Schooling*; Lortie, *Schoolteacher*.

CHAPTER 6. THE DEMANDS OF BECOMING A TEACHER

1. Spillane, *Standards Deviation*.

2. Coburn, "Beyond Decoupling"; Datnow and Castellano, "Teachers' Responses to Success for All"; Diamond, "Where the Rubber Meets the Road"; Everitt, "Teacher Careers and Inhabited Institutions"; Spillane and Burch, "The Institutional Environment and Instructional Practice."

3. Harris, *Value-Added Measurements in Education*; Jennings and Corcoran, "Beyond High-Stakes Tests"; Kelly, "Understanding Teacher Effects."

4. National Council on Teacher Quality, "State of the States 2015"; Porter, "Grading Teachers by the Test"; U.S. Department of Education, "Laws & Guidance."

5. See McCune, "Chicago Teachers Union Ratifies Deal that Ended Strike." In the Chicago case, even though CTU succeeded in preventing student test scores from influencing "merit pay," the deal did include measures of teacher influence on student test scores in teacher evaluations.

6. Strauss, "Resistance to Standardized Testing Growing Nationwide."

7. Rich, "Teacher Shortages Spur a Nationwide Hiring Scramble (Credentials Optional)"; Strauss, "Indiana's Got a Problem."

8. Strauss, "Teacher: 'Why I Just Can't Work in Public Education Anymore.'"

9. Hallett, "The Myth Incarnate"; Ingersoll, *Who Controls Teachers' Work?*

10. Hallett, "The Myth Incarnate."
11. See Kelly, "Understanding Teacher Effects," in particular where he writes: "While value-added models may control for students' initial level of achievement, they don't capture any of the affective and behavioral variables that affect learning and on which students vary greatly" (20).
12. Entwisle, Alexander, and Olson, *Children, Schools, and Inequality*; Lareau, *Unequal Childhoods*; Sewell and Hauser, "The Wisconsin Longitudinal Study of Social and Psychological Factors in Aspirations and Achievements."
13. Ingersoll, *Who Controls Teachers' Work?*
14. Goffman, "Gender Advertisements"; Ridgeway, "Framed Before We Know It"; West and Zimmerman, "Doing Gender."
15. In middle- and high-school contexts, for men to model an interest and passion for music, or the arts generally, is in fact an alternative to much of the local wisdom concerning masculinity (see Pascoe, *Dude, You're a Fag*).
16. Brundin, "A Teacher Retires After 25 Years, Dismayed At How His Profession Has Changed."
17. See Nunn, *Defining Student Success*, particularly her chapters on "Comprehensive High" that document how teachers routinely engaged in practices tantamount to "teaching to the test."
18. Everitt, "Teacher Careers and Inhabited Institutions."
19. Hallett, "The Myth Incarnate."
20. Hallett, "The Myth Incarnate," 62. See also Zuboff, *In the Age of the Smart Machine*, for a similar definition of "epistemic distress."
21. Hallett, "The Myth Incarnate," 70.
22. Ibid.
23. Porter, "Grading Teachers by the Test"; U.S. Department of Education, "Laws & Guidance."
24. Coburn, "Beyond Decoupling." See also Datnow and Castellano, "Teachers' Responses to Success for All."
25. Brundin, "A Teacher Retires After 25 Years, Dismayed At How His Profession Has Changed."
26. See Fligstein and McAdam, *A Theory of Fields*; Lawrence and Suddaby, "Institutions and Institutional Work"; Thornton, Ocasio, and Lounsbury, *The Institutional Logics Perspective*. All three represent emergent theories that extend new institutionalism by emphasizing the various ways that action and process at the micro level of analysis can serve to sustain, alter, and challenge elements of social institutions (see also Barley, "Coalface Institutionalism," for another example of such emphasis). Inhabited institutionalism is distinct from its theoretical peers in its orientation to social interaction as the vehicle for human sense-making and action, and the need to observe it directly in local settings. Inhabited institutionalism's foundations in symbolic interactionism make it distinct in this regard, as these other strands of institutional theory are not as firmly rooted in symbolic interactionist traditions, or Blumer's three premises of SI (Blumer, *Symbolic Interactionism: Perspective and Method*).
27. Fine and Hallett, "Group Cultures and the Everyday Life of Organizations."
28. Nunn, *Defining Student Success*, 12.
29. Hallett and Ventresca, "Inhabited Institutions."
30. Corsaro, *The Sociology of Childhood.*

31. Nunn, *Defining Student Success*.

32. Bidwell, "The School as a Formal Organization"; Lortie, *Schoolteacher*; Rosenholtz, *Teachers' Workplace*; Rosenholtz and Simpson, "Workplace Conditions and the Rise and Fall of Teachers' Commitment."

33. Britzman, *Practice Makes Practice*; Labaree, *The Trouble with Ed Schools*; Liston and Zeichner, *Teacher Education and the Social Conditions of Schooling*; Lortie, *Schoolteacher*.

34. Becker et al., *Boys in White*.

35. Everitt and Tefft, "Embedded Elaborations."

36. Levine, "Educating Schoolteachers."

37. Martin, "Gender as Social Institution"; Ridgeway, "Framed Before We Know It."

38. Institutional theory and gender scholarship can mutually benefit from this strand of empirical analysis, in my view. Institutionalism, in its various versions, tends not to emphasize micro-interaction as a mechanism through which multiple institutions interconnect, and thereby buttress each other's legitimacy in social life, something gender scholars have long emphasized (see Acker, "Hierarchies, Jobs, Bodies"; Martin, "Gender as Social Institution"; Ridgeway, "Framed Before We Know It"; and West and Zimmerman, "Doing Gender"). Likewise, gender scholarship tends to assume the institutional qualities of gender, at times sacrificing conceptual and empirical specificity in exactly how it functions as an institution, something that is a key strength of institutionalism, albeit in differing terms (see DiMaggio and Powell, "Introduction"; Fligstein and McAdam, *A Theory of Fields*; Hallett and Ventresca, "Inhabited Institutions"; Lawrence and Suddaby, "Institutions and Institutional Work"; Meyer and Rowan, "Institutionalized Organizations"; Thornton, Ocasio, and Lounsbury, *The Institutional Logics Perspective*).

39. Geertz, *The Interpretation of Cultures*.

40. This is a common unrecognized expense and effort among teachers, especially elementary teachers, who spend money out of their own pockets to supplement their classrooms with additional resources their school does not provide.

41. My subheading here is a play on words from the title of Christopher Hurn's, *The Limits and Possibilities of Schooling*.

42. Hallett and Meanwell, "Accountability as an Inhabited Institution."

43. Hallett, "The Myth Incarnate"; Hallett and Meanwell, "Accountability as an Inhabited Institution."

44. Lareau, *Unequal Childhoods*.

45. Hamilton, *Parenting to a Degree*; Calarco, "'I Need Help!'"

46. Bates, "How School Dress Codes Shame Girls and Perpetuate Rape Culture."

47. Eder, Evans, and Parker, *School Talk*; Pascoe, *Dude, You're a Fag*.

48. Becker et al., *Boys in White*; Cahill, "Emotional Capital and Professional Socialization"; Hallett and Gougherty, "Professional Education in the University Context"; Haas and Shaffir, "The Professionalization of Medical Students"; Merton, Reader, and Kendall, *The Student Physician*.

APPENDIX

1. U.S. Department of Education, *Preparing and Credentialing the Nation's Teachers*. This report, published in 2013, draws primarily on data from the 2009–2010 academic year, and as of the writing of this book, is the most recent report on nationwide trends in teacher education from the U.S. Department of Education. These data are just three

years removed from the academic year (2006–2007) during which I collected the ethnographic data for this study as well.

2. U.S. Department of Education, *Preparing and Credentialing the Nation's Teachers*, 25. It should also be noted here, though, that overall academic performance among education majors tends to be slightly lower than that of their peers in other academic majors (e.g., Levine, "Educating School Teachers").

3. U.S. Department of Education, *Preparing and Credentialing the Nation's Teachers*, 24. While this broad, descriptive statement is accurate if applied to the program at State University, it is also short on detail. For instance, course requirements for teacher candidates do include "academic content," but at times this proved woefully lacking. Teacher candidates in English education, as an example, received very little formal academic preparation in grammar and other concrete writing skills, and consequently often felt extremely unprepared to teach such subjects to high school students. Likewise, it is true that teacher candidates at State University took required courses in teaching students in "special education," but there was precious little training specific to teaching "English learners." Finally, while it is true that teacher candidates took sequential sets of courses on "pedagogy," very little of the formal content of these courses explicitly addressed techniques for managing student behavior in class or disciplinary strategies, something teacher candidates universally bemoaned as a shortcoming to their preparation.

4. U.S. Department of Education, *Preparing and Credentialing the Nation's Teachers*, 31. Again, while this description is generally accurate, it conflates diversity and variation among programs, as well as distinctions among requirements within programs. For example, at State University, elementary teacher candidates were required to complete a 15-week student teaching component, whereas secondary teacher candidates were required to complete a 12-week student teaching component.

5. U.S. Dept. of Education, *Preparing and Credentialing the Nation's Teachers*, 27–28.

6. Ibid.

7. Fraser, *Preparing America's Teachers*, 25.

8. Conant, *The Education of American Teachers*; Fraser, *Preparing America's Teachers*; Goldstein, *The Teacher Wars*.

9. Cremin, *The American Common School*.

10. Beecher, *The Duty of American Women to Their Country*.

11. Fraser, *Preparing America's Teachers*, 115.

12. Ibid., 142.

13. Ibid., 143.

14. It is important to note here that this process of legitimating university-based teacher education came with casualties. It contributed a great deal to the demise of the normal school and two-year "teachers colleges" that had emerged as similar to the normal school model. In addition, though, a number of historically Black colleges had teacher education programs for African American teachers that had to adopt more narrowly defined programs for accreditation purposes. This forced places like Howard and Fiske to adopt models exemplified by the Tuskegee Institute for funding and credentialing purposes, which indirectly forced them to drop a lot of the elements of their training programs that were rooted in more comprehensive liberal arts education.

15. Despite their institutionalization in higher education, schools of education have also long been treated as second-class citizens among academic departments in university settings (see Labaree, *The Trouble with Ed Schools*).

16. DiMaggio and Powell, "The Iron Cage Revisited."

17. Hallett and Gougherty, "Professional Education in the University Context."

18. Hallett and Gougherty ("Professional Education in the University Context") argue that linking science with the professional enterprise of these programs was instrumental in universities' capacity to assert claims that higher education was the appropriate environment for their training and credentialing, something similar to how early UBTE programs argued science was essential to teaching. For the managerial professions, the science of statistical analysis is a key basis for rationalizing them as professions, just as psychology has been for teaching and education.

19. I have modified the formal titles of the different academic units so as not to identify the particular School of Education or the university. I have replaced the specific names of these departments with general descriptors that both reflect the function of the department and represent very common types of units that could be found in a wide range of education schools (e.g., "educational psychology" and "curriculum and instruction").

20. The phrase "field experience" (also referred to as "supervised clinical experience" by the U.S. Department of Education) refers to a required component of this UBTE program in which teacher candidates must log so many observational hours in public schools while they fulfill coursework and prior to student teaching. For most teacher candidates, this meant roughly 40 hours of observation each semester during the junior year and first-semester senior year.

21. If these numbers seem odd, it is because of a program requirement by the university. Students pursuing a major in education were not labeled as such by the university until they had completed a number of course requirements in the major; until then they were counted as majoring in what many universities might call "general studies." In effect, this meant only students who were near the end of their academic careers (mostly seniors and some juniors) were counted in the university enrollment data as education majors. This is why it appears that seniors represent an unusual majority of the total number of education majors.

22. Licensure is distinct from, though linked to, teacher certification. Certification comes with the credential earned by completing a teacher education program. Licensure refers to a formal endorsement from the state making one eligible for employment as a teacher in public schools in that state. In most cases, fulfilling requirements for certification also satisfies eligibility requirements for licensure, but one must apply for licensure demonstrating certification credentials. It is this bureaucratic application process that the Teacher Education Office facilitates for teacher candidates upon completion of the program.

23. Indeed, this group was such an open and jovial one that it influenced my relationship with them. They insisted that I attend the bar crawl with them. I met them at one of their stops for a drink and conversation, but I did not follow them when they migrated to the next bar on their list. Though I was offered one, I respectfully declined a T-shirt of my own.

24. Corsaro, *Friendship in the Early Years*; Emerson, Fretz, and Shaw, *Writing Ethnographic Fieldnotes*.

25. Britzman, *Practice Makes Practice*; Herbst, *And Sadly Teach*; Labaree, *The Trouble with Ed Schools*; Liston and Zeichner, *Teacher Education and the Social Conditions of Schooling*.

26. Emerson, Fretz, and Shaw, *Writing Ethnographic Fieldnotes*, 215.

BIBLIOGRAPHY

Abbott, A. (1988). *The system of professions: An essay on the division of expert labor.* Chicago, IL: University of Chicago Press.

Acker, J. (1990). Hierarchies, jobs, bodies: A theory of gendered organizations. *Gender and Society, 4*(2), 139–158.

Adler, P. A., Kless, S. J., & Adler, P. (1992). Socialization to gender roles: Popularity among elementary school boys and girls. *Sociology of Education, 65*(3), 169–187.

Allan, J. (1993). Male elementary teachers: Experiences and perspectives. In C. L. Williams (Ed.), *Doing women's work: Men in nontraditional occupations* (pp. 113–127). Newbury Park, CA: SAGE Publications.

Armstrong, E. A., & and Hamilton, L. T. (2013). *Paying for the party: How college maintains inequality.* Cambridge, MA: Harvard University Press.

Arum, R., & Roksa, J. (2011). *Academically adrift: Limited learning on college campuses.* Chicago, IL: University of Chicago Press.

Aulette, J. R., & Wittner, J. (2011). *Gendered worlds* (2nd ed.). New York, NY: Oxford University Press.

Aurini, J. D. (2012). Patterns of tight and loose coupling in a competitive marketplace: The case of learning center franchises. *Sociology of Education, 85*(4), 373–387.

Barley, S. R. (2008). Coalface institutionalism. In R. Greenwood, C. Oliver, R. Suddaby & K. Sahlin (Eds.), *The SAGE handbook of organizational institutionalism* (pp. 491–518). Los Angeles, CA: SAGE Publications.

Barnett, B. G. (1984). Subordinate teacher power in school organizations. *Sociology of Education, 57*(1), 43–55.

Barr, R., & Dreeben, R. (1983). *How schools work.* Chicago, IL: University of Chicago Press.

Bates, L. (2015, May 22). How school dress codes shame girls and perpetuate rape culture. *Time.* Retrieved from http://time.com/3892965/everydaysexism-school-dress-codes-rape-culture/.

Becker, H. S., Geer, B., Hughes, E. C., & Strauss, A. L. (1961). *Boys in white: Student culture in medical school.* Chicago, IL: University of Chicago Press.

Beecher, C. (1845). *The duty of American women to their country.* New York, NY: Harper & Brothers.

Berger, P. L., & Luckmann, T. (1966). *The social construction of reality: A treatise on the sociology of knowledge.* New York, NY: Doubleday.

Bidwell, C. E. (1965). The school as a formal organization. In J. G. March (Ed.), *Handbook of Organizations* (pp. 972–1022). Chicago, IL: Rand McNally & Co.

Bidwell, C. E. (2001). Analyzing schools as organizations: Long-term permanence and short-term change. *Sociology of Education*, Extra Issue, 100–114.

Bidwell, C. E., Frank, K. A., & Quiroz, P. A. (1997). Teacher types, workplace controls, and the organization of schools. *Sociology of Education, 70*(4), 285–307.

Binder, A. J. (2007). For love and money: Organizations' creative responses to multiple environmental logics. *Theory and Society, 36*(6), 547–571.

Binder, A. J., & Wood, K. (2013). *Becoming right: How campuses shape young conservatives.* Princeton, NJ: Princeton University Press.

Blumer, H. (1969). *Symbolic interactionism: Perspective and method.* Edgewood Cliffs, NJ: Prentice-Hall, Inc.

Bourdieu, P., & Passeron, J-C. (1990). *Reproduction in education, society, and culture* (2nd ed.). (R. Nice, Trans.). London: SAGE Publications.

Bridwell-Mitchell, E. N. (2015). Theorizing teacher agency and reform: How institutionalized instructional practices change and persist. *Sociology of Education, 88*(2), 140–159.

Brint, S. (1994). *In an age of experts: The changing role of professionals in politics and public life.* Princeton, NJ: Princeton University Press.

Britzman, D. P. (1991). *Practice makes practice: A critical study of learning to teach.* Albany, NY: SUNY Press.

Brundin, J. (2016, Jun. 14). A teacher retires after 25 years, dismayed at how his profession has changed. *Colorado Public Radio.* Retrieved from www.cpr.org/news/story/teacher -retires-after-25-years-dismayed-how-his-profession-has-changed.

Cahill, S. E. (1999). Emotional capital and professional socialization: The case of mortuary science students (and me). *Social Psychology Quarterly, 62*(2), 101–116.

Calarco, J. M. (2011). "I need help!" Social class and children's help-seeking in elementary school. *American Sociological Review, 76*(6), 862–882.

Cavanagh, S. L. (2007). *Sexing the teacher: School sex scandals and queer pedagogies.* Vancouver: UBC Press.

Coburn, C. (2004). Beyond decoupling: Rethinking the relationship between the institutional environment and the classroom. *Sociology of Education, 77*(3), 211–244.

Common Core State Standards Initiative. (2017). Retrieved from http://www.corestandards .org.

Conant, J. B. (1963). *The education of American teachers.* New York, NY: McGraw-Hill.

Connell, C. (2015). *School's out: Gay and lesbian teachers in the classroom.* Berkeley, CA: University of California Press.

Connell, R. W. (1995). *Masculinities.* Berkeley, CA: University of California Press.

Corsaro, W. A. (1985). *Friendship and peer culture in the early years.* Norwood, NJ: Ablex Publishing.

Corsaro, W. A. (1992). Interpretive reproduction in children's peer cultures. *Social Psychology Quarterly, 55*(2), 160–177.

Corsaro, W. A. (1994). Discussion, debate, and friendship processes: Peer discourse in U.S. and Italian nursery schools. *Sociology of Education, 67*(1), 1–26.

Corsaro, W. A. (2003). *We're friends, right? Inside kids' culture.* Washington, D.C.: Joseph Henry Press.

Corsaro, W. A. (2014). *The sociology of childhood* (4th ed.). Los Angeles, CA: SAGE Publications.

Corsaro, W. A., & Molinari, L. (2000). Priming events and Italian children's transition from preschool to elementary school: Representations and action. *Social Psychology Quarterly, 63*(1), 16–33.

Corsaro, W. A., & Molinari, L. (2005). *I Compagni: Understanding children's transition from preschool to elementary school.* New York, NY: Teachers College Press.

Cremin, L. (1951). *The American common school.* New York, NY: Teachers College, Columbia University.

Cuban, L. (1993). *How teachers taught: Constancy and change in American classrooms, 1890–1990.* New York, NY: Teachers College Press.

Cuban, L. (2013). *Inside the black box of classroom practice: Change without reform in American education.* Cambridge, MA: Harvard Education Press.

Darling-Hammond, L. (2015). Can value added add value to teacher evaluation? *Educational Researcher, 44*(2), 132–137.

Darling-Hammond, L., Holtzman, D. J., Gatlin, S. J., & Heilig, J. V. (2005). Does teacher preparation matter? Evidence about teacher certification, Teach for America, and teacher effectiveness. *Education Policy Analysis Archives, 13,* 42–92.

Datnow, A., & Castellano, M. (2000). Teachers' responses to success for all: How beliefs, experiences, and adaptations shape implementation. *American Education Research Journal, 37*(3), 775–799.

Davis, F. (1968). Professional socialization as subjective experience: The process of doctrinal conversion among student nurses. In H. Becker, B. Greer, D. Riesman, & R. Weiss (Eds.), *Institutions and the Person.* Chicago, IL: Aldine.

Deering, T. E., & Stanutz, A. (1995). Preservice field experience as a multicultural component of a teacher education program. *Journal of Teacher Education, 46*(5), 390–394.

Dewey, J. (1899). *The school and society.* Chicago, IL: University of Chicago Press.

Dewey, J. (1902). *The child and the curriculum.* Chicago, IL: University of Chicago Press.

Dewey, J. (1916). *Democracy and education.* New York, NY: Free Press.

Diamond, J. D. (2007). Where the rubber meets the road: Rethinking the connection between high-stakes testing policy and classroom instruction. *Sociology of Education, 80*(4), 285–313.

DiMaggio, P., & Powell, W. W. (1983). The iron cage revisited: Institutional isomorphism and collective rationality in organizational fields. *American Sociological Review, 48*(2), 147–160.

DiMaggio, P., & Powell, W. W. (1991). Introduction. In W. W. Powell & P. DiMaggio (Eds.), *The new institutionalism in organizational analysis* (pp. 1–38). Chicago, IL: University of Chicago Press.

Dingwall, R., & Strong, P. M. (1985). The interactional study of organizations: A critique and reformulation. *Urban Life, 14*(2), 205–231.

Dorado, S. (2013). Small groups as context for institutional entrepreneurship: An exploration of the emergence of commercial microfinance in Bolivia. *Organization Studies, 34*(4), 533–557.

Dreeben, R. (2005). Teaching and the competence of occupations. In L. V. Hedges & B. Schneider (Eds.), *The social organization of schooling* (pp. 51–71). New York, NY: Russell Sage Foundation.

Eder, D. (1981). Ability grouping as a self-fulfilling prophecy: A micro-analysis of teacher-student interaction. *Sociology of Education, 54*(3), 151–162.

Eder, D., Evans, C. C., & Parker, S. (1995). *School talk: Gender and adolescent culture.* New Brunswick, NJ: Rutgers University Press.

Emerson, R. M., Fretz, R. I., & Shaw, L. L. (2011). *Writing ethnographic fieldnotes* (2nd ed.). Chicago, IL: University of Chicago Press.

Emirbayer, M., & Mische, A. (1998). What is agency? *American Journal of Sociology, 103*(4), 962–1023.

Entwisle, D. R., Alexander, K. L., & Olson, L. (1997). *Children, schools, and inequality.* New York, NY: Westview Press.

Etzioni, A. (Ed.). (1969). *The semi-professions and their organization*. New York, NY: Free Press.

Everitt, J. G. (2012a). Teacher careers and inhabited institutions: Sense-making and arsenals of teaching practice in educational institutions. *Symbolic Interaction, 35*(2), 203–220.

Everitt, J. G. (2012b). Teacher education and accountability: Adapting to prospective work environments in schools. In S. Kelly (Ed.), *Assessing teacher quality: Understanding teacher effects on instruction and achievement* (pp. 137–159). New York, NY: Teachers College Press.

Everitt, J. G. (2013). Inhabitants moving in: Prospective sense-making and the reproduction of inhabited institutions in teacher education. *Symbolic Interaction, 36*(2), 177–196.

Everitt, J. G., & Levinson, B. A. (2016). Inhabited institutions in new destinations: Local sense-making and institutional work in community response to new immigration. *Journal of Contemporary Ethnography, 45*(2), 115–142.

Everitt, J. G., & Tefft, T. (2015). Embedded elaborations: Adult socialization, experience, and institutional environments in teacher careers. Paper presented at the annual meeting of the Society for the Study of Symbolic Interaction, Chicago, IL.

Fairchild, E. (2014). Examining wedding rituals through a multidimensional gender lens: The analytic importance of attending to (in)consistency. *Journal of Contemporary Ethnography, 43*(3), 361–389.

Fields, J. (2008). *Risky lessons: Sex education and social inequality*. New Brunswick, NJ: Rutgers University Press.

Fine, G. A. (1987). *With the boys: Little league baseball and preadolescent culture*. Chicago, IL: University of Chicago Press.

Fine, G. A., & Hallett, T. (2014). Group cultures and the everyday life of organizations: Interaction orders and meso-analysis. *Organization Studies, 35*(12), 1773–1792.

Fligstein, N., & McAdam, D. (2012). *A theory of fields*. New York, NY: Oxford University Press.

Fraser, J. W. (2007). *Preparing America's teachers: A history*. New York, NY: Teachers College Press.

Friedson, E. (1970). *Professional dominance: The social structure of medical care*. New York, NY: Atherton Press.

Gamoran, A. (2012). Improving teacher quality: Incentives are not enough. In S. Kelly, *Assessing teacher quality: Understanding teacher effects on instruction and achievement* (pp. 201–214). New York, NY: Teachers College Press.

Gardner, H. (1983). *Frames of mind: The theory of multiple intelligences*. New York, NY: Basic Books.

Geertz, C. (1973). *The interpretation of cultures*. New York, NY: Basic Books.

Giddens, A. (1984). *The constitution of society*. Berkeley, CA: University of California Press.

Gieryn, T. F. (1999). *Cultural boundaries of science: Credibility on the line*. Chicago, IL: University of Chicago Press.

Goffman, E. (1967). *Interaction ritual*. New York, NY: Anchor Books.

Goffman, E. (1974). *Frame analysis*. New York, NY: Harper and Row.

Goffman, E. (1977). The arrangement between the sexes. *Theory and Society, 4*(3), 301–331.

Goffman, E. (1979). *Gender advertisements*. New York, NY: Harper and Row.

Goldstein, D. (2014). *The teacher wars: A history of America's most embattled profession*. New York, NY: Doubleday.

Greene, P. (2015, Aug. 12). Why a teacher "shortage"? *Education Week Teacher*. Retrieved from http://blogs.edweek.org/teachers/view-from-the-cheap-seats/2015/08/why_a_teacher _shortage.html?cmp=ENL-EU-NEWS2#.

Griffin, G. (1997). Teaching as a gendered experience. *Journal of Teacher Education, 48*(1), 7–18.

Haas, J., & Shaffir, W. (1977). The professionalization of medical students: Developing competence and a cloak of competence. *Symbolic Interaction, 1*(1), 71–80.

Haedicke, M. A. (2012). "Keeping our mission, changing our system": Translation and organizational change in natural foods co-ops. *The Sociological Quarterly, 53*(1), 44–67.

Haedicke, M. A. (2016). *Organizing organic: Conflict and compromise in an emerging market.* Stanford, CA: Stanford University Press.

Hallett, T. (2010). The myth incarnate: Recoupling processes, turmoil, and inhabited institutions in an urban elementary school. *American Sociological Review, 75*(1), 52–74.

Hallett, T., & Gougherty, M. (Forthcoming). Professional education in the university context: An inhabited institutional view of socialization. Chapter to be included in J. Mehta & S. Davies (Eds.), *Education in a New Society: Renewing the Sociology of Education.* Chicago, IL: University of Chicago Press.

Hallett, T., & Meanwell, E. (2016). Accountability as an inhabited institution: Contested meanings and the symbolic politics of reform. *Symbolic Interaction, 39*(3), 374–396.

Hallett, T., Shulman, D., & Fine, G. A. (2009). Peopling organizations: The promise of classical symbolic interactionism for an inhabited institutionalism. In P. S. Adler (Ed.), *The Oxford handbook for sociology and organizational studies: Classical foundations* (pp. 486–509). Oxford: Oxford University Press.

Hallett, T., & Ventresca, M. (2006a). Inhabited institutions: Social interactions and organizational forms in Gouldner's *Patterns of industrial bureaucracy. Theory and Society, 35*(2), 213–236.

Hallett, T., & Ventresca, M. (2006b). How institutions form: Loose coupling as mechanism in Gouldner's *Patterns of industrial bureaucracy. American Behavioral Scientist, 49*(7), 908–924.

Hallinan, M. (2008). Teacher influences on students' attachment to school. *Sociology of Education, 81*(3), 271–283.

Hamilton, L. T. (2016). *Parenting to a degree: How family matters for college women's success.* Chicago, IL: University of Chicago Press.

Hargreaves, A. (1993). Individualism and individuality: Reinterpreting the teacher culture. In J. W. Little & M. W. McLaughlin (Eds.), *Teachers' work: Individuals, colleagues, and contexts* (pp. 51–76). New York, NY: Teachers College Press.

Harris, D. N. (2011). *Value-added measurements in education: What every educator needs to know.* Cambridge, MA: Harvard Education Press.

Herbst, J. (1989). *And sadly teach: Teacher education and professionalization in American culture.* Madison, WI: University of Wisconsin Press.

Hochschild, A. R. (2012). *The managed heart: Commercialization of human feeling* (3rd ed.). Berkeley, CA: University of California Press.

Huberman, M. (1993). The model of the independent artisan in teachers' professional relations. In J. W. Little & M. W. McLaughlin (Eds.), *Teachers' work: Individuals, colleagues, and contexts* (pp. 11–50). New York, NY: Teachers College Press.

Hughes, E. C. (1958). *Men and their work.* Glencoe, IL: Free Press.

Hurn, C. J. (1993). *The limits and possibilities of schooling: An introduction to the sociology of education* (3rd ed.). Boston, MA: Allyn and Bacon.

Ingersoll, R. M. (2003). *Who controls teachers' work? Power and accountability in America's schools.* Cambridge, MA: Harvard University Press.

Ingersoll, R. M. (2011). Power, accountability, and the teacher quality problem. In S. Kelly (Ed.), *Assessing teacher quality: Understanding teacher effects on instruction and achievement* (pp. 97–109). New York, NY: Teachers College Press.

Ispa-Landa, S. (2013). Gender, race, and justifications for group exclusion: Urban black students bussed to affluent suburban schools. *Sociology of Education, 86*(3), 218–233.

James, W. (1890). *The principles of psychology*. New York, NY: Henry Holt & Co.

Jencks, C., Smith, M., Acland, H., Bane, M. J. , Cohen, D., Gintis, H., Heyns, B., & Michelson, S. (1972). *Inequality: A reassessment of the effect of family and schooling in America*. New York, NY: Basic Books.

Jennings, J. L., & Corcoran, S. P. (2012). Beyond high-stakes tests: Teacher effects on other educational outcomes. In S. Kelly (Ed.), *Assessing teacher quality: Understanding teacher effects on instruction and achievement* (pp. 77–95). New York, NY: Teachers College Press.

Johnson, S. M. (2005). The prospects for teaching as a profession. In L. V. Hedges & B. Schneider (Eds.), *The social organization of schooling* (pp. 72–90). New York, NY: Russell Sage Foundation.

Johnson, S. M. (2015). Will VAMS reinforce the walls of the egg-crate school? *Educational Researcher, 44*(2), 117–126.

Kanter, R. M. (1977). *Men and women of the corporation*. New York, NY: Basic Books.

Kelly, S. (2012). Understanding teacher effects: Market versus process models of educational improvement. In S. Kelly (Ed.), *Assessing teacher quality: Understanding teacher effects on instruction and achievement* (pp. 7–32). New York, NY: Teacher College Press.

Kimmel, M. (2012). *The gendered society* (5th ed.). New York, NY: Oxford University Press.

Konstantopoulos, S. (2012). Teacher effects: Past, present, and future. In S. Kelly (Ed.), *Assessing teacher quality: Understanding teacher effects on instruction and achievement* (pp. 33–48). New York, NY: Teachers College Press.

Kopp, W. (2001). *One day, all children . . . : The unlikely triumph of Teach for America and what I learned along the way*. New York, NY: Public Affairs.

Labaree, D. F. (2004). *The trouble with ed schools*. New Haven, CT: Yale University Press.

Lareau, A. (2011). *Unequal childhoods: Class, race, and family life* (2nd ed.). Berkeley, CA: University of California Press.

Lawrence, T. B., & Suddaby, R. (2006). Institutions and institutional work. In S. R. Clegg, C. Hardy, T. B. Lawrence, & W. R. Nord (Eds.), *The SAGE handbook of organization studies*, (pp. 215–254). London: Sage Publications.

Layton, L. (2015, Dec, 10). Obama signs new K-12 education law that ends No Child Left Behind. *The Washington Post*. Retrieved from https://www.washingtonpost.com /local/education/obama-signs-new-k-12-education-law-that-ends-no-child-left -behind/2015/12/10/c9e58d7c-9f51-11e5-a3c5-c77f2cc5a43c_story.html?utm_term= .0771eed9f7e5.

Levine, A. (2006). Educating school teachers. Report for The Education Schools Project.

Liston, D. P., & Zeichner, K. M. (Eds.). (1991). *Teacher education and the social conditions of schooling*. London: Routledge.

Lortie, D. C. (1968). Shared ordeal and induction to work. In H. Becker, B. Geer, D. Riesman, & R. Weiss (Eds.), *Institutions and the person* (pp. 252–264). Chicago, IL: Aldine.

Lortie, D. C. (1975). *Schoolteacher: A sociological study*. Chicago, IL: University of Chicago Press.

Lucas, S. R. (1999). *Tracking inequality: Stratification and mobility in American high schools*. New York, NY: Teachers College Press.

MacDonald, K. M. (1995). *The sociology of the professions*. London: Sage Publications.

Marsiglio, W. (2008). *Men on a mission: Valuing youth work in our communities*. Baltimore, MD: The Johns Hopkins University Press.

Martin, P. Y. (2004). Gender as social institution. *Social Forces, 82*(4), 1249–1273.

McCune, G. (2012, Oct. 4). Chicago teachers union ratifies deal that ended strike. *The Chicago Tribune*. Retrieved from http://articles.chicagotribune.com.

McPherson, C. M., & Sauder, M. (2013). Logics in action: Managing institutional complexity in a drug court. *Administrative Science Quarterly, 58*(2), 165–196.

Merton, R. K. (1968). *Social theory and social structure.* New York, NY: Free Press.

Merton, R. K., Reader, G. G., & Kendall, P. L. (Eds.). (1957). *The student physician: Introductory studies in the sociology of medical education.* Cambridge, MA: Harvard University Press.

Meyer, J. W., & Jepperson, R. L. (2000). The "actors" of modern society: The cultural construction of social agency. *Sociological Theory, 18,* 100–120.

Meyer, J. W., Ramirez, F. O., & Soysal, Y. N. (1992). World expansion of mass education, 1870–1980. *Sociology of Education, 65*(2), 128–149.

Meyer, J. W., & Rowan, B. (1977). Institutionalized organizations: Formal structure as myth and ceremony. *American Journal of Sociology, 83*(2), 340–363.

Meyer, J. W., & Rowan, B. (1978). The structure of educational organizations. In M. W. Meyer (Ed.)., *Environments and organizations* (pp. 78–109). San Francisco, CA: Jossey-Bass.

Muller, C. (2001). The role of caring in the teacher-student relationship for at-risk students. *Sociological Inquiry, 71*(2), 241–255.

National Council on Teacher Quality. (2015). *State of the states 2015: Evaluating teaching, leading, and learning.* Retrieved from http://www.nctq.org/dmsView/StateofStates2015

Nunn, L. M. (2014). *Defining student success: The role of school and culture.* New Brunswick, NJ: Rutgers University Press.

Oakes, J. (2005). *Keeping track: How schools structure inequality* (2nd ed.). New Haven, CT: Yale University.

Ormrod, J. E. (2010). *Educational psychology: Developing learners and human learning* (7th ed.). Pearson.

Owen-Smith, J. (2011). The institutionalization of expertise in university licensing. *Theory and Society, 40*(1), 63–94.

Padavic, I., & Reskin, B. (2002). *Women and men at work* (2nd ed.). Thousand Oaks, CA: Pine Forge Press.

Pascoe, C. J. (2011). *Dude, you're a fag: Masculinity and sexuality in high school* (2nd ed.). Berkeley, CA: University of California Press.

Piaget, J., & Inhelder, B. (1969). *The psychology of the child.* New York, NY: Basic Books.

Polakow-Suransky, S., Thomases, J., & DeMoss, K. (2016, Jul. 8). Train teachers like doctors. *The New York Times,* p. A27.

Porter, E. (2015, Mar. 24). Grading teachers by the test. *The New York Times,* p. B1.

Powell, W. W., & DiMaggio, P. J. (Eds.). (1991). *The new institutionalism in organizational analysis.* Chicago, IL: University of Chicago Press.

Pruit, J. C. (2015). Preschool teachers and the discourse of suspicion. *Journal of Contemporary Ethnography, 44*(4), 510–534.

RAND Corporation. (2012). Teachers matter: Understanding teachers' impact on student achievement. Retrieved from http://www.rand.org/pubs/corporate_pubs/CP693z1-2012-09.html.

Ray, R., & Rosow, J. (2010). Getting off and getting intimate: How normative institutional arrangements structure black and white fraternity men's approaches to women. *Men and Masculinities, 12*(5), 523–546.

Rich, M. (2015, Aug. 9). Teacher shortages spur a nationwide hiring scramble (credentials optional). *The New York Times,* p. A1.

Rich, M. (2015, Nov. 19). Negotiators come to agreement on revising No Child Left Behind law. *The New York Times,* p. A23.

Ridgeway, C. L. (2009). Framed before we know it: How gender shapes social relations. *Gender & Society, 23*(2), 145–160.

Risman, B. (2004). Gender as a social structure: Theory wrestling with activism. *Gender & Society, 18*(4), 429–450.

Rosenholtz, S. J. (1989). *Teachers' workplace: The social organization of schools.* New York, NY: Longman Group.

Rosenholtz, S. J., & Simpson, C. (1990). Workplace conditions and the rise and fall of teachers' commitment. *Sociology of Education, 63*(4), 241–257.

Rowan, B., & Meyer, H.-D. (Eds.). (2006). *The new institutionalism in education.* Albany, NY: State University of New York Press.

Sanchez, C. (2015). A vision for teacher training at MIT: West Point meets Bell Labs. *National Public Radio.* Retrieved from http://www.npr.org/sections/ed/2015/06/17/414980239/.

Schilt, K., & Westbrook, L. (2009). Doing gender, doing heteronormativity: "Gender normals," transgender people, and the social maintenance of heterosexuality. *Gender & Society 23*(4), 440–464.

Schleef, D. (2006). *Managing elites: Professional socialization in law and business schools.* Lanham, MD: Rowman & Littlefield.

Schneider, B. (2005). The social organization of schools. In L. V. Hedges & B. Schneider (Eds.), *The social organization of schooling* (pp. 1–12). New York, NY: Russell Sage Foundation.

Seron, C., Silbey, S. S., Cech, E., & Rubineau, B. (2016). Persistence is cultural: Professional socialization and the reproduction of sex segregation. *Work and Occupations, 43*(2), 178–214.

Sewell, W. H., & Hauser, R. M. (1980). The Wisconsin longitudinal study of social and psychological factors in aspirations and achievements. *Research in Sociology of Education and Socialization, 1,* 59–99.

Smith, A. C., & Kleinman, S. (1989). Managing emotions in medical school. *Social Psychology Quarterly, 52*(1), 56–69.

Spillane, J. (2004). *Standards deviation: How schools misunderstand education policy.* Cambridge, MA: Harvard University Press.

Spillane, J., & Burch, P. (2006). The institutional environment and instructional practice: Changing patterns of guidance and control in public education. In H.-D. Meyer & B. Rowan (Eds.), *The new institutionalism in education* (pp. 87–102). Albany, NY: State University of New York Press.

Strang, D., & Meyer, J. W. (1993). Institutional conditions for diffusion. *Theory and Society, 22*(4), 487–511.

Strauss, V. (2014, Mar. 25). Resistance to standardized testing growing nationwide. *The Washington Post.*

Strauss, V. (2015, Jan. 28). Researchers urge Arne Duncan to drop proposed teacher prep regulations. *The Washington Post.*

Strauss, V. (2015, Aug. 12). Teacher: Why "I can't work in public education anymore." *The Washington Post.*

Strauss, V. (2015, Aug. 13). Indiana's got a problem: Too many teachers don't want to work there anymore. *The Washington Post.*

Stuber, J. M. (2012). *Inside the college gates: How class and culture matter in higher education.* Plymouth, UK: Lexington Books.

Talbert, J. E., & McLaughlin, M. W. (1994). Teacher professionalism in local school contexts. *American Journal of Education, 102*(2), 123–153.

Thorne, B., & Luria, Z. (1986). Sexuality and gender in children's daily worlds. *Social Problems, 33*(3), 176–190.

Thornton, P. H., Ocasio, W., & Lounsbury, M. (2012). *The institutional logics perspective.* New York, NY: Oxford University Press.

Tolman, D. L. (1994). Doing desire: Adolescent girls' struggles for/with sexuality. *Gender & Society, 8*(3), 324–342.

Toppo, G., & Overberg, P. (2015). Fewer than half of teachers now covered by unions. *USA Today*. Retrieved from https://www.usatoday.com/story/news/nation/2015/02/10/teacher-unions-fewer-half/23195433/

Trudell, B. M. (1993). *Doing sex education: Gender politics and schooling*. New York, NY: Routledge.

United States Department of Education. (2014a). *Improving teacher preparation: Building on innovation*. Retrieved from http://www.ed.gov/teacherprep.

United States Department of Education. (2014b). *Laws & guidance*. Retrieved from http://www2.ed.gov/policy/eseaflex/secretary-letters/cssoltr8212014.html.

United States Department of Education, National Center for Education Statistics. (2015). *Digest of education statistics, 2013*. (NCES 2015–011).

United States Department of Education, Office of Postsecondary Education. (2013). *Preparing and credentialing the nation's teachers: The secretary's ninth report on teacher quality*. Washington, D.C.

United States Department of Labor, Bureau of Labor Statistics. (2017). *Union membership (annual) news release* [Press release]. Retrieved from https://www.bls.gov/news.release/union2.htm

Vygotsky, L. S. (1978). *Mind in society: The development of higher psychological processes*. Cambridge, MA: Harvard University Press.

Walkerdine, V. (1990). *Schoolgirl fictions*. London: Verso Books.

Waller, W. (2014). *The sociology of teaching* (Reprint). Eastford, CT: Martino Fine Books.

Weber, M. (1997). *The theory of social and economic organization* (reprint). New York, NY: Free Press.

Weick, K. E. (1976). Educational organizations as loosely coupled systems. *Administrative Science Quarterly, 21*, 1–19.

Weick, K. E. (1995). *Sensemaking in organizations*. Thousand Oaks, CA: Sage Publications.

Weiss, R. S. (1994). *Learning from strangers: The art of method of qualitative interview studies*. New York, NY: Free Press.

West, C., & Zimmerman, D. (1987). Doing gender. *Gender & Society, 1*, 125–151.

Williams, C. L. (1991). *Gender differences at work: Women and men in nontraditional occupations*. Berkeley, CA: University of California Press.

Williams, C. L. (Ed). (1993). Introduction. *Doing "women's work": Men in nontraditional occupations*. Newbury Park, CA: SAGE Publications.

Wolf, N. (2002). *The beauty myth: How images of beauty are used against women*. New York, NY: HarperCollins.

Zuboff, S. (1988). *In the age of the smart machine: The future of work and power*. New York, NY: Basic Books.

INDEX

ability tracking, 99–100

accountability, 4, 8, 12, 23, 72–94, 114, 117; compulsory education and, 145–148; enforcing, 4; goals of, 143; holding teachers accountable, 143–145; institutional myth of, 87, 95; intent of, 154; legitimacy of, 152; orientation to, 116; policies, 74; priming for accountability in public schools, 86–95; rise of, 73–74; satisfying requirements of, 74; standards, 87, 114, 118, 145, 154, 157; "turmoil" of, 152–154; validation of, 93–94

Acker, Joan, 105

active learning, 70

adapt/adapting, 3, 33–35, 85–86, 124, 156; "all students" as formal evaluation guide, 35, 37; assumptions regarding, 48–71; to bureaucratic contingencies, 74–86; challenges of, 48–71; curriculum standards, 87–94; diversity, 14, 34–35, 37; emphasizing, 27–33, 96; individual students, 49, 70, 98–99, 129–130; injunction to, 4, 19, 46, 57, 60, 95, 104, 115, 118–143, 156; scoring rubric, 35; student learning and, 49; training in, 143; trial and error, 33

ambivalence, 109, 149–150, 160–162; in autonomy, 134–141; professional culture of, 19–20, 94, 142–148, 156, 158–159; rationale for, 56–61, 70; about reaching all students, 48–61; shared sense of, 2–3, 19–20

anticipation guide, 28–30

arsenals of practice: developing, 118–124; diverse, 134

assessment, 87, 90

assimilation, 24

authority, 105–113, 116; administrative, 157; femininity and, 105–110; masculinity and, 110–113, 150

autonomy, instructional, 10–20, 73, 118–141, 145, 156, 159; ambivalence in, 134–141; experimenting with, 122–124; legitimacy of, 137; loss of, 145; prospective, 137–138; protecting, 148

baseball, 11

"Beauty Myth, the," 61

Beecher, Catherine, 166–167

behavioral disorders, 25, 34, 58–59, 99–105; bureaucracy/administration, 4, 72–95, 137; classes with high proportions of, 100–102; correcting, 107–108; diluting impact, 73; feeling comfortable with, 72; gendered forms of, 61, 131–133; increase in, 73; interactions with, 85–86; interruptions, 97–98; managing, 105–106, 111–113, 149; monitoring of teachers, 2; policy, 73, 148; priming for adaptation to bureaucratic contingencies, 74–86; strategies for dealing with, 100–103, 108–109; students' background and, 60–61, 70, 102, 139–141; students' reaction to, 102–103; tolerance for disrespectful, 108–109

Carnegie Foundation, 168

Carnegie Research I University, 169

child-centered instruction, 24, 37

classroom: composition, 99–105; disruptions, 58–60, 99–105; dynamics, 95, 99–100; management, 2, 58–59, 95–117, 124–134; practices, discrepancies in, 53

"Cluster Bar Crawl," 175–176

"coddling" students, 125–126

compulsory: attendance, 8; education, 12–14, 22–47, 86; education, institutional myth of, 26, 37, 46, 48; education, priming for, 26–37; education, realities of, 57–58; legitimacy of, 48; mandates, 35

constructionist pedagogy, 8, 22–47, 49, 70, 89, 151; agenda of, 55; challenging, 55; development of, 24; institutionalism of, 25, 53–54; limitations to, 54; models of instruction, 25, 31; partial buy-in to, 49–56; philosophy, 29, 60; priming for, 26–37; scoring rubric, 37; strategies, 135–136; tenets, 35, 49, 54–55, 119; utility of, 55–56

contingencies, 147–148; priming for adaptation to bureaucratic contingencies, 74–86

control, dilemmas of, 95–117

Corsaro, William, 18–19, 27, 69–70, 155

Course on Job Search Strategies for Beginning Teachers, 86

curriculum, 145–148; adjusting, 34–35, 86–87; coverage, 95–117; defining, 114; guides, 96; interruptions impacting, 102–104; orientations to, 113–116; planning, 113–116;

ABOUT THE AUTHOR

JUDSON G. EVERITT is an assistant professor in the Department of Sociology at Loyola University Chicago.

CPSIA information can be obtained
at www.ICGtesting.com
Printed in the USA
LVOW03s1552241117
557390LV00001B/1/P